MARXISM AND THE ORIGINS OF BRITISH SOCIALISM

The Struggle for a New Consciousness

MARXISM AND
THE ORIGINS OF
BRITISH SOCIALISM

The Struggle for a New Consciousness

STANLEY PIERSON

Cornell University Press
ITHACA AND LONDON

First published 1973 by Cornell University Press.
Published in the United Kingdom by Cornell University Press Ltd., 2-4 Brook Street, London W1Y 1AA.

International Standard Book Number 0–8014–0746X
Library of Congress Catalog Card Number 72–4571

Printed in the United States of America by Kingsport Press, Inc.

Librarians: Library of Congress cataloging information appears on the last page of the book.

FOR MY MOTHER

Acknowledgments

In the early stages of this study I benefited from the advice of three perceptive students of modern British history. The late David Owen introduced me to the history of Victorian society and guided my exploration of some aspects of the Socialist movement. H. L. Beales helped to orient me to British sources and offered a valuable criticism of an initial effort to formulate my ideas. The late G. D. H. Cole gave generously of his time and insight into Socialist development and directed me toward little-known materials. I have also benefited from correspondence and conversation with many British and American colleagues and friends. Carl Schorske provided a helpful reading of an earlier treatment of the growth of British Socialist ideas; Robert Worthington Smith commented on an earlier discussion of Victorian religious history; and Thomas P. Govan helped me to find a final form for the study. I am especially grateful to Val Lorwin, not only for a close reading of the manuscript, but for sharing with me over the years his rich understanding of European Socialist and labor movements.

A number of British and American librarians aided in locating research materials. I am grateful to the staffs of the following libraries: British Library of Political and Economic Science; British Museum Reading Room and the British Museum Newspaper Library at Colindale; University of London Library; Birmingham Central Reference Library; Leeds Central Reference Library; Brotherton Library, University of Leeds; Mitchell Library, Edinburgh; Sheffield Public Library; Bradford Public Library; Bodleian Library, Oxford; and the libraries of Harvard, Yale, Stanford, the University of California, and the University of Oregon.

viii   Acknowledgments

I wish also to express my appreciation to the following for permission to use and quote from collections of research materials: Manchester Public Libraries for the Robert Blatchford–A. M. Thompson Correspondence; Sheffield City Libraries for the Edward Carpenter Collection of correspondence and papers; Yale University Library and R. Walston Chubb for the Thomas Davidson Papers; International Institute of Social History, Amsterdam, for the Socialist League Correspondence and Papers, and other Socialist correspondence; the late Francis Johnson for the John Bruce Glasier Correspondence and other papers dealing with the history of the Independent Labour party (now deposited in the archives of the Independent Labour party, Bristol); the Passfield Trustees and Derek A. Clarke, British Library of Political and Economic Science, for the Passfield Papers; The Society of Authors on behalf of the Bernard Shaw Estate for the George Bernard Shaw correspondence; and May Wallas for the Graham Wallas Correspondence and Papers, British Library of Political and Economic Science.

I wish to thank Harvard University for a Sheldon Traveling Fellowship, the American Philosophical Society for three travel and research grants, the Social Science Research Council for a research fellowship, and Wesleyan University and the University of Oregon Graduate School for research funds.

Longer versions of the sections on the Labour churches, Edward Carpenter, and Ernest Belfort Bax have appeared elsewhere: "John Trevor and the Labour Movement," *Church History* (1960); "Edward Carpenter, Prophet of a Socialist Millennium," *Victorian Studies* (1970); and "Ernest Belfort Bax: The Encounter of Marxism and Late Victorian Culture," *Journal of British Studies* (1972). I am grateful to the editors of these journals for permission to present the accounts in revised form.

The staff of Cornell University Press provided valuable editorial aid. For her forbearance and many kindnesses I would like to thank my typist, Betty Stilwell. My deepest gratitude is to my wife, Joan, whose constant demand for more light in many obscure passages has spared the reader many difficulties.

STANLEY PIERSON

Eugene, Oregon

Contents

Introduction

The "great unresolved dilemma" of Marxist sociology, Daniel Bell observed, was the question of "how the proletariat achieves the consciousness of its role."[1] Marx, according to Engels, had complete faith in the "intellectual development of the working class."[2] The proletariat would lead mankind out of the "false consciousness" of the bourgeoisie into an understanding that would be fully adequate to the task of creating a humane social order. But nineteenth-century Marxists were unable to nurture a working class deeply informed about Socialist theory. Their failure is an important reason for the divergent strategies and outlooks that have characterized European Marxism in the twentieth century.

The struggle to develop a Socialist consciousness in Britain involved a process by which Marxist ideas were translated into familiar British terms and inspired a popular movement. During the course of the movement, from 1881 to 1900, the British Socialists attempted, through political and nonpolitical means, to implement their vision.

The first stage of the struggle was the encounter between Marxist ideas and native intellectual traditions. Marxist concepts filtered through three currents of nineteenth-century thought before taking root in British society. One originated in a century-long effort by leaders of organized religion to formulate the ideal of a Christian

[1] Daniel Bell, *The End of Ideology* (New York, 1960), p. 282. For a recent series of essays addressed to the problem, see Istvan Meszaros, ed., *Aspects of History and Class Consciousness* (London, 1971).

[2] See Friedrich Engels' preface to the 1888 edition of Karl Marx's *Communist Manifesto* (London, 1888).

community. The second derived from the writings of Carlyle and Ruskin. The third, utilitarianism, was given systematic expression by Bentham and the younger Mill and transmitted to the lower classes by the Owenites and the Secularists.

Marxist theory, in any strict sense of the term, disintegrated rapidly in the Britain of the eighties. But at the same time the major elements of this system of thought underwent new development. Through a complex process of mediation by British Socialist leaders, the rationalistic, the utopian, and what may be called the "realistic" strains in Marxism found new and distinctively British forms.

By the early nineties three different versions of Socialism had emerged—British Marxism, Fabianism, and a much less coherent school of thought that I have labeled Ethical Socialism. The last, strongly utopian in spirit, became the dominant form of British Socialism. It drew much of its vitality from moral and religious sentiments that had ceased to find satisfactory expression in the churches and the chapels. Through the blending of these feelings with the material aspirations of the working classes a new political party was born. But from the beginning the new Independent Labour party was characterized by a conflict between its utopian Socialist vision and its commitment to the immediate interests of the working classes. Indeed, some Socialists, fearing that their vision might be impaired, soon drew back from participation in the political process and sought other roads to Socialism. Their efforts paralleled those of the leaders of the Independent Labour party to accommodate their Socialist principles to existing political possibilities.

The term "consciousness" presents a problem of definition. Marx usually employed the term to emphasize the way in which men's ideas were shaped by their social setting.[3] His insights inspired later "sociologists of knowledge" to seek the connections between the

[3] See John Plamenatz, *Ideology* (London, 1970), pp. 23–27, 46–71. Also see Raymond Williams, *Culture and Society, 1780–1950,* Anchor Edition (New York, 1960), pp. 283–303. This book deals with several themes examined in the present study; Williams' use of the term "culture" corresponds at many points with my use of the term "consciousness."

thought of individuals or classes and their positions in the productive process or the social structure.[4] No study of a Socialist movement can ignore the influence of objective social or economic factors. But much that is crucial in explaining Socialist development—its relationship to inherited patterns of thought and feeling, the quality of enthusiasm or self-sacrifice it evoked, and the role of individuals— requires a sharper focus on the phenomenon of consciousness itself. Here the term is used to set off problems of theory and to include as well attitudes, sentiments, beliefs, purposes, and symbols, which were frequently only half formulated. So employed, the term "consciousness" lacks precision. Sometimes it applies to efforts to alter a few basic beliefs or values; at other times it relates to the hope for a comprehensive reconstruction of man's mental life. The term provides, however, a central orientation for the study.

There remains a problem of method. How does the historian describe the process through which new ideas become attached to deeply ingrained attitudes and feelings? I have relied largely on the technique of case studies. In my account of the critical stages in the growth of the Socialist movement I have presented biographical studies, or perhaps more accurately, intellectual portraits of those individuals who exemplified most clearly the shifts in emphasis or meaning. Their responses to the task of relating Socialist ideas to British life fall into patterns that enable one to trace with reasonable accuracy both the process of differentiating several forms of the Socialist consciousness and the main course of the movement. I have selected not only the most prominent figures in the various sections of the movement but a number of the men and women who were most active at the local levels of propaganda dissemination and organizational work. Often their development was idiosyncratic. Indeed, the lives of those Socialists who did not follow the main ideological and strategic paths of the movement, who attempted to steer it in new directions, or who held tenaciously to positions that most of their fellow Socialists were abandoning have a special importance in this inquiry. Their struggles,

---

[4] For a survey of this development see Peter L. Berger and Thomas Luckmann, *The Social Construction of Reality* (New York, 1967), pp. 1–18.

their defeats, and their isolation serve to delineate more sharply the dilemmas of the movement and the ways in which they were resolved.

Compared to its counterparts on the continent, the British movement was small. It never developed a genuine mass basis, and it failed, except insofar as it allied itself with non-Socialists, to become a significant political force. But the British movement represents an illuminating variant within the broader world of European Socialism. It demonstrated, even before the movements in Germany, France, Italy, and Russia, the instability as well as some of the diverse possibilities of the Marxist synthesis of ideas.

PART I
THE BRITISH SOURCES: QUEST FOR A NEW CONSCIOUSNESS IN NINETEENTH-CENTURY BRITAIN

1
Anglican and Nonconformist Visions of a Christian Commonwealth

An inquiry into the native sources of British Socialism leads back to the efforts of Christian thinkers, when faced with rapid and disruptive social change, to re-establish social life in sacred truths. Christian thinkers had responded ambivalently to the problem; some hoped to arrest or even reverse the changes under way, others set out to sanctify them. They helped to establish ambivalent patterns of response to social change which persisted in Victorian culture. Through their preoccupation with altering men's minds and providing a new basis for the traditional ideal of a "commonwealth," the Christian thinkers provided a model for those nineteenth-century intellectuals who had broken with orthodox religion and were seeking new foundations for society. The two other currents of thought which shaped the outlook of the Socialists—the social romanticism of Thomas Carlyle and John Ruskin, and the utilitarianism of John Stuart Mill, the Owenites, and the Secularists—tended to assume that the good society presupposed a common consciousness. A survey of the Christian efforts to define a new commonwealth, together with some attention to the internal changes which that approach underwent in the course of the century, provides a necessary background for understanding the struggles of the Socialists.

The great economic and social transformations under way in Britain during the late eighteenth and the early nineteenth centuries presented a serious challenge to the established church. Previously the church had "exercised the main part of her influence as an institution entwined in the structure of social life, acting less as an intellectual force than through her appeal to corporate feeling and

3

the associations which accumulate round an established usage." [1] For the lower classes gathering in the new urban and industrial centers, however, this older background of social custom and enforced conformity had disappeared. "They come," a Victorian investigator would write, "it may be from pious households, and for a time they persevere in their former good habits, but with no place in church, no pastor to recognize them, and exposed to all the evils of town life, all this soon passes away." [2]

Not until the period of reform between 1828 and 1832, when British political institutions began to accommodate many of the demands of the commercial and manufacturing classes, did the church respond to the current social changes. The reforms, most notably the repeal of the laws barring Catholics and religious dissenters from full legal access to public life, severely damaged the church's claim to spiritual supremacy. Anglican leaders reacted to the challenge by rationalizing endowment funds and starting a new building program.[3] These measures and renewed vitality at the parish level enabled the church to recover something of its former relevance and ensured its continued, if diminished, influence in national life.

Meanwhile Anglican thinkers had taken up the task of justifying anew the position of the church. They drew much inspiration from the later writings of Samuel Taylor Coleridge, who had, most notably in his *Aids to Reflection* (1825) and *On the Constitution of the Church and State* (1830), provided a fresh defense of the established form of religious life. Coleridge's strong sense of the corporate identity of the church and of its role as a "befriending opposite" to the state registered deeply on Anglican thought. But the subsequent development of British religious sensibilities may be

[1] A. E. Dobbs, *Education and Social Movements,* 1700–1850 (London, 1919), p. 17.

[2] George Huntington, *The Problem of the Churches in Our Large Towns* (London, 1871), p. 37.

[3] See Ursula Henriques, *Religious Toleration in England, 1787–1833* (Toronto, 1961); and Olive Brose, *Church and Parliament: The Reshaping of the Church of England 1828–1860* (Stanford, 1959).

seen most clearly in the light of his view of man's consciousness.

Coleridge had attempted in the *Aids to Reflection* to go beyond what he regarded as the specious clarity of the religious rationalists on the one hand and the obscurantist tendencies of the evangelicals on the other. Against the rationalists who, following John Locke, attempted to confine religion within the bounds of reason and common sense, Coleridge insisted that consciousness rested on deep and mysterious foundations: "The lower depths that the light of our consciousness can visit even with a doubtful glimmering, is still an unknown distance from the ground and so must it be with all truths and modes of being that can neither be counted, colored or delineated." [4] In opposition to the evangelicals, however, who stressed the miraculous workings of God's grace in the conversion experience, Coleridge viewed religious feelings as an integral part of man's nature. If deep reflection disclosed man's dependence on powers beyond his conscious self, it also revealed his capacity to act freely according to his own moral and rational resources. In conscience, which Coleridge saw as the union of will and reason, he found the assurance that man's nature could not be reduced to the laws of the physical or animal world. Conscience was the sovereign element in consciousness; it was also a first principle or intuition.

Coleridge's view of consciousness owed something to the Cambridge Platonists of the seventeenth century, but he turned mainly to the work of Immanuel Kant for philosophical support. He accepted Kant's division of reality into a phenomenal world of objects, explicable through natural understanding, and a noumenal realm of moral and spiritual truths, accessible only to "reason," or man's higher intuitive faculties. Where Kant, however, had viewed such ideas as God, freedom, and conscience as the "regulative" or practical necessities of man's moral life, not subject to demonstration or metaphysical statement, Coleridge gave these intuitions a constitutive or ontological status. "It was just in the realm of our common moral and religious experience," as one of his

[4] *The Complete Works of Samuel Taylor Coleridge,* ed. W. G. T. Shedd (London, 1860–1868), I: *Aids to Reflection,* p. 154.

commentators expressed it, "that we come into living contact with the supersensible realities of the spiritual world." [5]

The difference was crucial. While Kant, at least in the *Critique of Practical Reason,* sought to defend the autonomy of conscience and the sufficiency of man's moral and rational nature, Coleridge retained the traditional Christian emphasis on human weakness and dependence. Indeed, his sense of sin was almost Calvinistic. "The doctrine of Original Sin," he wrote, "gives all the other impulses of religion a common basis, a consciousness of dependence, an intelligibility of relationship, and a total harmony, which supersedes extrinsic proof." Man's conscience was not self-sustaining. Unless it was "taken up and transformed into the doctrines and mysteries of religion," it would fall into the "quicksand of prudential calculus." [6]

A revitalized religious consciousness was, for Coleridge, the primary remedy for the social ills of the age. Although he was a penetrating social critic, reasonably well-informed on economic questions and convinced of the need for state intervention to correct the evils of factory life, Coleridge did not grasp the fundamental nature of the institutional changes under way in British life. He had little sympathy for the economic and social values of the middle classes, even less for their political aspirations. The extension of the franchise, he feared, would destroy "the freedom of parliament" and fling it "open to the passions and follies of the people." [7] Indeed, Coleridge responded to the broad social challenge of his time by retreating to an idealized version of the old order. This restorative strategy, which envisioned the rebuilding of a religious community informed by common values and meanings, characterized Anglican social thought throughout the century.

Coleridge's successors elaborated particular aspects of his vision at the expense of others. The Tractarians, inspired in part by his defense of the church as an autonomous community, concentrated on renewing its liturgical, creedal, and ecclesiastical forms and the devotional life they expressed. In so doing they dissociated them-

[5] Vernon Storr, *The Development of English Theology in the Nineteenth Century* (London, 1913), p. 325.

[6] *Aids to Reflection, Complete Works,* I, 291– 293.

[7] *Table Talk, Complete Works,* VI, 383.

selves even more sharply from "the whole momentum of the contemporary world." [8] Thomas Arnold urged a different course. He attempted to enlarge Coleridge's ideal of the church to accommodate the actual movement of British society. His *Principles of Church Reform* (1833) urged changes to complement the recent political reforms. By lowering the creedal and ecclesiastical barriers, Arnold believed that the established church could assimilate the mass of religious dissenters and regain its spiritual supremacy.

Arnold's Christianity favored such a compromise because of its intensely moral emphasis. Convinced that "right doing" rather than "right thinking" was the basis of Christian fellowship, Arnold took little interest in the theological questions which occupied Coleridge. Indeed, he distrusted theology. The attempt to define religious truth with precision threatened to "rob it" of its living power. "The same truth," he wrote, "embodied in prayer, or confession, or even in catechism became more Christian just in proportion as it became less theological." Arnold thus followed what Coleridge regarded as the lower road of the practical understanding, avoiding the deeper mysteries of man's nature or leaving them to the formulae of evangelicalism, and he concentrated on the ethical task. "What is the good of a national church," he wrote, "if it be not to Christianize the nation and introduce the principles of Christianity into man's social and civic relations?" [9]

Arnold was friendlier toward the outlook and the aspirations of the middle classes than Coleridge, and he supported the Reform Bill. But he was hostile to proposals for radical social or economic change; even the efforts of the workers to organize trade-unions or benefit societies seemed dangerous to him.[10] To overcome social disaffection he urged education reform and a more systematic dissemination of moral and religious principles, which he believed, would provide the basis for a more humane society.

[8] W. G. Peck, *The Social Implications of the Oxford Movement* (New York, 1933), p. 41.

[9] A. P. Stanley, *The Life and Correspondence of Thomas Arnold* (New York, 1898), I, 312, 247.

[10] See T. W. Bamford, *Thomas Arnold* (London, 1960), p. 150.

Arnold also believed a renovated consciousness offered the chief corrective to the problems of the age. But a marked shift in religious judgment had occurred. In placing "a certain moral state" at the center of consciousness, Arnold exemplified and encouraged a trend in British religion which later became increasingly pronounced. Insofar as Arnold elevated man's moral sentiments to the supreme place in religious experience, he contributed to the tendency which Coleridge feared most—for men to "substitute shapeless feelings, sentiments, and impulses," developed in connection with former Christian virtues, for the "law and light of the church." [11] Yet Arnold's attempt to secure social harmony through common moral feelings sprang from recognition that the idea of a church commonwealth on any other terms was doomed. His moralistic approach to social unity would be extended in the later work of the "broad church-men" as well as in the thought of men who moved outside the estab-lished church, most notably Matthew Arnold and John Seeley.[12]

Frederick Denison Maurice, in contrast, renewed Coleridge's in-quiry into the nature of the religious consciousness and the "deep underground principles of society." He saw a profound crisis of belief approaching throughout Europe; men were questioning all systems of thought, secular as well as religious, and indeed, all social and political institutions. Western man had plunged back into the "ocean of being," and faced the fundamental alternative— "there is nothing or there is God." The great need of the age was not a liturgical revival or a new zeal in applying Christian moral principles, but "theological and metaphysical grubbing." Men must recover "a deep ground and source of faith—deeper than all the acts which proceed from it." [13]

---

[11] Coleridge, *Aids to Reflection, Complete Works,* I, 137.

[12] For the later development of this point of view, see R. T. Shannon, "John Robert Seeley and the Idea of a National Church," in *Ideas and Institutions of Victorian Britain,* ed. Robert Robson (New York, 1967), pp. 236–257.

[13] F. D. Maurice, *Modern Philosophy: A Treatise of Moral and Metaphysical Philosophy* (London, 1862), pp. 666, 657; Frederick Maurice, *The Life of Frederick Denison Maurice* (London, 1884), I, 246. Recent studies of Maurice include Alec Vidler, *Witness to the Truth: F. D. Maurice's Message for Today* (New York, 1948); and A. M. Ramsay, *F. D. Maurice and the Conflicts of*

In the Christian doctrine of the incarnation Maurice saw the decisive disclosure of the relationship of God to man and the assurance that God's love was an immediate resource open to all men. His love-centered theology replaced the older image of God as lawgiver and judge, stressed in Calvinism and much of evangelicalism, with the view of God the father giving the power of love to man through Christ. Maurice retained a strong conviction of man's sinfulness but also an overwhelming sense of God's grace— of a mysterious activity which overcame man's "lovelessness" and "powerlessness." This led him to reject the sharp division found in so much of conventional religious life between the sacred and the secular or the natural and the supernatural; and he invited the wrath of the orthodox by denying the doctrine of everlasting punishment. His theology also opened up a greatly enlarged prospect for God's redemptive work in society.

Maurice is best remembered for his association with the Christian Socialist movement at midcentury. In terms of his central theological mission, however, his Christian Socialist activity was probably ill-conceived. In attempting to demonstrate the social relevance of his theology he became involved in controversies which indicated both the difficulty of applying his theological ideas directly to society and his own captivity to older social institutions and values. The development of the Christian Socialist movement was marked by deepening disagreement between Maurice and the movement's founder, J. M. Ludlow. Ludlow, influenced by the struggles of the French working classes in 1848, carried forward the strong moralism of Arnold and the hope of applying Christian principles directly to social relations. He hoped to lead the church in a "holy warfare," in which each parish would "become a center of radiating life," gradually eliminating all pauperism and wretchedness and transforming England into "truly one Commonwealth and one Church." The Christian Socialists would "vindicate for Christianity its true authority over the realm of industry and trade" and dem-

Modern Theology (Cambridge, 1951). Also see Olive Brose, "Maurice and the Victorian Crisis of Belief," *Victorian Studies,* III (March 1960), 226-248.

onstrate the "true character" of Socialism "as the great Christian revolution of the nineteenth century." [14]

Ludlow's attempt to build a reform organization and develop practical experiments in working-class economic association struck at the heart of Maurice's convictions. They seemed to him to substitute human initiative, with its inescapable selfishness, for God's work. God's regenerative love, accessible to each individual whatever his condition, was pre-empted. The Christian Socialist should, according to Maurice, rather live to bear witness to a "Divine Order," a community of love which existed beneath all social forms. "Association" was not a principle to be implemented by party or program, but a divine fact or potentiality to be proclaimed. The kingdom of God should not be used as a measuring rod to test existing institutions; it was rather an underlying pattern of human relationships to be acknowledged. To seek this order through human "systems" or "notions" was to deny it, for such efforts divided men and disrupted society. Maurice had no sympathy for Ludlow's hope of destroying or radically altering existing social and political arrangements, and he feared that democracy would lead to military despotism or an "accursed sacerdotal rule." Not only was he convinced on religious grounds that institutional reforms were superficial, but he believed, like Edmund Burke and Coleridge before him, that the British social and political system was a divinely directed growth. "I must protest," he wrote, against "an attempt to create a new constitution of society when what we want is that the old constitution should exhibit its true function and energies" and carry out the "Divine Purpose." [15] The difference between the two leaders was irreconcilable and, together with the failure of the practical experiments in cooperative production, brought an end to the movement.

Maurice's political conservatism impaired his social message and

---

[14] See Torben Christensen, *Origin and History of Christian Socialism 1848–54* (Aarhus, Denmark, 1962), pp. 129, 154. See also N. C. Masterman, *John Malcolm Ludlow* (Cambridge, 1963), pp. 5–32, and P. R. Allen, "F. D. Maurice and J. M. Ludlow: A Reassessment of the Leaders of Christian Socialism," *Victorian Studies,* XI (June 1968), 461–482.

[15] Maurice, *Life,* II, 129, 42.

limited the openness to historical change which his theology seemed to demand. The disagreement with Ludlow also suggested his sharp separation from the developing sensibilities of his age. Maurice was one of the few Victorians to inquire deeply into the metaphysical or ontological underpinnings of conventional forms of thought. But his attempt to root man's consciousness in a new apprehension of divine power, to lead a theological reformation, gained slight response. His publicized debate with Dean Henry Mansel in 1859 on "The Limits of Religious Knowledge" saw Maurice defending a view or experience of God's immediacy which found little support among his fellow clergymen. The "good people," he conceded, found him unintelligible. In the years ahead he grew increasingly pessimistic and lamented the role of the educated classes in emptying "the words counted most sacred" of their old meanings and "urging on a revolution more terrible than anything yet witnessed." He anticipated "a terrible breakdown of notions, opinions, even of our most precious beliefs, an overthrow of what we call our religion—a convulsion greater than that of the seventeenth century—on our way to reformation and unity." [16]

A later generation of Anglican and Nonconformist thinkers found much to inspire them in the work of Maurice. They were attracted, however, not by his theological "digging," but by the ethical and social implications of his thought, and they usually fortified these implications with philosophical systems, Kantian or Hegelian, which he would have deplored, or with a High Church tradition which he had rejected.

By mid-century, however, the Anglican vision of a restored church commonwealth, rising out of a new religious or moral consciousness, had lost most of its earlier plausibility. During the second half of the century Anglicans were increasingly on the defensive. As their vision receded, the ideal of a national community informed by Christian beliefs and values found new spokesmen among the Non-

[16] See R. V. Sampson, "The Limits of Religious Thought: The Theological Controversy in 1859," in *Entering an Age of Crisis,* ed. Philip Appleman, William A. Madden, and Michael Wolff (Bloomington, Ind. 1959); Maurice, *Modern Philosophy,* p. 674.

conformists. The Nonconformist version of the commonwealth ideal more than any other influence nourished popular Socialism at the end of the century.

The major Nonconformist denominations, the Independents or Congregationalists, the Baptists, and the Methodists, had grown rapidly during the first half of the century. In 1851, when a religious census was taken, the Nonconformists, now concentrated in the middle classes, nearly equaled the adherents of the established church. Moreover, the reform legislation passed between 1828 and 1832 had opened the way for a much larger role by Nonconformists in public affairs. During the mid-Victorian decades they ceased to be "a separate and peculiar people" and played increasingly important parts in political and cultural life.[17]

The growth of a new Nonconformist vision of a Christian nation owed most to the work of Edward Miall. In 1839, Miall resigned his Congregational pastorate in Leicester in order to devote himself to the destruction of the "unholy alliance" of church and state, convinced that it was "the prolific parent of bigotry, cruelty, rapacity and hypocrisy—a terrible scourge to the nation—a tremendous obstacle to the progress of divine truth." [18] Miall was a new and outspoken champion of the conviction of earlier religious dissenters that the Christian life could flourish only when completely free from the interference of secular authority.

Miall's campaign to disestablish the Anglican church soon became entangled with the economic interests and political aspirations of the middle classes. The struggle to repeal the Corn Laws, in particular, indicated the close connection between Miall's religious voluntarism and the hostility of middle-class liberals to the older economic and political restraints.[19] The Liberal party in the fifties

---

[17] For a discussion of the census see K. S. Inglis, "Patterns of Worship in 1851," *Journal of Ecclesiastical History,* XI (1960), 74–86; see also Augustine Birrell, *Things Past Redress* (London, 1937), p. 38.

[18] Arthur Miall, *Life of Edward Miall* (London, 1884), p. 50; also see A. Temple Patterson, *Radical Leicester* (Leicester, 1954), pp. 247–259.

[19] See Norman McCord, *The Anti Corn Law League* (London, 1958), pp. 102–107; and Asa Briggs, "John Bright and the Creed of Reform," in his

and the sixties owned much to this developing blend of religious and economic impulses. When the Liberals triumphed in the parliamentary elections of 1867, the Nonconformists were, according to one observer, the "largest and most active, and most principled section" of the party's supporters. Miall's "Liberation Society" was still only a small element in that support, but Miall could look back over the years and discern a "providential direction" throughout the "civilized world toward a separation of the temporal and the spiritual." [20] Confident that his religious mission was nearing victory through the agency of the Liberal party, Miall and other Congregational leaders began to envision a larger conquest and contemplate a nation transformed by the values and methods of their own religious tradition. The vision found its most ardent and influential spokesman in J. Baldwin Brown.

Brown was, according to one of his followers, the "only Independent [Congregationalist] of his generation who might properly be described as a Maurician. . . . It is mainly through him that Maurice has acted upon us." But while Brown followed Maurice in viewing the incarnation as the central doctrine in the Christian faith and in affirming the sacredness of "our whole life in its interests and activities," his religious outlook corresponded more closely to that of Ludlow or Arnold. He was little concerned with theological or ontological questions; his bent was strenuously ethical and social. Confident, like Miall, that the campaign of the religious voluntarists was nearing final victory, Brown argued that it was time for the established church to surrender its traditional role in "the work of realizing the Christian national life." The Christian bodies had "grown strong enough to bear voluntarily what the State had been bearing wearily and painfully for ages." Brown also called on the Nonconformist bodies to recognize their "vital unities," widen the bounds of "Christian fellowship," and develop an "ever widening

---

Victorian People (Chicago, 1954).

[20] Spectator, Nov. 28, 1868; Miall, Edward Miall, p. 303. Also see J. Guinness Rogers, "Political Dissent," Fortnightly Review, XXII (Dec. 1877); John Vincent, The Formation of the British Liberal Party (New York, 1966), pp. 65–76.

conception of the nature and range of the Kingdom of the Lord." [21]

We too believe in the Christian Commonwealth. We too believe that the Kingdom of the Lord Jesus is to be sought not in the private domain of particular Christians, but in the social, political, and moral order of a Christian people. . . . The only adequate conception of a Christian state is that of a nation whose whole life is saturated with Christian ideas and influences; and which gives free play to its religious beliefs and impulses, that, like the higher intellectual life of the people, they may express themselves as they see fit.[22]

Miall, Brown, and other Nonconformist leaders were confident that a Christian society was growing up spontaneously out of man's "higher motives of action," rendering an established church unnecessary. But their hopes suffered a sharp setback with the passage of the Education Act of 1870, for this Liberal bill confirmed the dominant position of the established church in the new elementary education system. The Nonconformist political leaders attempted, without success, to mobilize their rank and file and force the Liberals to amend the act. But most Nonconformists, their grievances over church rates, burials, and entrance to the universities now removed, did not let appeals on behalf of the education and disestablishment causes override their other ties to the Liberal party. Indeed, those ties became stronger in the years ahead while the religious principles which had initially propelled Nonconformists into politics grew weaker. Nonconformists were, as one of their historians put it, tacitly abandoning a "distinct and higher ground of their own" and joining the Liberals on the ground of social and moral principle.[23]

21 P. T. Forsyth, *Baldwin Brown: A Tribute, a Reminiscense, and a Study* (London, 1884), p. 4; J. Baldwin Brown, *First Principles of Ecclesiastical Truth: Essays on the Church and Society* (London, 1871), p. 190; J. Baldwin Brown, "The English Church and Dissenters," *Contemporary Review*, XVI (Jan. 1871), 298–320; "The Religious Life and Christian Society," in *Ecclesia*, ed. H. R. Reynolds (London, 1870), pp. 133–191; J. Baldwin Brown, "Our Theology in Relation to the Intellectual Currents of our Time" (Chairman's Address, Congregation Union, 1878), *Congregational Yearbook* (London, 1878), p. 40.

22 Brown, "English Church and Dissenters," p. 306.

23 H. J. Hanham, *Elections and Party Management* (London, 1959), p. 119; Henry Clark, *History of Nonconformity* (London, 1913), II, 403.

They could respond enthusiastically to William Gladstone's insistence that "all important political questions" involved "clear cut moral decisions." To one clergyman the Nonconformist spirit seemed the "very essence of Liberalism," [24] and a leading Nonconformist newspaper, *The Nonconformist and Independent,* identified the Liberal party as the "party of Christ":

It is the party of moral principles as against that of selfish and corrupt interests, the party of peace as against that of violence, the party of popular improvement and reform as against that of resistance to progress, the party of justice as against that of despotic force or social disorder. [It is] a party whose object it is to rule man's action by moral principles in legislation and government.[25]

At the local political level during the seventies and eighties it was the Nonconformists who "nearly everywhere made up the rank and file of the caucus," the new organization by means of which Joseph Chamberlain was wresting control of the Liberal party from its older Whig leadership.[26]

The individualistic, libertarian, and philanthropic values stressed by the Liberals appealed strongly to the politically active Nonconformists. These values served both their religious aspirations and their economic and social interests. During the eighties, however, a series of new problems, stemming from economic recession, relations with Ireland, and challenges in international affairs, raised doubts as to the continuing relevance of the old liberal attitudes to the issues of the day. Political Nonconformists, who were less and less inclined to distinguish their religious concerns from their social or political faith, were little prepared for the sharp disagreements which now developed within the Liberal party. Indeed, those disagreements soon entered the denominational assemblies.

The great bulk of its Nonconformist supporters, which included

---

[24] Philip Magnus, *Gladstone: A Biography* (London, 1954), p. 175; Rogers, "Political Dissent."

[25] Quoted by John Glasier, "Nonconformity and Liberalism, 1868–1885," Ph.D. dissertation, Harvard University, 1949, p. 9.

[26] M. Ostrogorski, *Democracy and the Organization of Political Parties* (New York, 1922), I, 196.

by the eighties the majority of the Methodists as well as most of the Baptists and the Congregationalists, remained faithful to the Liberal party. But a number, like Robert Dale, the Birmingham Congregationalist who had joined his friend Chamberlain in breaking with Gladstone over the Irish issue, were now forced to re-examine the relationship of Nonconformist religion to political life. Having been denounced at a meeting of the Congregational Union as one "chained to the Tory chariot," Dale concluded that the denomination was dividing "into two hostile camps" on a purely political issue. In the years immediately following he opposed the efforts of prominent Nonconformists, who were seeking, through the creation of "Free Church Councils," to concert Nonconformist opinion on social and political issues. They had reached, according to Dale, a "parting of the ways on the great question of how the Christian church should attempt to regenerate the social life of the nation," and he worried lest Nonconformists become involved in a "premature attempt to apply to the political order the laws of a diviner kingdom" through "direct political action." [27]

Most Nonconformist leaders disagreed. As the Methodist Hugh Price Hughes expressed it, they were "rising above sectarian rivalries" and all narrow conceptions of their "duty" and were "uniting to reconstruct human society on a Christian basis." Indeed, during the closing decades of the century Nonconformists, like their Anglican counterparts, were engaged in a variety of experiments designed to overcome the religious estrangement of the lower classes and to cope as well with the social breakdown which had attended economic and demographic changes. To one Nonconformist writer, Richard Heath, it even seemed as though organized religion had "gone so far in its effort to get in touch with the British people as to become a mere chameleon, reflecting the colour and hue of the social and political atmosphere." [28] Heath exaggerated, but he pointed to the

[27] A. W. W. Dale, *Life of R. W. Dale* (London, 1899), pp. 583–588, 649, 670. Also see P. T. Forsyth, "Dr. Dale," *London Quarterly Review* New Series, I (April, 1899), 214–216.

[28] *Methodist Times*, March 9, 1893; Richard Heath, *The Captive City of God* (London, 1905), p. 208. For a critical analysis of Hughes's political role see J. H. S. Kent, "Hugh Price Hughes and the Nonconformist Conscience,"

virtual disappearance for many Nonconformist leaders of the former tension between the claims of religious doctrine and the main movement of British cultural and political life.

The loss of the older sense of separatism and the new hope that Nonconformists were staking out the course of the nation's future development were most evident among the Congregationalists.[29] Firmly settled in the more prosperous and politically active sections of the middle classes, the Congregationalists also possessed a clergy that was particularly sensitive to secular thought and culture. They were also less restrained by central authority than their Baptist or Methodist counterparts. In the alteration of religious sensibilities taking place within Congregationalism one can discover a major source of inspiration for popular Socialism. Men and women of Congregationalist background would play key roles in developing an idiom which made the new social creed congenial to important sections of the working classes.

Congregational liturgy, sermons, and theology all seemed to dilute the aspects of religious experience that fostered a strong sense of an objective power or authority. The Holy Communion, for example, had long since ceased to evoke, as it had for earlier Congregationalists, a sense of a divine presence. It had become purely symbolic; it was essentially a "commemorative rite," a "picture lesson of Christ's sacrifice." This didactic bent and the appeal to the moral feelings were countered to some extent during the seventies and eighties by "aesthetic modifications" in Congregational forms of worship. But the aesthetic turn also tended to diminish further the objective content of worship. It reflected, one contemporary writer concluded, religious uncertainty and a desire to "embody the higher

---

Essays in Modern English Church History, ed. G. V. Bennett and J. D. Walsh (London, 1966). The responses of organized religion to social problems are discussed in K. S. Inglis, *Churches and the Working Classes in Victorian England* (London, 1963); Peter d'A Jones, *The Christian Socialist Revival, 1877–1914* (Princeton, 1968); and Stephen Mayor, *The Churches and the Labour Movement* (London, 1967).

[29] The development of Congregationalism is examined in J. W. Grant, *Free Churchmanship in England, 1870–1940* (London, 1955).

tendencies of religious feeling without . . . any very distinct intellectual conclusions." [30]

A similar movement away from traditional religious authority was evident in the development of Congregational preaching. In the early period of religious dissent the minister had expounded the "word of God" as found in the Scripture. He was a medium through whom God's truth reached the congregation; the act of preaching was charged with numinous overtones or charismatic power. Under the impact of evangelicalism the style of chapel preaching had become more impassioned and popular; it also became more dependent on the personal style of the preacher. During the second half of the nineteenth century as the pulpits of the Congregationalists, like those of the other Nonconformist denominations, gained their greatest influence on national life, their leading preachers tended to seek fresh inspiration in secular culture or in matters of social and political concern. As Brown explained, the end of Nonconformist "insularity" and the "increased circulation of ideas" meant that the minister could hold his own only through the "force of superior character and culture" or by giving greater attention to social problems.[31] He might, like George Dawson, the Birmingham Baptist turned Unitarian, become an "effective retailer of the ideas of Carlyle and Ruskin" or of other secular prophets. One Congregational minister during the eighties even began preaching the "gospel of Kropotkin." [32] While these tendencies indicated an effort to make their religious message more relevant to the social problems of the day, they also reflected a deepening loss of confidence by Congregationalists in their own doctrinal or theological tradition.

Theological developments provided the clearest evidence of the growing crisis of religious authority within Congregationalism. By

[30] Dale, *Life of Dale,* pp. 358–359; "Aesthetic Modifications of Dissent," *Spectator,* May 22, 1875; "The Increasing Love of Religious Symbol," *ibid.,* June 29, 1889.

[31] "Is the Pulpit Losing Its Power," *Nineteenth Century,* I (March 1877), 97–112.

[32] See the *Spectator,* Dec. 2, 1877: R. W. Dale, "George Dawson, Politician, Lecturer, Preacher," *Nineteenth Century,* Aug, 1877, pp. 44–61; *British Weekly,* Nov. 19, 1886.

the middle of the century the Calvinist system, on which Congregationalists had traditionally relied, was disintegrating. Many of the denomination's clergymen had retreated to a "moderate Calvinism" in which the harsh doctrines of predestination and election had been softened, partly under the influence of evangelicalism, to permit a larger place for personal decision. But "moderate Calvinism," as Dale observed, was "Calvinism in decay." It had "neither the logic of the older theory to satisfy the understanding, nor its tremendous solemnity and awfulness to command the fear and wonder of the heart." [33] The "broken tradition" seemed to Dale to encourage new variety and freedom. But for many of the denomination's younger clergymen at the end of the century it also meant a widespread revolt against theology.

Meanwhile, the reliability of the Bible, so important in the Protestant tradition, had been undermined by Darwinian biology and the new historical criticism coming from Germany. While some Nonconformists retreated to the shelter of an inerrant Scripture, most Congregational leaders set out to reconcile their faith with the new disclosures of science and scholarship.[34] In the words of A. M. Fairbairn, the denomination's most influential thinker during the final third of the century, a "timely removal of the more antiquated and obnoxious portions" of their creed was necessary:

It is an evil thing for any church to fall behind the intellect of a country, or to float out of sympathy with it in its most earnest and religious endeavor to discover whatever of God's true nature, or Man, which Scripture may reveal. It is a thing no less evil for any church to swear by the standards of the past when its faith has been permeated and almost transformed by the thought of the present. . . . And the question for the Churches to consider is whether they are to estrange and drive into unwilling antagonism men who are Christian at heart but are too conscientious to subscribe to a burdensome and oppressive creed.[35]

[33] R. W. Dale, *A History of English Congregationalism*, ed. A. W. W. Dale (London, 1907), p. 538.

[34] See especially Willis B. Glover, *Evangelical Nonconformity and Higher Criticism in the Nineteenth Century* (London, 1954).

[35] Quoted by W. B. Selbie, *The Life of Andrew Fairbairn* (London, 1914), p. 68.

Fairbairn, like a growing number of Anglicans, drew on G. W. F. Hegel to provide new theological support for Christian doctrines. Other Congregationalists borrowed from Maurice and the Anglican broad church tradition or turned to the ethically centered theology of Albrecht Ritschl, the most influential German religious thinker during this period.

But whatever the source, this theological reorientation saw the evangelical stress on man's sin and his radical dependence on God giving way to a belief in divine immanence and God's redemptive activity in history. The doctrine of the atonement yielded centrality to the doctrine of the incarnation; the suffering Christ of the cross was increasingly displaced by the Jesus of love and moral perfection as the primary object of the religious feelings. By the 1890s one of the denomination's leading thinkers, P. T. Forsyth, observed that a "religious man" meant "a man of a particular way of feeling rather than a man with a special relation to reality." [36]

What was characteristic of the Congregationalists was increasingly true of the late Victorian religious climate generally. Moral feeling rather than belief in doctrines was more and more seen as the measure of one's religious faith. Indeed, for Mrs. Humphry Ward, author of the most popular religious novel of the period, the "dissociation of moral judgment from a specific religious formula" was the "crucial, epoch making fact of the day." To some spokesmen for organized religion, like Mandell Creighton, Bishop of London, it seemed clear that men were living on a "moral sense" or "Christian conscience without the faith which formed it" and gradually substituting for Christianity the notion that the "spiritual man is merely the 'natural man' at his best." [37] There was inescapable opposition between the traditional Christian stress on sin, grace, and redemption and an outlook in which the moral feelings had been elevated to the supreme place.[38] Examined in the light of these feelings the Christian doctrine of the atonement, for example, appeared

[36] Forsyth, "Dr. Dale," p. 196. Also see Henry Clark, *Liberal Orthodoxy* (London, 1911), pp. 271–273.

[37] Mrs. Humphry Ward, *Robert Elsmere* (London, 1888), II, 378; Louise Creighton, *Life and Letters of Mandell Creighton* (London, 1913), II, 190, 247.

[38] For a discussion of the tension between ethics and religion, see Gerhard Ebeling, "Theology and the Evidentness of the Ethical," in Rudolf Bultman

barbaric. Many Victorian unbelievers had been estranged from Christianity, not on intellectual grounds, but because its doctrines violated their consciences; it seemed "immoral in its cardinal tenets." During the closing decades of the century the churches were increasingly judged and condemned, often most passionately by their own clergymen, mainly in terms of their failure to implement the moral ideals which were becoming for many the essence of Christianity. Fairbairn, who, as principal of the major Congregational college in Yorkshire, influenced many younger clergymen in the northern industrial counties, expressed this increasingly moralistic outlook in a series of lectures to the working classes of Bradford in 1883. He argued "that the whole past life of the Christian religion had been a series of efforts to embody itself in a higher social and economic order." Christianity, he insisted, possessed the power to "create a perfect state through perfect men. . . . The Christian religion supplies us for all civil and social questions with constructive and regulative principles of the noblest kind. In their light politics becomes the science of working out a perfect order in which every man shall achieve virtue and attain happiness, that is, realize the ideal of humanity latent within him." [39] During the closing decades of the century the promise of a Christianized society, held out by Fairbairn and other Nonconformist leaders, was heard in countless chapels and particularly in the "Brotherhood" and "Pleasant Sunday Afternoon" meetings—those extensions of chapel life designed to retain contact with an increasingly alienated working class. Through these and other channels the altered religious outlook merged with the new social and political aspirations which informed the Socialist movement.

---

et al., Translating Theology into the Modern Age (New York, 1965), pp. 96–129.

[39] Beatrice Webb, My Apprenticeship (London, 1926), p. 97; A. M. Fairbairn, Religion in History and Modern Life (New York, 1893), pp. vi, 252. Also see Noel Annan, "Strands of Unbelief," in Ideas and Beliefs of the Victorians (London, 1949); and Howard R. Murphey, "The Ethical Revolt against Christian Orthodoxy in Early Victorian England," American Historical Review, LX (July 1955), 800–817. For an example of a young Congregational minister from the Airedale Independent College who entered the Socialist movement, see J. W. Dixon, Pledged to the People: A Sketch of the Reverend Richard Westrope (London, 1896).

2

The Romantic Social Vision:
Carlyle and Ruskin

In the shift, so apparent by the end of the century, from a doctrinal to a moralistic orientation in religious life, the writings of Ruskin and Carlyle have special significance. Their lives record in particularly sensitive ways the alteration of consciousness and the reordering of values which attended that change. Moreover, by projecting their intense moral and aesthetic feelings into vivid pictures of transformed social relations they provided many Victorians with compelling new interpretations of the main problems of the age. They played crucial roles in the translation of the Christian ideals of community into its Socialist forms.

No one can read extensively in the autobiographies of the Socialist and labor leaders of the end of the century without being struck by the frequent references to the influence of Carlyle and Ruskin.[1] After their popularity among the upper classes had subsided, the writings of these two Victorian prophets retained their appeal for many young men and women in the lower classes, especially to those occupational groupings—shop assistants, commercial travelers, and clerks—which provided much of the cadre for the Socialist movement. Carlyle's *Past and Present* and Ruskin's *Unto This Last* often touched members of these sectors of society as revelations. They shattered existing notions about the social system, awakened new aspirations, and strengthened the will toward action.

[1] See "The Labour Party and the Books that Helped Make It," *Review of Reviews,* XXXIII (June 1906), 568–582, in which labor members of the House of Commons report on their early reading. Carlyle and Ruskin are mentioned most frequently, but Mill, Henry George, Charles Dickens, Giuseppe Mazzini, and Ralph Waldo Emerson are prominent.

To understand the distinctive features in the thought of these two men is to enter in some measure into the popular Socialist mentality of the early nineties.

In *Sartor Resartus,* Carlyle relates the story of his loss of orthodox religious faith and his "spiritual rebirth." Yet, he assures his readers that his moral convictions "remained in my heart . . . legible and sacred." [2] Carlyle's resolute moralism, derived from his Scottish Calvinist background and centering on work and duty, provided a sheet anchor as he set out, like his Puritan forebears, to gain a fresh and unmediated relationship with God. His unique position among the Victorian sages and his influence on the Socialists came largely from the exceptional force of his moral character. Yet his own development led into a social and political impasse which anticipated some of the dilemmas of the later movement.

As a young man Carlyle had turned to German writers for aid in his spiritual quest. For over a decade, between 1818 and 1830, he was occupied with the works of Kant, Goethe, Herder, Fichte, Schiller, Jacobi, and others. Carlyle approached their writings, not as a convert, but as one "innocently wandering among complex systems of thought . . . seeking here and there an echo of his own convictions." [3] German thought assured Carlyle that ultimate reality was spiritual and that man's conscience was a trustworthy point of contact with the divine, and it greatly enlarged his range of sympathies. In the work of Goethe and Schiller particularly he discovered a new ideal of human fulfillment which stressed man's capacity for aesthetic enjoyment and creativity. Schiller's aesthetic ideal challenged Carlyle's ascetic moral view that the good life would be found through the repression of man's natural desires. For some time Carlyle struggled with this opposition, but his Puritanism prevailed.[4] He remained distrustful of aesthetic satisfactions and the

---

[2] Thomas Carlyle, *"Sartor Resartus" and "On Heroes and Hero Worship,"* Everyman's Edition (London, 1908), p. 124.

[3] C. F. Harrold, *Carlyle and German Thought, 1819–1834* (London, 1934), pp. 18, 235.

[4] This conflict is analyzed by Hill Shine, *Carlyle's Fusion of Poetry, History and Religion by 1834* (Chapel Hill, N.C., 1938). Also see C. F. Harrold, "The Nature of Carlyle's Calvinism," *Studies in Philology,* XXXIII (1936), 475–486.

free play of the imagination unchecked by moral purpose. The "aesthetic tea," he concluded, was a "feast of chickenweed." [5] But the tension between a purely aesthetic appreciation of the world and his Puritan sense of moral purpose became a basic feature of his writing and entered strongly into later Socialism as well.

By 1830, at the age of thirty-five, Carlyle had redefined his calling, inspired by Fichte's image of the "hero" as a man of letters charged with the task of spiritual enlightenment. Carlyle now began to see, like the earlier romantics, the possibility of a "new religion" in literature. Contemporary literature possessed "fragments of a genuine Church homiletic, even a liturgy." The "artist or poet" was rising to the position of "prophet" and with "heaven made implements" conquering "Heavens for us." Literary journalists and newspaper editors were forming the "true church of England." Carlyle displayed in these early writings both a continuing religious sense of wonder and a feeling that his world was becoming "disembellished and prosaic." He set out, therefore, to bestow new religious value on the world around him. But soon he began to concentrate on the problem of recovering community which occupied so many of the leading minds of the 1830s. Carlyle's quest reflected in part his own strong sense of being a "limb torn off from the family of men" and his own yearning for human "fellowship." [6]

Carlyle was convinced that the efforts of Coleridge and his followers to nurture a new commonwealth through a revitalized established church was futile. But he shared their belief that religion was the "life essence of society." The decline of the religious attitudes of reverence and awe meant that society in the true sense was becoming "extinct." Only "gregarious feelings and old inherited habitudes . . . hold us from Dispersion and universal, national civil, domestic and personal war." Carlyle was not completely unsympathetic to the utilitarian celebration of economic progress and the efforts of political radicals to free the individual from older social restraints. Indeed, he conceded that the utilitarians and the

[5] Carlyle, *Sartor Resartus,* p. 96.

[6] *Ibid.,* pp. 190, 171, 52; Charles Eliot Norton, ed., *The Two Notebooks of Thomas Carlyle* (New York, 1898), p. 65.

radicals were carrying out a necessary task in exposing conventions which had ceased to correspond to the real needs of men. But this work was purely negative, a kind of "dog madness" of destruction. Their logic-chopping, their reliance on external and mechanical contrivances, and their view of the soul as a "kind of stomach" disqualified utilitarians for the vital work of "retexturing the spiritual tissues." [7] Carlyle dedicated himself, therefore, to the task of nurturing a new religious consciousness in opposition to the secular and pluralistic tendencies of the age.

Carlyle recognized that man's inner life was much more complicated than the simple picture held by most Christians or the new model offered by Jeremy Bentham and the utilitarians. In his notion of the "unconscious," he possessed a much fuller appreciation of the hidden forces beneath the conscious level of man's existence. He retained, moreover, a strong Calvinistic sense of sin and of the menace of man's own nature. Carlyle did not go beyond the recognition of the dark and morally ambiguous depths of consciousness. He drew back from deep theological or psychological exploration into the "mineshaft," recoiling from such inquiry as a violation of the "holy of holies" and standing firmly on his moral intuitions as "messages of the divine" and not "fantasms." [8]

The deliverances of Carlyle's conscience held much besides the simple Christian ethic that he carried over from the past. In his prophetic pronouncements on contemporary life he invested the social norms of his youth with sacred or absolute value. Alongside the Puritan notions of work and duty were the older emphases of a more organic and hierarchical society based on personal loyalty and deference to superiors. These preindustrial social values would persist as dominant elements in Carlyle's outlook. They were most explicit in *Past and Present* (1843), the work of Carlyle which most influenced the Socialists.

In *Past and Present,* Carlyle presented a mythical picture of a religious community in twelfth-century England possessing the kind of

---

[7] Carlyle, *Sartor Resartus,* pp. 174, 162.

[8] For Carlyle's notion of the "unconscious" see "Characteristics," in *Critical and Miscellaneous Essays,* III (London, 1904), 1-43.

spiritual unity lacking in contemporary life. It was a community animated by a spirit of charity, personal loyalty, and reverence for authority, a hierarchical order in which all the members dutifully performed their allotted tasks under the leadership of Abbot Samson, who relied solely on his intuition of God's law. This vision of society as a community of the faithful, a church, drew together the main elements of Carlyle's moral and social outlook. In the light of this ideal he launched his well-known indictment of the classical theory of political economy and attacked those who would make the "cash nexus" the sole relationship between men.

Carlyle had reached back into history to find a social model which corresponded to his innermost convictions. Yet he did not completely reject the emerging industrial society, for there was much in the new middle-class world, particularly its productive energy and the leadership provided by the captains of industry, which he admired. His ethic of work offered a new sanction for the middle-class way of life and he envisioned, like the Saint Simonians, the possibility of informing industrial life with a new faith. As early as *Sartor Resartus,* Carlyle had looked forward to a social rebirth or "palingenesis," and yet the vision he offered in *Past and Present* remained essentially archaic. He did not seek to understand the social and economic changes of his time. The contrast with Marx, who in these years shared something of Carlyle's ethical concern, is striking. While Carlyle sought to call men back to the social values and forms of an earlier period, Marx attempted, however one may judge the result, to grasp the inner dynamic of the new industrial world. Carlyle, much like Marx, located the peculiar "misery" of contemporary man in the sense of being "crushed under a juggernaut," a "dead mechanical idol," but this was for him simply another sign of the "unfathomable, all-pervading domain of mystery." [9] In the face of the complexities of social and economic life, as well as those presented by the "unconscious," Carlyle fell back on his moral and religious feelings.

From these feelings Carlyle derived a power which established him as a social prophet during the forties. His writings and lectures,

[9] Carlyle, *Sartor Resartus,* p. 51.

delivered in a style reminiscent of the Old Testament, found a ready response among the Victorian middle and upper classes. He registered especially strongly on those troubled by religious doubt, and he often gave them a new sense of spiritual truth without the embarrassing encumbrances of dogma or church. "In Carlyle's writings," James Froude observed, "dogma and tradition melted like a mist, and the awful central fact [of God] burnt clear once more." And yet Carlyle's affirmation of the primacy of conscience begged the central religious questions, for he evaded the problem of the status of the Christian faith. His teachings implied that its church, liturgy, and creeds were "old clothes," which must be set aside so that the true spirit of religion could find new forms. At one point Carlyle seemed ready to attack orthodox religion directly and lead his generation in the "Exodus from Houndsditch." But he drew back, perhaps as Froude suggested, because "the good which he might do would be out balanced by the pain he would inflict." [10] If so, it was a strange capitulation to the utilitarian test of action which he deplored.

Carlyle's development was marked by deepening metaphysical uncertainty. The study of history to which he had turned as the only "Bible of Revelation" possessing "plenary inspiration," did not provide the spiritual certainty formerly supplied by religious revelation. Indeed, history threatened to dissolve all values in a relativistic flux. Carlyle warded off the danger by his doctrine of the hero, who was blessed with a "direct vision of reality" and capable of re-establishing the links between the transcendental order of God and temporal circumstances. The hero became, therefore, the proper object of man's most exalted feelings, the focus of awe and reverence. He was a corrective to democracy, which, according to Carlyle was a "self-cancelling business," a mere interim marked by the absence of genuine leaders. [11]

Carlyle's vision of community—organic, spiritually unified, and

[10] J. A. Froude, *Thomas Carlyle: A History of His Life in London, 1834–1881* (2 vols.; London, 1884), I, 293; II, 31.

[11] See "On History Again," *Critical and Miscellaneous Essays*, II; "Chartism," *ibid.*, II, 158.

authoritarian—increasingly separated him from the dominant trends
of the time. His estrangement was recorded most sharply in the
eight *Latter-Day Pamphlets,* published at mid-century. In the years
ahead the pathos of his quest for a new moral community deepened
as he studied Frederick the Great. This was not a labor of love.
"Why," Carlyle wrote to a friend, "have I not a more pious task to
end with?" Yet he seemed to feel that his study of the Prussian
ruler was the inescapable outcome of his life's work. In a world
which, he believed, now faced "centuries of spiritual anarchy,"
where God was "allowing his existence to be obscured," men would
have to find order not through a common faith but through coercion.
Frederick, skilled in the use of political and military power, became
the prototype of the modern hero. He was not, as Carlyle's biographer observed, "spiritual," but he believed in "facts," the "nearest approach to a religious" man possible in modern times. Unable
to discern any integrating force within the developing liberal and
industrial system, Carlyle could envision social unity only in terms
of a community of faith or alternatively of a harmony secured
through external power. In the absence of any new religious faith,
Prussian militarism, as revitalized by Bismarck, became the future
"center of European stability." [12]

It was a strange conclusion for the prophet of a new spiritual
community, and the Socialists largely ignored it. But Carlyle offered
an ambivalent legacy of ideas, influencing not only the Socialists
but the Fascists who followed. A number of the latter, in fact, turned
to right-wing movements only after having become disillusioned with
the Socialist and democratically inspired struggle toward a new organic society.

For many of those who played central roles in the development
of British Socialism, however, the early writings of Carlyle provided
a great inspiration. "I mark the reading of *Sartor Resartus,*" Keir
Hardie said, "as a real turning point and went through the book
three times in succession until the spirit of it somewhat entered
into me." [13] The spirit which Hardie and many other young men

[12] Froude, *Carlyle,* II, 242, 260, 87.
[13] "Labour Party and Books," pp. 570–571.

and women of the lower classes received from Carlyle was both critical and constructive. He provided an indictment of the competitive and individualistic ethos of capitalism; he also fortified the moral feelings. Thus Robert Blatchford, by far the most effective popularizer of Socialist ideas in the nineties, had steeped himself in Carlyle a few years earlier. He indicated his reliance on Carlyle in a letter to a friend: "I think that all work . . . should have a foundation of solid truth, deep thought, and earnest purpose. . . . I have read some five of Carlyle's works over and over again. . . . I have read 'Heroes and Hero Worship' through about six or seven times, slowly and carefully. I have studied 'Sartor Resartus.' " [14]

To Hardie and Blatchford, the two most influential spokesmen for popular Socialism, Carlyle conveyed a strong moral passion enlisted on behalf of an alternative though archaic social vision. But Carlyle retained a Calvinistic belief in human imperfection which imposed strong restraints on the aspiration after a radically different society. A much more optimistic and humanistic version of the aspiration emerged in the work of John Ruskin who became, in the words of Frederic Harrison, an "apostle for a sort of moral and religious Socialism." [15]

Ruskin's early development expressed the tension, so strong in Carlyle, between the traditional religious claims and the aesthetic possibilities of life. For a time he found in the notion of the "landscape feeling" a way of reconciling his evangelical faith and his extraordinary sensitivity to natural and artistic beauty. In this notion Ruskin restated the romantic view that nature was sacramental and offered a continuing revelation of God and a channel of grace. Whether experienced directly or through painting, nature could serve as a "gigantic moral" instrument. The landscape artist and the art critic as well could take their places alongside the preachers as "commentators on infinity." Ruskin's own commentary, presented in the

---

[14] Robert Blatchford to Alexander Thompson, Oct. 1885, Robert Blatchford–A. M. Thompson Correspondence, Manchester Public Libraries, Manchester.

[15] Frederic Harrison, *Tennyson, Ruskin and Mill and Other Literary Estimations* (London, 1899), p. 101.

first two volumes of *Modern Painters*, published in 1843 and 1846, exhibited the "sentimental naturalism" common even among scientists at this time as he attempted to demonstrate the ways in which nature displayed the attributes of God.[16]

The account of consciousness presented in these early writings indicated Ruskin's strong susceptibility to feelings which some students of comparative religion see as the innermost core of religious experience.[17] He sharply differentiated the sense of awe and wonder, or the "holy," evoked by certain natural settings, from experiences of aesthetic, ethical, and rational significance. He was acutely sensitive to those destructive forces in life, sometimes referred to as the demonic, that defy normal categories of explanation. Probably no other Victorian thinker equaled Ruskin in his appreciation of the "grotesque" forms through which artists at various times have acknowledged the power and the menace of the irrational.[18] The fading out or perhaps displacement of this sensibility provides one clue to the growth of Ruskin's later outlook. The attenuation of the ideas of sin and evil, still strong in Carlyle, prepared the way for Ruskin's more optimistic social vision.

The vision began to emerge in the early fifties as Ruskin extended his interests beyond landscape art to religious art in general and then to architecture. His study of architecture, particularly that of medieval and Renaissance Venice, brought a growing interest in society as a whole. The leaders of the contemporary Gothic revival argued that architecture represented a mirror of the spiritual life of a peo-

16 Ruskin discusses the conflict between his religious commitments and his aesthetic feelings in a letter to his tutor Thomas Dale in September 1841. See *The Works of John Ruskin*, ed. E. T. Cook and Alexander Wedderburn (London, 1902–1912), I, 395; Ruskin to Osborne Gordon, March 10, 1844, *ibid.*, III, 66, 665. For Ruskin's view of art see Henry Ladd, *The Victorian Morality of Art: An Analysis of Ruskin's Aesthetic* (New York, 1932).

17 Ruskin's perception of the "holy" is examined in the context of his religious development in Rudolf Dalhoff, *Studien über die Religiosität John Ruskins* (Marburg, 1935), pp. 1–15. Also see Rudolf Otto, *The Idea of the Holy* (Oxford, 1938), who draws on Ruskin to illustrate his analysis. For Ruskin's account see Cook and Wedderburn, eds., *Works*, V, 364ff, and IV, 371–381.

18 See especially the chapters "Renaissance Grotesque" and "The Mountain Gloom," in Cook and Wedderburn, eds., *Works*, XI, 135–195; VI, 385–417.

ple.[19] Ruskin discerned in the development of Venetian architecture a cycle of social health and decay. His studies of Venice helped him to formulate both a criticism of his own society and a new ideal of community.

Ruskin, like Carlyle, discovered in medieval society a blend of spontaneity and order, of creative diversity and unity, made possible by a common faith. In the building of a Gothic cathedral he saw the result of a great variety of talents expressing themselves freely according to a single spiritual purpose. The decline of Venetian architecture, attended by a growing uniformity of sculpture and decoration, also provided Ruskin with a new interpretation of English social development. He began to view the work process associated with industrialization as destructive of human dignity and freedom:

> It is verily this degradation of the operative into a machine, which more than any other evil of the times, is leading the mass of the nations everywhere into a vain, incoherent, destructive struggle for a freedom of which they themselves cannot explain the nature to themselves. . . . It is not that men are ill fed but that they have no pleasure in their work. . . . It is not that labor is divided, but the men . . . broken into small fragments. . . . We manufacture everything except men. . . . To brighten, to strengthen, to refine or form a single living spirit, never enters into our estimate of advantages.[20]

These words provided many Socialists with their central criticism of capitalism and a new view of human and social fulfillment. For Ruskin, however, the attainment of a more humane order still depended mainly on the growth of a common moral and religious consciousness. Yet the nature of that consciousness was increasingly problematical, for his Christian faith was ebbing.

Ruskin's Christianity, based initially on a simple Biblical literalism, had been weakened owing to his increased historical perspective and his growing awareness of the range of spiritual expression in art. He did not explicitly discard Christianity until the late fifties, but he

---

[19] Ruskin's relationship to the "Gothic Revival" is discussed in Kenneth Clark, *The Gothic Revival* (London, 1928), and Graham Hough, *The Last Romantics* (London, 1961), pp. 32–39.

[20] "The Nature of Gothic," Cook and Wedderburn, eds., *Works*, VI, 19, 4-6.

began to suffer from religious doubts a decade earlier. One outcome of these doubts was a tendency to emphasize the moral mission of the established church. In his pamphlet *Notes on the Construction of Sheepfolds* (1851), he proposed, much as Arnold had a few years earlier, that the creedal and liturgical features of church life be de-emphasized so as to accommodate the Nonconformists. At the same time, however, he called for a tightening of moral discipline within the church; clergymen should exercise powers of "excommunication" and "exclude thieves, liars, busybodies, people who didn't pay their debts" and the "avaricious," all those, in short, whose conduct was clearly in conflict with Christian morality. Ruskin still viewed men in evangelical fashion as sharply and clearly divisible into saints and sinners. The evangelical concern for individual souls, however, was giving way to the aspiration for a righteous nation.[21]

By the mid-fifties Ruskin had lost the earlier harmony between his religious, moral, and aesthetic feelings. The landscape feeling which had previously united them was dead; he had become convinced that it was escapist, a symptom of religious decline. This feeling, he wrote, was peculiar to "persons not of the first order of intellect, but of brilliant imagination, quick sympathy, and indifferent religious principles, suffering also usually under strong and ill governed passions." The loss of a harmonious balance or relationship between the various forms of human awareness now seemed to Ruskin to be a fundamental tendency of his age. The most "dangerous and attractive" form of "modern infidelity" was the inclination to ignore the "occult and subtle horror belonging to many aspects of creation" by "dwelling chiefly on the manifest appearances of God's

---

21 See the letters to his father in January and April 1852, in Cook and Wedderburn, eds., *Works,* XXXVI, 126ff; X, xxxviiiff. He describes his religious development in the autobiographical *Praeterita,* and in *Fors Clavigera,* Letter 76. *Notes on the Construction of Sheepfolds* is in Cook and Wedderburn, eds., *Works,* XII, 531. To Maurice, Ruskin's proposals seemed to eliminate both the heights and depths of the Christian faith. "I never read any scheme," he wrote Ruskin, "better conceived for enthroning, if not canonizing, respectability and decency; and any scheme which less levels the hills and exalts the valleys, which less affronts the scribes and the Pharisees" (*ibid.,* pp. 561–562).

kindness." [22] Ironically, Ruskin was anticipating his own development.

Ruskin remained acutely sensitive to the aspects of existence that eluded normal rational or moral categories. He retained a strong sense of evil, and his writings occasionally exhibited profound pessimism. But with the final loss of his religious convictions in the late fifties his darker perceptions tended to be suppressed. Writing to the Robert Brownings shortly after the final collapse of his faith in 1858, he confessed that the "truth as far as I can make it out is too terrible to be the truth." [23] Ruskin now adopted an ethically centered "religion of humanity," and the sense of the nonrational forces in life and nature largely disappeared from his writings.

This narrowing of the range of his consciousness was countered to some extent by the larger role which Ruskin gave to the artist as the interpreter of reality, releasing the artist as such from conventional moral restraints:

In order to the pursuit of beauty rightly, our great painter must not shrink in a timid way from any form of vice or ugliness. . . . [It] is not possible for him to nourish his (so-called) spiritual desires, as it is to an ordinary virtuous person. . . . This continued mechanical toil, this fixed physical aim, occupies his intellect and energy at every spare moment, blunts his sorrows, restrains his enthusiasm, lifts his speculation, takes away all common chances of his being affected by the feelings or imaginations which lead other men to religion.[24]

But while Ruskin came to see religious faith as indifferent, even antagonistic, to the work of the artist, he continued to believe that true art presupposed a strong moral commitment. Morality was a "certain

[22] See Francis G. Townsend, *Ruskin and the Landscape Feeling,* Illinois Studies in Language and Literature, XXXV, No. 3 (Urbana, 1951), p. 74; also the discussion of awe or "holy fear" in Cook and Wedderburn, eds., *Works,* IV, 198–200; XI, 164.

[23] Ruskin to Mr. and Mrs. Browning, March 29, 1848, Cook and Wedderburn, eds., *Works,* XXXVI, 279.

[24] "Notes on a Painter's Profession Ending Religiously," *ibid.,* IV, 287–298. The editors suggest that the essay was written after 1855.

and unalterable . . . instinct in the hearts of all civilized men."
With art it performed the work of perfecting man's nature.[25]

Ruskin's developing outlook was fortified by his friendship with
Carlyle. Writing to Carlyle in 1855, Ruskin expressed his surprise
and vexation "at finding that what I really had and knew I had
worked out for myself, corresponded very closely to the things you
had said much better." [26] In the years just ahead, as he passed through
his crisis of faith, Ruskin drew strength from the older man's character. Carlyle also encouraged Ruskin to carry forward the attack,
launched in the *Stones of Venice*, on the dominant economic tendencies of the time.

The attack was renewed in 1860 in the *Cornhill* magazine with
the publication of the first essay of *Unto This Last*, the work which
gave Ruskin his greatest influence among the Socialists. To his attack
on the developing capitalistic world and its economic theory Ruskin
brought a prophetic style which, much like Carlyle's, was laced with
Biblical phrases, displayed great powers of invective, and refused to
recognize any nucleus of truth in the position of his opponents. Ruskin also demonstrated a great gift for piercing through the claims of
current economic doctrine in order to raise fundamental human and
social issues. His quarrel with the defenders of the classical theory of
political economy was not so much with their arguments as with
their first principles. He scorned the spirit in which thinkers from
Adam Smith through the younger Mill had approached economic
and social phenomena. To their struggle toward an economic science
based on an abstract "economic man," Ruskin opposed his concerns
as a moralist. They sought to analyze actual social practices; he
measured those practices against his ideal conceptions of man and
society. Hence his attempt in *Unto This Last* to redefine such key
terms in the classical theory as wealth, value, and utility. For Ruskin,
political economy was not mainly analytical and descriptive, but
rather the art of designing a new social order.

He worked out his own design in *Munera Pulveris, Time and Tide,*

---

[25] John Ruskin, *Lectures on Art* (London, 1872), p. 30.

[26] Ruskin to Carlyle, Jan. 23, 1855, Cook and Wedderburn, eds., *Works,*
XXXVI, 183.

and the four volumes of *Fors Clavigera*. Ruskin, like so many Christian and romantic social thinkers, saw reform not as a dynamic and adaptive process, but as a problem of restoration and primarily as a task of moral conversion. Ruskin emphasized the preindustrial values of cooperation, loyalty, obedience, and reverence for authority, along with the aesthetic satisfactions in work which he discerned in medieval society. He envisioned an order, essentially agricultural, with a quasi-feudal subordination of most men to an aristocracy. The guild system would be restored, together with a spiritual hierarchy made up of clerical and secular leaders. The plan owed something to Plato's *Republic*. For a time Ruskin even hoped that enlightened "captains of industry" would initiate the work of reform. Then in 1871 he founded the Guild of St. George to put his ideas in practice, and a few years later he started a communal experiment on a few acres near Sheffield. The project did not prosper and exercised only slight influence on the development of Socialism.[27] By the mid-seventies Ruskin was concentrating more and more on the task of disseminating his ideas and creating a body of morally committed men, particularly in the working classes, who would carry the cause forward.

Ruskin's archaic social vision increasingly estranged him from his age, and he was less able than Carlyle to bear the pain of isolation. The inner connections between his pathetic and abortive love for Rose La Touche, the strange medley of ideas he expressed in these later years, and his gradual decline into insanity have resisted satisfactory analysis. But the perceptions of the grotesque and menacing aspects of life, so evident in his early writings, returned to haunt him in dreams and bring periods of deep melancholy in which nature itself appeared as evil. Ruskin called on Carlyle in vain for spiritual guidance.[28] In 1870 he turned back to Christianity, but his reconversion brought little peace of mind and did not alter his outlook on

[27] See W. H. G. Armytage, *Heavens Below: Utopian Experiments in England, 1560–1960* (London, 1960), pp. 289ff, for an account of the venture.

[28] See *The Diaries of John Ruskin*, ed. Joan Evans and John Howard Whitehouse (Oxford, 1956–1959), II, 1848–1873, and III, 1873–1884; Ruskin to Carlyle, June 27, 1844, Cook and Wederburn, eds., *Works*, XXXVII, 116.

society. His vision of a morally regenerate body of men, removed from a wicked world, gained in force. Many of his bitterest attacks in these last years, before he lost his sanity completely, were leveled at the churches and their clergy. Their compromises with the world, he felt, had totally disqualified them as agents of the coming social reformation.

Ruskin strongly influenced the thought and the form of the popular Socialist movement of the nineties. Some of the new Socialist leaders, like Fred Jowett or Katharine Conway, looked back to their reading of *Unto This Last* as an event which changed their lives. Others, like Tom Barclay and Tom Mann, brought a strong commitment to Ruskinian ideas into their early work as Socialist propagandists. But Ruskin's specific social and economic ideas were probably no more important than the sense of moral righteousness with which he imbued his followers, who received a deep sense of being a band of righteous men engaged in a crusade to regenerate society. A Socialist recruiter in Liverpool in the eighties observed that many of the members of the Ruskin Society had "advanced to our position" and were "hesitating to join us only because they wish to make certain that our League is one of righteous men resolved to win by righteous methods." [29] The same insistence on their high moral calling permeated popular Socialist propaganda.

Ruskin and Carlyle had reached back into the collective experiences recorded in history and in art to find ways of ordering the bewildering social changes of the nineteenth century. They had constructed social myths which condemned the ethos of industrial capitalism and held the promise of a new and more humane community. They had made visible some of those "pre-capitalistic dispositions" which Henry De Man, the most penetrating analyst of European Socialism, saw as its primary source:

The Socialist labor movement is not a product of capitalism. We must look upon it as the product of a reaction which occurs when capitalism (a new social state) comes into contact with a human disposition which

[29] Socialist League Correspondence and Papers No. 3251/2, International Institute of Social History, Amsterdam.

may be termed pre-capitalist. This disposition is characterized by a certain fixation of the sense of moral values, a fixation which can only be understood with reference to the social experiences of the days of feudalism and the craft guilds, to Christian ethics, and to the ethical principles of democracy.[30]

In their fixation on the older social and moral values Carlyle and Ruskin had largely divorced themselves from the dominant economic and political tendencies of their age. Indeed, both of these social prophets discouraged in their followers any attempt to grasp the meaning of objective social forces. Carlyle, with his residual Calvinism, was much less inclined to ignore what one of Ruskin's critics called the "innumerable principles of growth which are quite independent of the will of man." [31] But both men tended to make their followers scornful of parliamentary political practice, which assumed, as they did not, the existence of legitimate conflicts of interest and the need for compromise.

The readers of *Past and Present* or *Unto This Last* received, however, a powerful stimulus to conscience and to new forms of collective action. Many young men and women, middle and lower class alike, would brush aside the authoritarian features of these works, blend their moral and social teachings with democratic values, and recover in secular terms the evangelical view of the world as a struggle between the righteous and the unrighteous. Carlyle and Ruskin thus helped to redirect late Victorian moral and religious sentiments toward the Socialist cause.

The British Socialists did not tap these sentiments immediately. Socialism entered England during the early eighties in a form inspired by Marx, which was profoundly hostile to the priority Christians and romantics placed on the growth of a moral or religious

---

[30] Henry De Man, *The Psychology of Socialism* (New York, 1928), pp. 38–39. Gustave Le Bon, *Psychology of Socialism* (New York, 1899), p. 91, argued that the vitality of Socialism depended on its capacity to attach itself to a sentiment which survived the religious beliefs which "had first maintained it." Also see Joseph Schumpeter's discussion of "pre-capitalist strata" and the persistence of older social and cultural norms in *Capitalism, Socialism and Democracy* (London, 1950), pp. 121–163.

[31] *The Spectator,* Sept. 22, 1877.

consciousness. Marxism was quickly assimilated into a century-long tradition of radical thought which ran counter to the Christian and romantic ideals of community. The nineteenth-century utilitarians together with their Owenite and Secularist popularizers provided a third legacy of ideas on which the Socialists drew.

3

Aspirations for a Rational Community:
Utilitarians, Owenites, and Secularists

In its tendency to reduce social life to simple relations of economic exchange, utilitarianism expressed the outlook of those classes whose lives were dominated by business transactions. The utilitarian moral code, Elie Halévy observed, was the economic psychology of the bourgeoisie "put into the imperative." Through the writings of Jeremy Bentham, utilitarianism became a new approach to social reform. Bentham himself was preoccupied with administrative and legal reforms and little disposed to investigate the more obscure problems of man's inner life or to challenge prevailing moral conventions. He did, however, launch an anonymous attack on the established church and he projected, most clearly in his plan for a model prison, the Panopticon, a new ideal of social organization.[1] Bentham left a dual legacy to his nineteenth-century utilitarian successors. Some would employ his test of utility, or the greatest happiness of the greatest number, in their efforts for public reform; others would seek to translate utilitarianism into a more radical vision of social transformation. These latter were engaged in their own version of the quest for a new community informed by a new consciousness.

James Mill took the first important step in this direction when he

[1] Elie Halévy, *The Growth of Philosophic Radicalism* (London, 1928), pp. 477–478. An excellent general treatment of the utilitarians is John Plamenatz, *The English Utilitarians* (Oxford, 1958). A provocative reinterpretation of the liberal and utilitarian traditions is in Sheldon Wolin, *Politics of Vision* (Boston, 1960). See also Talcott Parsons, *The Structure of Social Action* (Glencoe, Ill., 1949); Robert Denoon Cumming, *Human Nature and History* (Chicago, 1969), Vol. II; and Gertrude Himmelfarb, "The Haunted House of Jeremy Bentham," in her *Victorian Minds* (New York, 1968).

published his *Analysis of the Phenomena of the Human Mind* (1829).[2] Mill employed the principle of association, the basic premise of Bentham's psychology, and virtually completed the effort, initiated in the seventeenth century, to explain consciousness in terms of the action of external sensations. Only the postulate of an instinctive drive toward pleasure survived the relentless analysis through which Mill attempted to do away with the conventional explanations of man's mental life. The will, the conscience, the imagination, faith, the moral sentiments, even reason, were reduced to the mechanical collocation of physical impressions. By virtue of repeated associations, so the argument went, men tended to act so as to attain pleasure and avoid pain. Man was essentially egoistic and hedonistic, but also rational. Society arose out of the self-conscious and calculated interrelationships of its members.

Beneath the ostensible hedonism of Mill's creed was an austere sense of duty as unbending as that of his Scottish Covenanter forebears. His philosophy has been related to his need, as an apostate Calvinist, to "restore the old vision of the one and the many on a secular foundation." [3] But the further development of the vision was left to John Stuart Mill. In the younger Mill and his followers the utilitarian confidence in reason, or science, was transformed into the ideal of a new order of rational men. The hope would inform much of nineteenth-century British thought, find popular expression in Owenism and Secularism, and enter deeply into the Socialist movement.

"If it were possible," Bentham had declared, "to suppose a new people, a generation of children in which the legislator would find no ready made expectation to contradict his vision, he might fashion them to his will like a sculptor deals with a block of marble." The severe educational regimen which the elder Mill imposed on his son followed from this dream of giving human nature a new rational

---

[2] The differences between Bentham and James Mill are emphasized in Shirley Letwin, *The Pursuit of Certainty* (Cambridge, 1965), pp. 186–202. David Baumgardt, *Bentham and the Ethics of Today* (Princeton, 1952), pp. 478–487, argues that Mill simply carried out the logic of his master's position.

[3] Letwin, *Pursuit of Certainty,* p. 200.

shape. According to the subject, however, the experiment nearly destroyed him. The mental crisis which the younger Mill experienced in 1826, at the age of twenty, lends itself to various interpretations, but through his crisis Mill confronted a dilemma which would trouble utilitarians throughout the century. He discovered that the utilitarian goal of the general good was not the self-sustaining ideal which his father had assumed. He found that his consciousness, having become "irretrievably analytic," was emptied of motivation.[4] The dilemma recurred in the early development of British Socialism and led to a rapid conquest of its initial utilitarian form by romantic modes of thought.

Mill recovered his will power, but only after finding through poetry and the romantic literature of the period new nourishment for his feelings. He began to discover in the works of Coleridge and Carlyle, the German idealists, and the French disciples of Saint Simon ideas about man and society which profoundly altered his utilitarian outlook. He became aware of society as a complex historical growth of institutions, ideas, and feelings, not resolvable into the simple dualism of the individual and the state. He came to believe, with Saint Simon, that he lived in an age of critical transition, marked above all by the loss of any generally accepted system of principles. "What passes as the virtues of liberalism," he suggested at one point, might be "no more than the delusions of such a transition period" prior to a time when "the most virtuous and best instructed of the nation" would acquire a new "ascendance over the opinions and feelings of the rest." [5] During the 1830s, like his Anglican contemporaries and Carlyle, Mill began to envision a spiritual authority capable of overcoming "intellectual anarchy" and checking as well the tendencies

---

[4] Bentham is quoted in Halévy, *Philosophic Radicalism*, p. 503. See J. S. Mill, *Autobiography* (London, 1879), pp. 138–139.

[5] Mill's development in these years can be followed through his letters. See Hugh Elliot, ed., *The Letters of John Stuart Mill* (2 vols.; London, 1910); *The Collected Works of John Stuart Mill*, ed. F. E. L. Priestley (Toronto, 1963–1969), XII, XIII: *The Earlier Letters, 1812–1848*, ed. Francis Mineka; Iris Mueller, *John Stuart Mill and French Thought* (Urbana, Ill., 1956); R. C. K. Pankhurst, *The St. Simonians, Mill, and Carlyle* (London, 1957); J. S. Mill, *The Spirit of the Age*, ed. Friedrich von Hayek (Chicago, 1942), p. 93.

toward social breakdown and class strife. Equipped with this new historical and cultural perspective, Mill resumed the utilitarian mission.

His father's utilitarianism had been expanded to include a large part of the opposing religious and romantic currents of thought. Mill presented his revised utilitarianism in two essays, "Bentham" (1838) and "Coleridge" (1840). Here he argued that Bentham had ignored the problem of the "culture of the inward man" and those "depths of character quite independent of any influence of worldly circumstances." Bentham had also failed to recognize that calculations of individual self-interest were not sufficient to integrate men into society. Without common "spiritual interests," society would decline into anarchy and a "mutual conflict for selfish ends." Mankind needed "binding forces," including a fixed principle or an institution, and feelings "of sympathy or common interest among those who live under the same government." [6] In its true and healthy state, Mill concluded, society was a community of shared values, principles, and loyalties.

The philosophical inconsistencies which followed Mill's effort to reconcile the traditions of Bentham and Coleridge have been subject to extensive critical commentary.[7] But on the basis of his enlarged utilitarianism, in which the rigorous rationalism and associationism of his father were combined with Coleridge's insistence on man's self-forming spiritual constitution, Mill raised his own vision of a mental and social reconstruction.[8] *A System of Logic* (1843) was its

[6] J. S. Mill, *Bentham and Coleridge,* ed. F. R. Leavis (London, 1950), pp. 70, 121–124.

[7] See R. P. Anschutz, *The Philosophy of J. S. Mill* (Oxford, 1953), pp. 164–182; and Karl Britton, *John Stuart Mill* (Harmondsworth, 1953), pp. 45–78.

[8] Maurice Cowling, *Mill and Liberalism* (Cambridge, 1963), emphasizes this side of Mill's thought; a milder version of this approach appears in Letwin, *Pursuit of Certainty.* For the earlier stages of a developing "Cambridge critique" of Mill see Noel Annan's essay in *The English Mind,* ed. Hugh Sykes Davies and George Watson (Cambridge, 1964). The view that Mill was primarily and increasingly dedicated to the values of individuality, creative freedom, and social diversity is restated by Isaiah Berlin, "John Stuart Mill and the Ends of Life," *Four Essays on Liberty* (Oxford, 1969). Also see Cumming, *Human Nature and History,* II, Part VI.

foundation. For not only did *Logic* present the rules of correct or scientific thinking; it offered an approach to the total renovation of man's consciousness and his political life:

The concluding book is an attempt to contribute towards the solution of a question, which the decay of old opinions, and the agitation that disturbs European society to its inmost depths, render as important in the present day to the practical interests of human life, as it must at all times be to the completeness of our speculative knowledge—viz: Whether moral and social phenomena are really exceptions to the general certainty and uniformity of the course of nature; and how far the methods by which so many of the laws of the physical world have been numbered among truths irrevocably acquired and universally assented to, can be made instrumental to the formation of a similar body of received doctrine in moral and political science.[9]

Although Mill was occupied in *Logic* mainly with the methodological difficulties in the way of scientific understanding of man's moral character and social relations, he also outlined his ideal of a society of rational men. The ideal was similar in its general form to Coleridge's, for social and cultural unity would be recovered through a "body of received doctrine" and a group of spiritual or philosophical leaders. But in place of Coleridge's religious solution to the deficiencies of human consciousness, Mill envisioned the progressive conquest of man's irrationality and selfishness through education. Scientific attitudes and procedures would gradually replace the deeply ingrained habits and sentiments derived from tradition. Science, viewed as the ordering of phenomena according to Newtonian principles, provided the sole test of truth and ruled out any fixed notion of a soul or self beneath the "thread of consciousness." "I have often had moods," he wrote his friend John Sterling, "in which I would gladly postulate like Kant a different foundation," but "my way is founded on the methods of the physical sciences and entirely a posteriori." [10]

Logic, Mill informed Auguste Comte in 1842, was simply the "first blow" against the "ontological" or "essentially theological"

[9] J. S. Mill, *A System of Logic* (New York, 1884), I, v.
[10] Elliot, ed., *Letters of Mill*, I, 114.

school of thought which provided the main support of the "ancient social order." But while he agreed that the new philosophy was radically incompatible with all theology, he was also convinced that a direct assault on the authority of religion was not yet possible in England. He regretted that the English were not, in this respect, as far advanced as the French. An open attack, Mill believed, would "compromise our cause" and even give "a new force to the religious reaction." It would be much better to "quietly eliminate it from all philosophical and social discussions," to treat their chosen subjects "as if religion did not exist." [11]

Yet Mill's own mental crisis had convinced him that a simple rationalism, or the utilitarianism of his father, did not in itself supply adequate motive force for social reform. He welcomed Comte's suggestion that it would be necessary to develop feelings or "higher sentiments" which could take the place in consciousness formerly occupied by religious beliefs. Mill felt that he was especially well qualified for this task because he had never believed in God. Moreover, he had experienced personally the "capacity of positive philosophy to take full possession" of the higher social aims; he foresaw the "inevitable substitution" of the "idea of Humanity" for that of God.[12]

Mill's close relationship with Comte ended in 1846, but he remained "entirely at one" with Comte in seeking a "philosophical regeneration" and an "entire renovation of social institutions and doctrines." The work on political economy which followed *Logic* was one side of this larger mission. It dealt, however, with what Mill called the "secondary" level of progress. At this level Mill moved, in subsequent editions of his economic treatise, to a form of Socialism and influenced the thought of the Fabians. But his main goal was the reconstruction of moral and metaphysical beliefs. He lamented the tendency of contemporary leaders of the "proletarian movements" to associate their reforms with an outmoded metaphysics, and for a

[11] Mineka, ed., *Earlier Letters, Collected Works,* XIII, 530, 657, 671 (my translations). Mueller, *Mill and French Thought,* devotes a chapter to the relations between Mill and Comte. Also see W. M. Simon, *European Positivism in the Nineteenth Century* (Ithaca, N.Y., 1963), pp. 172–201.

[12] Mineka, ed., *Earlier Letters, Collected Works,* XIII, 560.

time he encouraged those who were preaching rationalism to the lower classes. In 1847 he even suggested the necessity for a violent revolution in England to "break up the old associations" and overcome the "extreme difficulty of getting any ideas into her stupid head." [13] The continental upheavals of 1848 dispelled whatever enthusiasm Mill might have had for violence, but he continued to reflect on the need for a new "spring and regulator of energetic action." The problem increasingly drew him to the phenomenon of religion which provides an important theme through his major essays of the fifties—"Nature," "The Utility of Religion," "Utilitarianism," and "On Liberty." Mill developed the idea of a new humanity-centered religion most fully in "Utilitarianism."

Although he felt that Comte had been premature in trying to "define in detail the practices" of a new religious cult, Mill held that the French thinker had demonstrated its possibility. Through education, Mill argued, certain habitual associations or "social feelings" could bring "to the service of humanity, even without the aid of belief in providence, both the psychological power and the social efficacy of a religion." Indeed, once grasped, the new ideal might "take hold of human life and color all thought, feeling and action in a manner of which the greatest ascendancy ever exercised by any religion may be but a type and foretaste." [14]

Beyond this hope, which became a fundamental part of his program for a rational society, Mill did not go. Indeed, he was reluctant to propagate his religious views. The essays in which he attacked orthodox religion most sharply were not published until after his death, and "Utilitarianism" did not appear until 1862. "On Liberty" contained a strong criticism of Christianity, but in the year it was published, 1859, he told a friend that he was "not anxious to bring over any but really superior intellects and characters" to the "whole" of his opinions. As for all others, he "would rather, as things are now, try to improve their religion than to destroy it." [15]

[13] *Ibid.*, pp. 739, 698; Elliott, ed., *Letters of Mill*, I, 131, II, 362.
[14] J. S. Mill, "Utilitarianism," in Marshall Cohen, ed., *The Philosophy of John Stuart Mill* (New York, 1961), pp. 360–361.
[15] Elliot, ed., *Letters of Mill*, I, 223.

In the last decade of his life Mill became much more conciliatory toward those moral and religious sentiments which he had earlier set out to displace. He informed a correspondent in 1862 that "neither in the *Logic* nor in any other of my publications had I any purpose in undermining Theism" and that he accepted as a "very probable hypothesis" the view that "the world was made in whole or in part by a powerful Being who cared for man." [16] He developed this view in his final discussion on religion, the essay "Theism." While he continued to insist that religious doctrines such as the existence of God or personal immortality possessed only "one of the lesser degrees of probability" when tested by the canons of science and logic, he defended the role of the imagination in providing a "wider range and greater height of aspiration" for human life. He concluded that Christianity held up to "believers and unbelievers alike a standard of excellence, an ideal representative and guide of humanity," which had never been surpassed.[17]

Mill had thus acknowledged the need for a religious or imaginative augmentation of rational consciousness, first through the notion of a religion of humanity and later through his ethically centered theism. To one of Mill's most influential disciples, John Morley, the outcome seemed an "intellectual scandal," a "fatal relaxation of his own rules and methods of reasoning." [18] But another of Mill's followers, Leslie Stephen, after a systematic treatment of the utilitarian tradition of thought, recognized Mill's fundamental dilemma:

There was somewhere a gap in the Utilitarian system. Its attack upon the mythological statements of fact might be victorious; but it could not supply the place of religion either to the vulgar or to the loftiest minds. Then the problem arises whether the acceptance of scientific method, and of an empirical basis for all knowledge, involves the acceptance of a lower moral standard and of a materialism which denies the existence or the

[16] Quoted by Michael St. John Packe, *The Life of John Stuart Mill* (London, 1954), p. 43.

[17] J. S. Mill, *Three Essays on Religion* (London, 1924), pp. 242, 245, 249. Also see Robert Carr, "The Religious Thought of John Stuart Mill: A Study in Reluctant Scepticism," *Journal of the History of Ideas*, XXIII (Oct.–Dec. 1962), 475–495.

[18] John Morley, *Recollections* (New York, 1917), II, 106ff.

value of all the unselfish and loftier elements in human nature? Can we adhere to facts without abandoning philosophy; or adopt a lofty code of ethics without losing ourselves in a dreamland? [19]

Mill had sacrificed philosophical consistency and, indeed, much of his earlier vision of a utilitarian community to his empirical grasp of psychological and social realities. He had also retreated, at least part way, to the position of those Benthamites who set aside ethical and metaphysical problems in order to concentrate on legislative and administrative reforms.

Like Bentham, Mill left an ambiguous legacy to his utilitarian successors. Some, like Stephen, would carry on the search for a scientifically grounded personal and social ethic. Others, like Frederic Harrison and the British Positivists, would recapture the broader utilitarian vision of a rational community in the movement inspired by Auguste Comte. They would also carry this mission to the working classes through the trade-union leaders and exercise an important influence on many of those who participated in the Socialist movement of the eighties.[20] But the utilitarian tradition entered the British Socialist movement more directly and more deeply through popular forms of the creed. In Owenism and Secularism the lower classes had received simpler versions of the ideal of a rational commonwealth.

Until the end of the eighteenth century, leaders of lower-class social protest in Britain had normally expressed their grievances and hopes in traditional Christian terms.[21] Free-thinking and deistic ideas were common in the upper classes, but there was little effort to disseminate them among the masses. With the renewal of political radicalism in the closing decades of the century and the growth of a rationalist wing of religious dissent, however, the materials for a popular ideology outside the old religious framework were at hand. Thomas Paine, combining deistic views with democratic ideas, became its most effective publicist. The new radicalism inspired the

---

[19] Leslie Stephen, *The English Utilitarians* (London, 1900), III, 477.

[20] See Royden Harrison, *Before the Socialists* (London, 1965), pp. 251ff.

[21] This tradition is surveyed in William Dale Morris, *The Christian Origins of Social Revolt* (London, 1949).

London Correspondence Society, which was organized during the 1790s and became a "sort of democratic and social reform seminary" for the agitators for reform after 1815.[22] Several of its members carried forward the tradition of popular rationalism along with their struggle to secure a cheap and unfettered press. In these years Robert Owen also advanced his vision of a social reformation.

Owen's vision, developed during his experiences as a factory and educational reformer, took systematic form in a series of essays written in 1812 and 1813 and published under the title *A New View of Society, or Essays on the Principle of the Formation of the Human Character.* The "new view" was actually a forceful restatement of ideas which had become common to the radical social thinkers of the period—to Paine and William Godwin as well as to the Benthamites—but Owen displayed a new boldness in developing their religious and social implications.[23]

Owen was convinced that he had looked into the "secret recesses" of man's consciousness and "delineated the whole . . . as on a map." If, Owen wrote, one could "hold up the mirror to man" without the "intervention of any false media," man would learn "what he is, and . . . be better prepared to learn what he may be." Owen's ideas opened up the prospect of a new age. When "the minds of all men . . . [were] born again . . . a race of rational or superior beings" would arise. "In short, when these great errors shall be removed, all our evil passions will disappear; no ground of anger or displeasure from one human being toward another will remain;

22 See John M. Robertson, *A History of Free Thought in the Nineteenth Century* 2 vols; (London, 1929); F. B. Smith, "The Atheist Mission, 1840–1900," in *Ideas and Institutions of Victorian Britain,* ed. Robert Robson (New York, 1967); Henry Collins, "The London Corresponding Society," in *Democracy in the Labour Movement,* ed. J. Saville (London, 1954), p. 129. An account of the society is in E. P. Thompson, *The Making of the English Working Class* (London, 1965), pp. 152–157.

23 Owen's relationship to the other utilitarians is discussed in Halévy, *Philosophic Radicalism,* pp. 220–224. Frank Podmore, *Robert Owen* (London, 1924), remains the fullest account of his life. Owen's ideas and movement are examined in the context of the period by J. F. C. Harrison, *Quest for the New Moral World* (New York, 1969).

the period of the supposed millennium will commence, and universal love prevail."

Underlying the hope was a doctrine of natural harmony, cosmic as well as social, which characterized much of eighteenth-century deist thought. This harmony had been broken by the delusion of free will or personal responsibility. Until men recognized that their character was formed for them by their social environment and that education could impart almost "any habit or sentiment" desired, there could be little improvement.[24]

Impelled by this vision to devote his life "to relieving mankind from . . . mental disease, and all its miseries," Owen struck out at what he regarded as the bastion of accumulated error. In August of 1817 he delivered "A Denunciation of All the Religions of the World," in which he blamed traditional religious notions for making man "the most inconsistent and the most miserable being in existence."[25] The "denunciation" proved to be a turning point in Owen's career as a reformer. He was ostracized by the governing classes, to whom he had looked to initiate the work of re-education. Henceforth he found his most receptive audience among the lower classes, particularly the artisans of London and the workers of the North.

In this new context Owen's ideas rapidly took a practical direction. His experience as a manufacturer had already led him to view economic competition as a major source of social disharmony and to propose, in 1817, "villages of cooperation" as a solution to the social problem. Several London radicals, most notably William Thompson, adopted his cooperative ideal and developed a critique of the new industrial order.[26] Owen's ideas also helped to inspire the growth of trade unions in England during the twenties, and in 1829, after his return from the abortive New Harmony experiment in America, he attempted to mobilize the newly awakened workers.

[24] Robert Owen, *A New View of Society, Or Essays on the Formation of the Human Character* (London, 1817), pp. 24, 82.

[25] Quoted by Podmore, *Owen*, p. 246. See Owen's account in Robert Owen, *The Life of Robert Owen* (London, 1920), pp. 219ff, 282ff.

[26] See Werner Stark, *The Ideal Foundations of Economic Thought* (London. 1943); and Richard K. Pankhurst, *William Thompson* (London, 1954).

But Owen was little concerned with the goals of increased economic benefit which preoccupied the trade union leaders. He still pursued his aim of "a great moral revolution of the human mind." Indeed, his co-workers in the campaign to build a national confederation of trade-unions urged him to stop pursuing "the phantoms of theology" since the people were "frightfully sensitive . . . on this point." Owen, however, was little disposed to compromise his principles or to regard the trade-unions as other than instruments to hasten the coming of the new moral order. Following the collapse of the trade-union organization his path diverged from the main course of working-class reform effort. Although the Chartist movement of the thirties absorbed many of his ideas, Owen was hostile to its efforts to secure political rights for the lower classes. He regarded the existing political machinery as obsolete. The new moral order would "sweep constitutional machinery into oblivion." Owen wanted to draw the "germ of all party from society," for he saw "political or religious parties or sects" as the "source of dissension and irritation." Power conflicts were relics from the past; coercion would not exist among those initiated into the new truths.[27]

Owen adopted a twofold strategy. He continued to promote the building of model communities outside the existing framework of social institutions in order to convert the world by force of example. But he concentrated mainly on propagating his ideas. Convinced that he alone possessed the truth, he demanded autocratic powers from his associates. Owen's movement grew steadily during the thirties, as societies dedicated to his teachings sprang up in most of the larger towns of England. By 1842 there were sixty-two of these, organized as The Universal Society for Rational Religionists. Ten "social missionaries" and other Owenite speakers were visiting three hundred and fifty towns and reaching, according to one estimate, fifty thousand hearers in Sunday morning meetings. The meetings were often held in Owenite "Halls of Science" or "Social Institutes" and featured lectures, hymns, and readings.

During these years Owen intensified his opposition to conven-

---

[27] Podmore, *Owen,* pp. 431, 425; Owen, *New View of Society,* p. 26.

tional moral and religious ideas. He attacked the institution of marriage for he was convinced that it had "perverted and degraded a natural and lawful instinct" and thus prevented the reign of "pure affection." He blamed the priests for the "fall of man from innocence" and assured his readers that in the new moral world the clergy would be abolished and "all works of theology destroyed." There would be "no temples, no forms and ceremonies, no mortifications of the flesh and spirit, no religious persecution, no hard tasks to be done by man for the glory of God." Owen's regenerated man was, despite a Rousseauistic gloss, the economic man of the utilitarians: "To produce happiness will be the only religion of man; the worship of God will consist in the practice of useful industry; in the acquisition of knowledge; in uniformly speaking the language of truth, and in the expression of the joyous feelings which a life in accord with nature and truth is sure to bring." [28] Some of Owen's followers decided, however, that his view of character eliminated spiritual qualities which were essential to the good life, and they added the idea of an "internal love spirit" as the "spring of action." [29] Others, among whom Minter Morgan was the most prominent, sought to reconcile Owenism and Christianity.[30]

Owen's attempt to combine a utilitarian or rationalist creed with religious and millennial forms foundered in the early forties. The attacks on orthodox religion brought civil prosecution and led Owen and other leaders to defend their movement as a form of religious dissent, much to the dismay of their more militantly rationalist members. Meanwhile, the last of the Owenite experiments in community building, that at Queenwood in Scotland, was failing. In the face of these and other difficulties the movement disintegrated, but its main impulses were soon renewed in other forms. The practical drive toward new means of economic security found expression in the consumer cooperative movement, pioneered in 1845 by a group of working men in Rochdale. Owen's own visionary and millennial bent

[28] Podmore, *Owen*, pp. 489, 495.
[29] The so-called "Sacred Socialist"; see the *New Moral World*, Jan. 16, 30, 1841.
[30] See Harrison, *New Moral World*, pp. 58–59.

was revived in his spiritualist faith. And the educational mission was reformulated by one of Owen's "social missionaries," George Jacob Holyoake, who had become convinced that the community experiments had failed mainly because the "old habits of thought . . . utterly disqualified the majority" of the participants.[31]

Holyoake started a weekly, the *Reasoner*, in 1846, which affirmed the "sovereignty of reason" and the determination to test all speculative and practical issues by the "tangible standard of utility." He also set out to emancipate morality from "the interference of religion" or, alternatively, to develop a "religion independent of theology." Yet he sought to avoid the opprobrium attached to strict atheism and in 1853 coined the term "Secularism" to describe his point of view. The term was, Holyoake wrote, "a new word for a new conception. . . . We maintained that morality resting on material and social facts was a force among all people. We were the first who taught that the secular was sacred." [32] Holyoake submitted a set of principles to Mill for approval:

[I] asked him if we had made such a statement of secularist principles as were worthy to stand as self defensive principles of the working classes . . . as an independent mode of opinion which should no longer involve them in the necessity of taking on their shoulders the responsibilities of an Atheistic or Infidel propaganda. . . . It was not until we had the sanction of one so competent to judge that these principles were promulgated in a definite manner as the principles of a party.[33]

Under Holyoake's leadership Secularism began to gain a new following, but his creed came under attack from two directions within the movement. One group regarded Secularism as excessively intellectual and wished to make it more religious, to root it more deeply

[31] *The Reasoner and Herald of Progress*, Sept. 16, 1846.

[32] *Ibid.*, June 3, Oct. 7, 1846; George Jacob Holyoake, *Sixty Years of An Agitator's Life* (London, 1892), I, 255.

[33] G. J. Holyoake and Charles Bradlaugh, *Secularism, Scepticism, and Atheism* (London, 1870), p. 49. Mill also loaned Holyoake money when he was in difficulty, but did not wish his name connected with Holyoake's paper, which, he told the latter, he did not like (Mill to Holyoake, April 11, 1864, Mill-Holyoake Correspondence, British Library of Political and Economic Science, London).

in the feelings. Others, led by Charles Bradlaugh, wished to return to the more outspoken free thought and republican tradition of Paine and Richard Carlile. "Our real work," Bradlaugh argued, "is war against religion . . . clearing away the structure based on ignorance which the Church has piled on the people in order that we may enable them to go on with the work of political redemption and the work of social emancipation." [34] Supported by the bulk of the London Secularists, Bradlaugh wrested the leadership of the movement from Holyoake in 1858.

Under Bradlaugh's leadership the main body of the Secularists, organized as the National Secular Society, concentrated on undermining the authority of the Bible and the doctrines of the churches. Until the "uselessness of the sacred machinery was brought to the popular mind" there could be no true "civilization of the masses." [35] Bradlaugh and his associates also attempted to disseminate a "scientific" view of life, drawing mainly on the works of Ludwig Büchner, the German popularizer of a materialistic cosmology.

The Secularist movement spread slowly during the sixties and seventies. At its peak during the early eighties the movement embraced nearly a hundred branches and a total membership of between six and seven thousand. Its support corresponded closely to the pattern of industrialization and developed mainly among the more literate and skilled sections of the working classes. To one observer, it seemed to express the outlook on life which came naturally to the new urban working classes. But the Secularist lecturers were usually men and women who had at some time been active in organized religion and carried into their espousal of Secularism evangelical habits of mind. They appealed most readily to younger members of the working classes for whom chapel or church had been an important influence; where this influence had weakened, the simple versions of Biblical criticism or science presented by the Sec-

[34] "Recent Aspects of Atheism in England," *Christian Examiner*, July, 1859, pp. 339–379; Holyoake and Bradlaugh, *Secularism*, p. 64.
[35] Hypatia Bradlaugh Bonner, *Charles Bradlaugh: A Record of His Life and Work* (London, 1908), II, 141–142.

ularist lecturer completed the process of severing their ties with organized religion.[36]

The outlook fostered by the Bradlaugh school of Secularists stopped short of a radical critique of the social order. Bradlaugh did help to revitalize the older cause of republicanism. On major economic and political questions he was a strong liberal ready to cooperate with middle-class radicals and Nonconformists within the Liberal party. Indeed, Bradlaugh encouraged the tendency, so pronounced among the mid-Victorian working classes, to adopt the prudential, competitive, and self-help ethos of the middle classes. Even his work for the unpopular cause of Malthusianism, or birth control, as a solution to the problem of poverty indicated how fully Bradlaugh accepted the classical theory of political economy, for Malthus' warning of overpopulation had been the only serious challenge to the classical theory's assumption of a natural social harmony. Firmly committed to that theory, Bradlaugh insisted that "an acquaintance with political economy" was as "necessary to the working man as knowledge of navigation to the master of a ship. It is the science of social life." [37]

The absence of any dramatic new social vision helps to explain why so many Secularists passed over into the Socialist movement during the mid-eighties. Its rapid decline also suggested its failure, as one student of the movement concluded, to give men "living in an industrial society a higher purpose and a new morality." Many of those who did become active soon left to join one of the other movements which were proliferating in late Victorian society. An observer in the seventies noted the disposition of Secularists to go over to the most eccentric of the new faiths.[38] Malcolm Quin, who became

36 See John Edwin McGee, *A History of the British Secular Movement* (Girard, Kan., 1948), pp. 92ff; John Eros, "The Rise of Organized Free Thought in England," *Sociological Review*, II (July 1954), 98–120; William Molesworth, *The History of England from the Year 1830 to 1874* (London, 1874), II, 236; Smith, "Atheist Mission," pp. 228–229; and Susan Budd, "The Loss of Faith. Reasons for Unbelief among Members of the Secularist Movement in England, 1850–1950," *Past and Present*, No. 36 (April 1967), 122.

37 Bonner, *Bradlaugh*, II, 171.

38 Eros, "Free Thought in England," p. 118; "The Religious Heresies of the Working Classes," *Westminister Review*, LXXVIII (Jan. 1862), 47.

a prominent provincial leader of British Positivism, recalled that Secularism had been only a brief resting place in his quest for a new faith:

It had no beauty for me. It seemed a home of forlorn souls struggling amidst the flood of modern religious revolution and desperately seeking a new land of promise. . . . I wanted something deeper and wider— something to fill the mind, and take the place of the religion which I had outgrown and which had left me a persisting deposit of memories, affections, imaginations and ideals. Secularism could not do this.[39]

In Positivism Quin found new meaning for memories and feelings which traditional religion had deposited in the consciousness, as many later discovered in Socialism. George Bernard Shaw made the point in his somewhat cynical account of the popular appeal of Socialism:

The working man who has been detached from the Established Church or the sects by the Secularist propaganda, and who, as an avowed Agnostic or Atheist, strenuously denies or contemptuously ridicules the current beliefs in heavens and devils and bibles, will, with the greatest relief and avidity, go back to his old habits of thought and imagination when they reappear in this secular form.[40]

Socialism engaged this deeper structure of sentiments and attitudes, however, only after a complex process of mediation. Marxism entered Britain during the early eighties in a utilitarian form. The assimilation of Marxism to the utilitarian tradition was the first stage in the rapid disintegration of Marxist theory in Britain. In the new political and intellectual climate the major elements of the Marxist system of thought, the rationalistic, the utopian, and what I have called the "realistic," broke apart and developed independently. At the same time they found new points of growth in British life. The chapters that follow will examine this process.

[39] Malcolm Quin, *Memoirs of a Positivist* (London, 1924), p. 48; also see F. J. Gould, *The Life Story of a Humanist* (London, 1923).
[40] George Bernard Shaw, "The Illusions of Socialism," *Forecasts of The Coming Century,* ed. Edward Carpenter (Manchester, 1897), p. 157.

PART II
TRANSFORMATIONS
OF MARXISM

4

The Reception of Marxism in Britain

Marxist theory challenged the basic assumption underlying the main schools of nineteenth-century social thought in Britain—the primacy of consciousness. In developing the radical humanistic wing of Hegelian philosophy, Marx had rejected as utopian the preoccupation of middle-class reformers with changes in man's consciousness; they failed to appreciate the extent to which one's outlook was conditioned by his social or class situation. Marx had attempted, by means of a dialectical understanding of history, to develop a theory which grasped the relationship between consciousness and the social process in integral or reciprocal terms. His theory also claimed to provide a realistic guide for political practice.

Marx's synthesis of theoretical consciousness and revolutionary strategy broke down in the face of the political developments in Europe during the sixties and the seventies.[1] In the closing decades of the century the various Marxist-inspired Social Democratic movements all faced the problem of relating their theoretical picture of social change to the actuality of economic and political life. The early development of Marxists in Britain reflected the uncertain state of their theory. From the beginning they had few inhibitions against combining the new theory with ideas and values drawn from their native traditions. For Marxism the outcome was a rapid loss of theoretical coherence. The process began with the work of the pioneer Marxist propagandist in England, Henry Mayers Hyndman.

[1] See George Lichtheim, *Marxism* (London, 1961), Part III.

Henry Mayers Hyndman and the Formative Years of British Social Democracy

Hyndman turned to Marxism out of a growing conviction that the old political parties in Britain were bankrupt. Raised in a conservative upper middle-class family, he had as a young man developed a "great admiration for John Stuart Mill" and adopted utilitarianism. But he had little sympathy for the liberalism of Gladstone, having developed in his travels as a journalist and company promoter an enthusiasm for the civilizing role of the British empire. In 1880, aroused by the exploitative policies of the British in India, Hyndman decided to run for Parliament. He stood as an independent and appealed to working-class radicals in London on behalf of a "really liberal policy at home" and a more humane imperial administration. He failed to gain much support and withdrew from the contest. This failure, together with an abortive move in the direction of the Conservatives a year later, led Hyndman to consider the possibility of a new political party.[2]

Hyndman met Marx in 1880 and later in the year, on a trip to America, read a French translation of *Capital*. "I learned more from its perusal," he wrote Marx, "than from any other book I ever read." During the months which followed he cultivated Marx, seeking from him "some little encouragement" in guiding "to good . . . the movement . . . for which you have so long waited." Meantime Hyndman contacted the political radicals in London and in March of 1881 promoted the first of several meetings which issued in a new organization, the Democratic Federation. At the same time he began to propagate his version of Marxism.[3]

---

[2] H. M. Hyndman *et al., How I Became a Socialist* (London, 1894), p. 3. In his first letter to Marx, Feb. 19, 1880, Hyndman expressed his belief that "the bust up of parties has already begun" (Karl Marx Correspondence, International Institute of Social History, Amsterdam).

[3] Hyndman to Marx, Oct. 1, 1880, Jan. 1881, and Oct. 29, 1881, *ibid.* The best study of Hyndman's career is Chushichi Tsuzuki, *H. M. Hyndman and British Socialism* (London, 1961). Also see H. M. Hyndman, *The Record of An Adventurous Life* (London, 1911), and *Further Reminiscences* (London, 1923); F. J. Gould, *Hyndman: Prophet of Socialism* (London, 1925); and H. W. Lee and E. Archbold, *Social Democracy in England* (London, 1935).

The Reception of Marxism in Britain   61

It was not a version which pleased Marx and Engels.[4] Hyndman's Socialism was set firmly within a national framework, much like that of Ferdinand Lassalle, from whom he drew some inspiration. The dominant note in his early writings was not the emancipation of the proletariat, but the development of a healthier and more harmonious national life. Indeed, for a brief period Hyndman appeared to be using Marxist ideas to warn the ruling classes of their peril. Even when he took a more radical path Hyndman remained, as George Bernard Shaw described him, "a politician in the higher sense," one who was primarily interested in "societies, states and their destinies." [5] His deep concern for what he believed to be the civilizing mission of Great Britain at times greatly hampered Hyndman's work as a Socialist leader.

Hyndman was not a subtle or rigorous theoretician, he did not present any systematic statement of his Marxism, or carefully work out his social and political philosophy. He simply accepted the tradition of British radicalism as the basis for the new party.[6] The older radicalism had emphasized the political values of liberty and equality and drawn its ideas from various sources—from the dissenting religious tradition, from Paine and William Cobbett, and from the utilitarians and the Secularists. The newer radicals stressed such goals as a fully democratic political order, in Ireland as well as at home, and under the influence of Henry George they turned to the cause of land reform. George's writings and lecture tours did much to sensitize men in the eighties to the problem of economic justice,

[4] The hostility of Marx and Engels toward Hyndman has been attributed mainly to their anger over the latter's failure to give proper credit to Marx for using his ideas in the initial statement of Hyndman's Socialism, *England for All,* published in 1881. See Tsuzuki, *Hyndman,* p. 42. Max Beer, *British Socialism* (London, 1920), II, 228, discusses the theoretical issues behind the estrangement. Also see Henry Collins, "The Marxism of the Social Democratic Federation," *Essays in Labour History, 1886–1923,* ed. Asa Briggs and John Saville (London 1971).

[5] H. M. Hyndman, "Dawn of a Revolutionary Epoch," *Nineteenth Century,* IX (Jan, 1881) 1–18. See Shaw's review of Hyndman's autobiography reprinted as an appendix in R. T. Hyndman, *The Last Years of H. M. Hyndman* (London, 1924).

[6] The radical tradition has been traced in great detail by Simon MacCoby, *English Radicalism* (6 vols.; London, 1935–1961). Also see the series of essays

but George himself was put off by the intolerance of the Socialists and lamented the fact that a man of such force as Hyndman should "follow so blindly such a superficial thinker as Karl Marx." [7]

Hyndman's Marxism centered on the theory of surplus value and its corollary doctrines of working-class exploitation and the class struggle. "He who writes the history of class wars," Hyndman observed in 1882, "writes the history of civilized peoples." Convinced that English politicians should "study the history of their own country and especially working class movements," he attempted in *The Historical Basis of Socialism in England* (1883) to apply Marxist ideas to his country's past. He described the process through which "laborers became more and more blood and flesh mechanisms, at the mercy of a great mechanical force." They had become "literally and truly slaves of their own production," their "bodies and minds stunted and enfeebled by the very nature of their employment." [8]

Although Hyndman attempted to build on the native radical tradition, his Marxism clashed with many of the older attitudes toward society. The Marxist emphasis on conflict and power introduced a note of political realism while its stress on the class struggle and the organic character of society contrasted sharply with the individualistic outlook of the radicals. The shift from the individual to the class as the primary social reality, moreover, necessitated for Hyndman a revision of the classical utilitarian premise of hedonistic individualism: "It is not the individual who forms the judgement as to the utility; but the class, or social position in which he is placed, forms it for him. There is, strictly speaking, no real freedom of choice

---

by John W. Derry, *The Radical Tradition* (London, 1967). Some continuity with the utilitarian tradition was sugested by the presence of Mill's stepdaughter, Helen Taylor, in the Federation's early membership. Miss Taylor left the group in 1884 after a quarrel with Hyndman. She thought him arrogant and morally blind, "as yet only half a socialist" (Taylor to Hyndman, July 25, 1884, John Stuart Mill and Helen Taylor Correspondence, British Library of Political and Economic Science, London).

[7] Henry George to Walker, June 20, 1884, Henry George Correspondence, British Library of Political and Economic Science, London.

[8] H. M. Hyndman, "The Coming Revolution in England," *North American Review*, CXXXV (Oct., 1882), p. 302; H. M. Hyndman, *The Historical Basis of Socialism in England* (London, 1883), pp. 69, 239.

in the matter. Even our needs arise from the system of production, or from the state of things based on the production below." [9]

To view working-class interests in utilitarian terms also entailed a revision of Marxism. Marx had employed the dialectic to overcome the divergence in Western thought between materialism, of which utilitarianism represented one variant, and idealism. He had sought to incorporate into a new monistic outlook both the scientific or deterministic depiction of the external world and the moral or volitional qualities of man's inner life. Marx believed that he had superseded philosophy, in the sense of an abstract understanding divorced from social development, and achieved a new integration between man's knowledge and his practical activity. The reformer or revolutionary, armed with a dialectical understanding of the laws of economic development, would be able to cooperate fruitfully with objective social forces.

Marx's dialectical fusion of science and ethics, of the subjective and objective aspects of experience, and of theory and practice has been described in various ways—as a "scientific substitute for the religious systems of the past," as a "naturalistic vitalism," and as a "myth." But whatever the philosophical or metaphysical status of Marxism, it had entered something of an impasse by the seventies. In this situation, recent commentators have argued, Engels attempted to develop Marxism into a comprehensive world view and produced a system of philosophical materialism emptied of ideal and ethical content.[10]

Hyndman's Marxism may be seen as a variant of this later tendency to revert to a more consistently materialistic view of life. Moreover, Hyndman failed to grasp the importance of the dialectic. Perhaps, as Marx concluded, the British Socialist leader lacked the patience necessary to "study a matter thoroughly." But without the

[9] Hyndman, *Historical Basis*, p. 102.

[10] Rudolph Schlesinger, *Marx, His Time and Ours* (London, 1950), p. 14; George Sabine, *History of Political Theory* (London, 1951), p. 634; Robert Tucker, *Philosophy and Myth in Karl Marx* (Cambridge, 1964); Lichtheim, *Marxism*, pp. 244–258. Eugene Kamenka writes of Engels' "blindness for alienation, his crude evolutionism and his utilitarian concern with economic satisfactions" (*The Ethical Foundations of Marxism* [London, 1962], p. ix).

dialectic Hyndman's Socialism rested on a simple utilitarianism which Marx himself had earlier condemned as a "sophistical rationalization of existing society." [11] Without the dialectical drive toward a constant negation of existing forms of society, Marxism also lost much of its critical force. Hyndman had gone far to eliminate from Socialism the impulse toward a qualitatively different way of life.

Hyndman continued during the eighties to view English development as a fulfillment of the goals of the political radicals, adding only a much more collectivistic view of national policy. He approached the gradualist position which the Fabians later adopted. Hyndman noted the "growing disposition of the state, even in its bourgeois form, to take control of various departments" of life and substitute "collective in some degree . . . for individual effort." [12] He stressed as well the need for strengthening local governing bodies and decentralizing political life. When Hyndman used the term "revolution" in these years he normally meant a peaceful transformation of society, distinguished from reform merely by an increase in tempo and a clear shift of power to the working classes. He expected the propertied classes to surrender power before the rising strength of the proletariat, due either to fear or to an enlightened sense of their own interests. He also appealed to conventional British ideas of justice and fair play.

At times, particularly in the late eighties, Hyndman felt that Britain might pass through a "fiery furnace." But while he entertained the possibility of violence, his view of the Socialist future lacked the utopian note, the expectation of a sudden release of new human capabilities, which characterized most versions of Marxism. Hyndman quickly dissociated himself from those Socialists who sought "to transcend all previous experience of human motives . . . at one bound." He did believe that a Socialist order would

[11] Marx to Friedrich Sorge, Dec. 15, 1881, *Marx and Engels: Selected Correspondence, 1846–1895*, tr. and ed. Dona Torr, (New York, 1942), p. 397. Marx discusses utilitarianism in *German Ideology* (1845–1846). The relevant passages are reprinted in translation as an appendix to Sidney Hook, *From Hegel to Marx* (Ann Arbor, Mich., 1962).

[12] Hyndman, *Historical Basis*, p. 261.

bring an unprecedented flowering of culture, and in a rare departure from his common-sense utilitarianism, insisted that a "truer morality," a "spirit of communism," was emerging among the "most materialized" and "hopeless class" in the slums of the large cities. Usually, however, Hyndman emphasized the need for educational reform and "the habit of work." "In the present condition of production," he wrote, "it is the habit of work at machines which is in effect chiefly needed." Hyndman was not even sanguine about achieving a proper distribution of wealth, for "centuries [might] pass before" the goal was reached.[13] Few Marxists could have accepted such conclusions.

Hyndman organized the Democratic Federation in 1881 because he was convinced that a Socialist society could be achieved only through the independent political force of the workers. Most working-class radicals in London during the early eighties still looked to Bradlaugh and to Charles Dilke for political leadership. But for a time the Federation made headway, resting its appeal on the narrow bases of sympathy for the Irish cause and for land reform. Hyndman's ever sharper criticism of the Liberal party leaders, however, antagonized the working-class members, whose old political loyalties did not die easily. By 1883 most of the working-class radicals had withdrawn. The organization then became the Social Democratic Federation, with an explicit Socialist program and a largely middle-class membership.

Hyndman continued to appeal mainly to the radicals. He even attempted to take advantage of Joseph Chamberlain's effort to re-orient the Liberal party toward a more positive social program, which he saw as a move toward Socialism. On the eve of the general election of 1885, after Chamberlain had presented his "unauthorized program" for more vigorous social action, Hyndman declared that the "difference between us and the radicals is merely one of time and opportunity. . . . The Radicals who follow Mr. Chamberlain

[13] H. M. Hyndman, "Something Better than Emigration," *Nineteenth Century,* XV (Dec., 1884), 998; Hyndman, "Revolutionary Epoch," p. 10; Hyndman, *Historical Basis,* pp. 450–451, 457, 469.

are . . . thoroughly committed to perspectives which lead inevitably to Socialism." [14]

The ensuing split among the Liberals over the home rule issue, Chamberlain's break with the party, and their growing disagreements about social policy presented the Social Democrats with a great opportunity. Many radicals, stranded between the alternative courses of Gladstone and Chamberlain, were receptive to a new program and political strategy. The inability of the Social Democrats to exploit this opportunity to any great extent indicated in part the tenacity of old political allegiances and in part a growing rigidity in the outlook of the Federation. Although its policies directly appealed to working-class interests, Hyndman's organization developed a narrowly rationalistic view of the process through which the working classes attained a consciousness of Socialism. This became clear during 1884 and 1885 as Hyndman's leadership came under attack from two directions within the Federation.

One group, which included William Morris, objected to Hyndman's emphasis on piecemeal reforms, such as the eight-hour day and better housing, as well as the political opportunism associated with these appeals. Late in 1884 this group broke away to form the Socialist League based on the propagation of pure Socialist principles. Meanwhile, a number of Social Democrats, including some who joined the Socialist League, opposed Hyndman on the ground that his principles and tactics were too rigid. They began to desert the Federation to seek more practical opportunities for working-class economic and political action. These two deviations from Hyndman's course will be examined later. To some extent they reflected social or class impulses: middle-class members tended toward a purist and educational policy, while working-class members were drawn toward practical work. But here the defections helped to

[14] H. M. Hyndman, "The Radicals and Socialism," *North American Review,* CLXI (Nov., 1885), 838. Also see the discussion in G. D. H. Cole, *History of Socialist Thought* (London, 1953–1960), II: *Marxism and Anarchism, 1850–1890,* 387ff. On the relationship between the Social Democrats and the radicals in London see Paul Thompson, *Socialists, Liberals, and Labour* (London, 1967), chapters 4, 5, and 6.

clarify Hyndman's Marxist strategy with its curious blend of political opportunism and theoretical dogmatism.

Although Hyndman had restated Marxism in his own terms, he was also convinced that Marx's *Capital* provided a unique and unassailable analysis of British social development. The crucial feature of that development, given the ripening of economic conditions, was an organized and class-conscious proletariat. To develop such a class and provide leadership for it was the primary task of the Federation. At the outset, however, Hyndman faced a fundamental question—to what extent should the British Marxists cooperate with existing working-class organizations and accept the interests they fostered? The immediate practical problem for the Federation was its relationship to the trade-union movement.

Hyndman had no doubt about the answer. From the beginning he saw the "trade union fetish" as the "chief drawback to our progress." [15] He was willing to support the demands of the trade union leaders for immediate reforms such as the eight-hour day, but he firmly opposed close alliance between the Social Democrats and the trade-unions for political purposes. A compromise here would be disastrous for the new party because the trade unionists were only "a small fraction of the total working population." They were "an aristocracy of labor, who in view of the bitter struggle now drawing nearer" represented a "hindrance to that complete organization of the workers which alone can obtain for the workers their proper control over their own labor." [16] The mentality of the typical trade union leader seemed to Hyndman poor soil for the growth of a Socialist outlook. In 1885, when Tom Mann appealed to the Federation's executive to show that they "attached great importance to the trade union and cooperative movement," Hyndman exploded: "What were the precious unions? By whom were they led? By the

[15] Hyndman to Marx, Oct, 29, 1881, Marx Correspondence.

[16] Hyndman, *Historical Basis,* p. 261. He also accepted the Lassallean view of the "iron law of wages," which maintained that the wages going to the working classes under capitalism tended toward the subsistence level. See Tsuzuki, *Hyndman,* pp. 55–56.

most stodgy-brained, dull-witted, and slow-going time servers in the country. To place reliance upon these or go out of our way to conciliate them, would be entirely wrong, and the same applied to the cooperative movement." [17]

Hyndman's refusal to work closely with the trade unionists, on the ground that their organization and outlook hindered working-class solidarity, had considerable justification. The unions were often jealous rivals of each other, and the strong tendencies toward minute and subtle stratifications among the workers had long impeded broader conceptions of working-class economic and political cooperation. Indeed, some younger working-class leaders, particularly in industrial areas without strong unions, were attracted to the Federation mainly because it promised a broader basis of unity. Members or former members of the Federation were prominent in organizing unskilled workers into the new general unions which rose spectacularly at the end of the decade. Social Democratic propaganda also appealed to those workers who either were outside the unions or had lost confidence in them. During 1886 the Federation headed significant agitation on behalf of the unemployed in London. Social Democratic organizers were effective also among workers involved in prolonged labor disputes, as in Lancashire during 1884 and the northeastern mining areas during 1887. After the settlement of these strikes branches of the Federation remained as tangible expressions of a new and more militant spirit among the workers.

Hyndman viewed the development of a Socialist consciousness in terms of Marx's assurance that "as history proceeds, and with it the conflict of the proletariat is shown more plainly . . . they have only to take account of what is passing under their eyes and make themselves the expression of it." [18] Through propaganda he attempted to present to the workers a clear picture of their interests. Frequently he employed invective and taunts to bring home to his working-class audiences the "economic and political malefactions" of the capital-

---

[17] Tom Mann, *Memoirs* (London, 1923), pp. 56–58. Also see Dona Torr, *Tom Mann and His Times*, I: *1856–1890* (London, 1956), 205ff.

[18] Quoted in Hyndman, *Historical Basis*, p. 192, from Marx's *Misery of Philosophy*.

istic class. On occasion Hyndman would chide the workers for their "wooden headed ignorance and stupidity." To some of his fellow Socialists, Hyndman's speeches seemed "almost wholly critical and destructive." [19] But he was concerned above all with inculcating the central Marxist doctrines of economic exploitation and the class struggle. Within the Federation he largely succeeded, and its local branches became noted for their classes in economics and their catechism-like exercises in Marxist theory.

Marxists who retained a belief in the dialectical interaction between consciousness and political practice were especially willing to participate directly in the immediate struggles of the workers. Engels, for example, urged British Marxists to take an active role in the trade unions and other forms of working-class self-help. Hyndman, however, held back. His concern for theoretical rectitude prevented him, despite his strong political opportunism, from entrusting the cause of Socialism to the customary forms of working-class action. Nor was Hyndman willing to enhance the Socialist appeal by pitching his propaganda strongly to the moral sentiments. Many middle-class Socialists, including some of his own associates, increasingly relied on this kind of appeal. But Hyndman's Marxism remained essentially rationalistic; it suffered from the limitations of its utilitarian basis. Hyndman was much less aware than Mill of the inner deficiencies of strict utilitarianism and of the need for moral or emotional reinforcement.

Yet, even in Hyndman's rather narrow terms, British Social Democracy made headway. By 1888 the Federation had started more than forty branches in England and Scotland and gained an active membership of perhaps a thousand. In these years the dry abstractions of Hyndman's Marxism took on life; they proved capable of kindling new hopes in small though scattered bands of followers. The first stage in this process witnessed a struggle between the Social

[19] J. Bruce Glasier, *William Morris and the Early Days of British Socialism* (London, 1921), p. 29. Glasier was highly critical of Hyndman, but a similar description of Hyndman's platform work is in Frank Harris, *Latest Contemporary Portraist,* Series 5 (New York, 1927), p. 324.

Democrats and the Secularists for the allegiance of the more radical sections of the lower classes.

Bradlaugh had recognized the Socialist challenge to the Secularist movement. Early in 1884 he delivered a series of lectures attacking Socialism, and in April he met Hyndman in a public debate.[20] Here Bradlaugh used the stock arguments of orthodox political economy to refute Socialist claims. In response, Hyndman acknowledged that his opponent had "worked many years for the cause" and done "great good." But he insisted that Secularism did not grapple with basic social and economic problems. Although Bradlaugh gained most of the applause, the resulting publicity was a boon to the Federation, and the main issues in the debate were soon being discussed in branch meetings of the National Secular Society up and down the country.

The relations between these "unconscious brothers in arms," as one Socialist recalled, remained for some time "strained and frequently bitter."

Secularists asserted that there could be no substantial social progress until the power of the priest and the Church, with their endeavors to divert the attention of povery-stricken men from their earthly sufferings to the problematical consolations of a better world beyond the skies, had been broken. . . . The Social Democrats on the other hand declared that Christian orthodoxy was already derelict and would soon disappear, and that by attacking it the Secularists were themselves guilty of diverting the attention of the workers from the one thing that mattered, the destruction of the capitalistic system and the establishment of an organic social democracy.[21]

In some areas the Socialist propagandists even blamed their difficulties in making headway on the prevalence of "the atheistic individualistic school of thought." [22]

Yet Socialism appealed strongly to many Secularists. Several of its leaders and a growing number in the rank and file joined the new

20 See Charles Bradlaugh and H. M. Hyndman, *Will Socialism Benefit the English People?* (London, 1884).

21 Lord Snell, *Men, Movements and Myself* (London, 1934), p. 91.

22 *Commonweal*, Dec. 18, 1886.

movement. Edward Aveling and Annie Besant, both vice-presidents of Bradlaugh's organization, were the most prominent converts.[23] Both had turned to the work of popularizing free thought after unhappy marriages occasioned sharp breaks with many of the values and conventions of their middle-class backgrounds. Aveling's desertion of the Secular cause may have been prompted as much by a romantic attachment to Eleanor Marx as by ideological convictions, but during the eighties he became an important interpreter of Marxist theory. Annie Besant, having been personally wounded by Aveling's apostasy, was converted somewhat later by the argumentative powers of George Bernard Shaw. She then offered her great skills as a propagandist to the new Fabian Society.

Other prominent Secularists who joined the Federation were Herbert Burrows and John Burns, who became members of its executive, and A. P. Hazell, a frequent contributor to its organ *Justice*. But the close relation between the old movement and the new was most evident outside of London. As Socialist propaganda began to touch the working classes in the Midlands and the North after 1885 it owed much to the preparatory work of the Secularists. Young Socialist organizers and propagandists like Tom Maguire in Leeds, Ben Turner in Huddersfield, John Bruce Glasier in Scotland, Tom Barclay in Leicester, H. Musgrove Reade in Manchester, and Percy Redfern in Nottingham had all been active Secularists. The pioneer of Socialist propaganda in the Colne Valley, George Garside, had fallen "under the spell of Charles Bradlaugh" as a young man. In the unpromising town of Hastings, a local "freethinker," Toby King, took up Socialism and "gathered some pupils around him." Most of the first Socialists in Bradford were also Secularists; and when Tom Mann traveled to Birmingham in 1886 to start a branch of the Federation his first converts were eight youths from the local Secular Sunday School. Elsewhere, scattered Secularist societies offered the first local hospitality and audiences to Socialist speakers. In the years ahead such prominent Secularist writers and speakers as George

---

[23] See Arthur Nethercot, *The First Five Lives of Annie Besant* (Chicago, 1960), pp. 147ff.

Standring, H. Percy Ward, F. J. Gould, and Chapman Cohen contributed at least part of their energies to the Socialist cause.[24]

Ten years after the founding of the Federation the Secularist movement in Great Britain was moribund. Its decline resulted only partly from the superior appeal of Socialism. Bradlaugh's death in 1891 deprived the movement of a leader of great force. The growing secularization of life, reflected in the decline in church attendance and the growth of popular forms of entertainment, together with changes within organized religion, diminished the relevance of the Secularist attacks. But many of its ideas and aspirations were rechanneled into the Socialist movement. "Instead of Secularism making no headway," a correspondent in *Justice* observed in 1894, "the very opposite is true—the doctrine is making rapid progress in all countries . . . but it is known by the name of Socialism." A few years later the *Labour Annual* explained the "disintegration" of Secularism by noting that "many of the active workers in local societies turned their attention to the Socialist agitation." For "many of the best members of Labor and Socialist societies . . . the first call to public service came from the great leaders of the Secularist movement." [25]

While the Marxism of the Federation appealed strongly to many Secularists it also gave fresh meaning to forms of thought and feeling

[24] See Edward Carpenter *et al., Tom Maguire: A Remembrance* (Manchester, 1896); Ben Turner, *About Myself* (London, 1930); Wilfred Whiteley, *J. Bruce Glasier* (London, 1920); Tom Barclay, *Memoirs of a Bottle Washer* (Leicester, n.d.); H. Musgrove Reade, *From Socialism to Christ* (London, 1909); Percy Redfern, *Journey to Understanding* (London, 1946); D. F. E. Sykes, *The History of the Colne Valley* (Straithwaite, 1906), p. 371; F. C. Ball, *Tressell of Mugsborough* (London, 1951), p. 60; Fenner Brockway, *Socialism over Sixty Years* (London, 1946), pp. 37ff. Mann's converts are described in the *Labour Mail* (Birmingham), Dec. 1906. Early Socialist lectures before Secular societies in Sheffield and other Midland centers are reported in *Justice,* Aug. 30, 1884, and in *Commonweal,* April 1886. The volumes of *Labour Annual* are a rich source of information about figures in the various reform movements at the close of the century. Its biographical sketches frequently indicate a shift of interest from Secularism to Socialism. For Gould see his *Life Story of a Humanist* (London, 1923). Standring, a prominent Secularist printer and editor, became one of the most active Fabians. Also see Chapman Cohen, *Almost a Biography* (London, 1936).

[25] *Justice,* July 24, 1894; *Labour Annual* (Manchester, 1900), p. 84.

which had been shaped by organized religion. The Federation's middle-class converts had often, like Edith Nesbit, "drifted further and further from the conventional world" and had seized on Socialism as a new "gospel of salvation for . . . all the people of the world." [26] The tendency for Socialism to engage sentiments and aspirations loosened from the traditional religious forms became more pronounced in the late eighties and early nineties. Within the Federation, no figure illustrated the transference more clearly than the minister of the Free Christian Church in Croydon, Edmund Martin Geldart. In an early issue of *Justice* he gave lyrical expression to his new Socialist faith:

We Socialists like the early Christians know that we have passed from death unto life since the Socialist gospel sounded in our ears and was embraced in our hearts. We have passed from listlessness to action, from apathy to energy, from despair to hope. From indolent opportunism and from cynical pessimism we are alike delivered. . . . From the pool of perdition, from the curse of this crazy warfare of every man against his brother, Socialism has come to save us.[27]

Geldart's fate, however, was tragic. A congregation which could tolerate his extremely liberal theology was unwilling to countenance his radical social heresy, and he was compelled to resign. In the spring of 1885 Geldart disappeared while crossing the Channel, presumably having jumped to his death.[28]

The extent to which Social Democracy began to replace older religious beliefs was suggested too in the debate, periodic in the early growth of the Federation, over the relationship between Socialism and Christianity. Many Social Democrats were intent on preaching

[26] Doris L. Moore, *Edith Nesbit: A Biography* (London, 1933), p. 58; *Justice,* Sept. 12, 1885.

[27] *Justice,* Nov. 1, 1885.

[28] A writer in *Commonweal,* March 1886, suggested that "the mental depression brought on a sensitive temperament by the worry and brow beating [connected with his resignation] led to . . . the final catastrophe." Hyndman referred to Geldart as one of the "most brilliant" men he had ever known. Geldart's religious and intellectual development is discussed briefly in a memoir by C. B. Upton in *Ethics of Truth: Sermons by the Late E. M. Geldart,* ed. Mrs. Geldart (London, 1886).

Socialism as a new religion or a comprehensive world view. They were opposed by Hyndman and others who wished to build a new political force, for the latter recognized the political liabilities which would attach to explicit anti-Christian propaganda, and they attempted to avoid the issue. They stated their position in *Justice:* "In reply to many inquiries from friends of the cause asking whether Socialism commits its supporters to dogmatic atheism . . . our manifesto should be sufficient answer; there we ask the help of men and women of all creeds and nationalities. We have nothing to do with the religious opinions of anyone who is willing to work with us honestly." [29] But for the former Secularists and for those who attached to Socialism many of the attitudes and feelings drawn from their religious past, the question could not be disposed of so easily. It arose frequently in the heated polemic of the open-air platform, where Social Democratic speakers often had to reply to assertions that God had ordained poverty or that individual regeneration must precede social improvement. The question erupted periodically in the correspondence columns of *Justice.* On several occasions, after extensive discussion, the editors refused to print any more letters dealing with "socialism and religion." Typical was the editorial comment early in 1885: "Our sole aim is to upset the present economic conditions. We shall do this without prejudice against any existing form of religion itself." [30] Later the Federation's leaders attempted to meet the dilemma by adopting a position which, though admittedly antichurch, was not necessarily anti-Christian. But such a tactic, characteristic of much Socialist propaganda in the years ahead, heightened the confusion. Thus, Harry Quelch, a workingman, a strong voice in the executive, and later editor of *Justice*, made the following observation:

Social Democracy is a theory of social organization based upon complete democratic industrial organization as a result of economic development. As such it is purely material; it is concerned neither with religion nor ethics, it is neither atheistic nor theistic. . . . Clericalism is undoubtedly

[29] *Justice,* May 3, 1889.
[30] *Ibid.,* Jan. 3, 1885.

the enemy, not Christianity. Christian ethics are not taught in the churches. . . . Religion, morality and philosophy, and sexual relations are all modified by the material circumstances of life; they do not appreciably modify the material conditions. Christianity has adapted itself to many forms of society. . . . There is nothing in Christianity as far as we can see that militates against its disciples advocating Social Democracy.[31]

The debate on the religious question continued among the Social Democrats, a persistent sign not only of the strong Secularist element within the Federation, but also of the desire of many of its members to expand the meaning of their Socialism beyond Hyndman's conception. Indeed, to the extent that this impulse toward a larger Socialism continued, the Federation's outlook became more sectarian and its capacity for political compromise was further limited.

The aspiration for a broader and deeper conception of Socialism had early built up intolerable pressures within the Federation. In William Morris the impulse toward a more radical change in the quality of existence found a spokesman of great personal force and creative imagination. His challenge to Hyndman in terms of the legacy of ideas from Carlyle and Ruskin opened a new path for the development of British Marxism.

William Morris: The Marxist as Utopian

When Morris arrived as a student at Oxford in 1850 he aspired, with his close friend, Edward Burne-Jones, to form an Anglican religious brotherhood and found a new monastery. Something of this hope for a new brotherhood would persist in a life which became, as a contemporary described it, a "series of splendid enthusiasms." At Oxford the influence of Carlyle and Ruskin soon eclipsed that of the Tractarians. Morris discovered in *Past and Present* and in *Modern Painters* "inspired and absolute truths." Religious aspirations gave way to social and aesthetic ideals. Ruskin became "not only a master of art but throughout the whole sphere of life." Abandoning his plan to enter the church, Morris chose first architecture and then painting as a vocation before discovering his versatile

[31] *Ibid.*, Oct. 15, 1887.

talents in the decorative arts, for which the firm he founded in 1861 meant "the beginning of a new era." [32]

Morris' new vocation centered on the ideal of the "home beautiful," a dwelling filled with useful and aesthetically pleasing objects. The home would become the "visible form of life itself." His ideal appealed to an increasing number of prosperous members of the middle classes who were discarding earlier ascetic values and discovering the aesthetic possibilities of life. Ruskin had done much to form a new middle-class taste. Morris supplied that taste with objects of beauty and superior design—woven and printed fabrics, wallpapers, stained glass, furniture, carpets, and handsomely printed books. He also displayed his appreciation of the purely aesthetic side of life in his poetry. When his highly romantic poem about medieval wanderers, "The Earthly Paradise," was published in 1870, Henry James described it as "an effective antidote for the overwrought self-consciousness of this generation." "It offers," James added, "a glimpse into a world where [men] will be called upon neither to choose, to criticize, nor to believe, but simply to feel, look, and listen." Walter Pater was prompted by the same poem to praise "the love of art for its own sake" and provide a manifesto for a new aesthetics, liberated from religious, moral, or social concerns.[33]

Morris had not abandoned his hope of advancing a Ruskin-inspired "aesthetic revolution" which would bring a new art "by and for the people." Yet it had become clear to him by the early seventies that such a change in English society was not likely, for handicrafts cost "time, trouble, and thought," and only the wealthy classes could afford them. Meanwhile, Morris was experiencing deep personal unrest. An unhappy turn in his married life was perhaps a

---

[32] R. D. Macleod, *Morris without Mackail* (Glasgow, 1954), p. 7; J. W. Mackail, *Life of William Morris* (London, 1889), I, 38; Nicholas Pevsner, *Pioneers of Modern Design* (New York, 1949), p. 9.

[33] Oscar Maurer, Jr., "William Morris and the Poetry of Escape," *Nineteenth Century Studies* ed. Herbert Davis (New York, 1940), pp. 252–254. For the significance of "The Earthly Paradise" in Morris' development see Edward Thompson, *William Morris: Romantic to Revolutionary* (London, 1955), pp. 140–163.

major cause,[34] but he also felt a deepening sense of the spiritual confinement of Victorian life. This mood underlay his growing absorption in Icelandic literature. His trip to the island in the summer of 1871 and greater familiarity with Icelandic mythology introduced into his outlook a heroic element which registered strongly on his Socialism. He was deeply stirred by the primitive character of the remote land and even more by the savage and violent world revealed by the sagas, which pictured life as a heroic struggle of men against the gods and each other, a life of strife, destruction, and renewal. Of this outlook on life, Morris wrote, "I think one could be a happy man if one could hold it, in spite of the wild dreams and dreadful imaginings that hung about it here and there." He began to view his age in terms of its possibilities for heroic achievement. In his poetic work, as Edmund Gosse observed of the translation of "Sigurd the Volsung," Morris had left "escapist" poetry and become the "interpreter of high desires and ancient heroic hopes." [35]

Morris became a social activist in 1877, when he plunged into a campaign to protect ancient buildings and assumed a leading role in the political agitation aroused by the Turkish massacres in the Near East. In a series of lectures on art and social subjects, he began to elaborate an aesthetic gospel, which, with new conclusions to some of the root ideas of Carlyle and Ruskin, would make up the core of his Socialism.

Following Ruskin, Morris judged social development in terms of the vitality of the decorative arts; their decay was both a symptom and a cause of social breakdown. England, he held, had reached such a point. Its pervasive man-made ugliness and vulgarity were closely related to the greed of the commercial system and growth of class antagonism. The solution to these problems lay in the renewal of craftsmanship and of man's capacity to "beautify the familiar matters of everyday." The "great office of decoration" was "to give

[34] The apparent love affair between Janey Morris and Rossetti is discussed in Oswald Doughty, *Dante Gabriel Rossetti: A Victorian Romantic* (2nd ed.; London, 1960), Book III.

[35] Mackail, *Morris,* I, 334; Maurer, "Morris," p. 267.

people pleasure in the things they must perforce use" and also "in the things they must perforce make." The recovery of man's "delight in beauty," his "god-like part," required, however, that the gulf between the handicraftsman and the major artists, painters, sculptors, and architects be overcome: "For as the arts sundered into the greater and the lesser, contempt on the one side, carelessness on the other arose. . . . The artist came out from the handicraftsmen, and left them without hope of elevation, while he himself was left without the help of intelligent understanding sympathy." [36] Without a popular basis in craftsmanship, all the arts, including poetry and music, died, and the "loss of peace and the good life" followed.

The distance Morris had traveled from the social romanticism of Carlyle was evident in his pivotal notion of work. For Carlyle, still strongly puritan in outlook, work was a duty, usually painful and unpleasant, but inevitable. Through work men checked the anarchic tendencies of their natural desires. Work also assumed liturgical qualities for Carlyle; it was a form of worship and a source of grace. Ruskin, however, de-emphasized the negative or repressive aspects of work. He virtually erased the distinction between artists and workers and stressed the way in which man might fulfill himself through his labor. Morris went even further in discarding the older ascetic attitudes. He hated puritanism with a passion and thought Calvin "quite the worst man that ever lived." For Morris, work properly understood was synonymous with art. The disposition of earlier romantics to set the artist off from ordinary men seemed to him "sheer nonsense." "What is an artist but a worker who is determined that . . . his work should be excellent?" Work and art should be regarded simply as the "pleasurable exercise of man's faculties." No work, he wrote in 1881, "that cannot be done with pleasure in the doing is worth doing." [37] For Morris, artistic activity became the primary source of human happiness and the chief end in life.

[36] "The Lesser Arts," *William Morris: Selected Writings and Designs,* ed. Asa Briggs, Penguin Edition (Harmondsworth, 1962), pp. 84–105.

[37] Ernest Belfort Bax, *Outlooks from the New Standpoint* (London, 1891), p. 33; Mackail, *Morris,* I, 186, II, 63.

By the early eighties, however, Morris had come to despair of the possibility of a "new dawn of the arts" and a social "rebirth." Having lost confidence in conventional political methods, he was also becoming convinced that "disaster and misfortune" might be necessary to "cure us." [38] At this point he turned to Marxism and Hyndman's Democratic Federation. Later he recalled his state of mind:

Apart from the desire to produce beautiful things, the leading passion of my life has been and is hatred of modern civilization. . . . What shall I say concerning . . . its stupendous organization for the misery of life . . . and its contempt of simple pleasures which everyone could enjoy but for its folly? Its eyeless vulgarity which destroyed art, the one solace of labour? . . . The hope of past times was gone; the struggle of mankind for many ages had produced nothing but this sordid, aimless, ugly confusion; the immediate future seemed to me likely to intensify all the present evils by sweeping away the last survivals of the day before the dull squalor of civilization had settled down on the world. . . . So there I was in for a fine pessimistic end of life, if it had not somehow dawned on me that amidst all the filth of civilization the seeds of a great change, what we others call Social Revolution, were beginning to germinate. The whole face of things was changed for me by the discovery that all I had to do in order to become a Socialist was to hook myself onto the practical movement.[39]

The heroic and visionary qualities in Marxism struck deep chords in Morris. A decade earlier in Iceland he had begun to conceive of social regeneration on an epic scale. The hope now found new meaning:

I have no more faith than a grain of mustard seed in the future history of "civilization," which *I know* now is doomed to destruction and probably before very long; what a joy it is to think of: and how often it consoles me to think of barbarism once more flooding the world, and real feelings and passions, however rudimentary, taking the place of our wretched hypocrisies.[40]

[38] Philip Henderson, ed., *The Letters of William Morris* (London, 1950), p. 113.
[39] "How I Became a Socialist," in Briggs, ed., *Morris,* p. 36.
[40] Henderson, ed., *Letters,* p. 236.

The Marxist interpretation of history promised an upheaval; it also fit into the scheme of aesthetic and social degeneration which Morris had drawn from Ruskin. Marx explained, as Ruskin did not, the causes of the changes which had degraded the arts and reduced the craftsman to a machine. Marx also disclosed the class struggle as the source of the energy to destroy the blight of "commercialism." Morris embraced Marxism as a new revelation. "I cannot conceive," he wrote in 1884, "of anyone who loves beauty, that is to say the crown of a full and noble life, being able to face it unless he has full faith in the religion of socialism." [41]

Although Marxism provided Morris with a new explanation of social development, it did not mesh easily with his aesthetic gospel. The new system of thought was superimposed on his earlier ideas rather than integrated with them.[42] This was ironic in a sense, for Marx's early thought was deeply rooted in a German humanist tradition which ran parallel to the social romanticism of Carlyle and Ruskin. Marx's initial emphasis on man's "alienation" expressed an ideal of human nature which, in its ethical and aesthetic concern, had much in common with the views of Ruskin and Morris. In the later development of Marxism these concerns tended to fade. The Marxism of the eighties, whether in the form developed by Engels or that of Hyndman, left little room for the questions which engaged Morris most deeply. On the problems of art and the artist and the quality of life under Socialism, this Marxism was silent. Just as Hyndman had translated Marx into familiar terms, so too Morris, even less a theoretician than the Federation leader, inserted his own ideas and values into the Marxist framework. The resulting conflict between these two versions of British Marxism helped to split the Social Democrats.

[41] Morris, "The Exhibition of the Royal Academy," *Today,* July 1884; reprinted in May Morris, *William Morris* (2 vols.; New York, 1966), I, 225–241.

[42] Edward Thompson argues that Morris "grafted Ruskin to the stem of Marx" (*Morris,* p. 773). G. D. H. Cole was more accurate when he stated that Morris "grafted a sort of Marxism upon" his "artistic gospel" (*Socialist Thought,* II, 421). See also Cole's essay on Morris in his *Selected Writings of William Morris* (London, 1944). Morris apparently recognized the disjunction between his Socialist commitments and his aesthetic aspirations. As late as 1889 he spoke

Morris had joined Hyndman's organization in 1883. Within six months he was complaining privately that Hyndman was "too sanguine of speedy change happening somehow" and "too inclined to intrigue and the making of a party." The schism, which occurred at the end of 1884, owed something to clashes of temperament; it also expressed growing resentment at Hyndman's autocratic tendencies. But the fundamental disagreements lay in the areas of aims and tactics. Morris believed that the Federation had "neglected education for agitational" work and had not looked after its branches properly. Hyndman's emphasis on "adventure, show and advertisement," he feared, would at best bring only a "mechanical" or "Bismarckian" Socialism:

I cannot stand all this, it is not what I mean by Socialism, either in aim or in means: I want a real revolution, a real change in Society: Society a great organic mass of well regulated forces used for bringing about a happy life for all. And means for attaining it are simple enough, education in socialism and organization for the time when the crises shall force action upon us: nothing else will do us any good at present: the revolution cannot be a mechanical one, though the last act of it may be civil war, or it will end in reaction after all.[43]

Early in 1885 Morris and other dissident Social Democrats founded the Socialist League in an attempt to develop an alternative strategy to that of Hyndman. It was soon deeply divided. Some members, like Morris, regarded Hyndman as simply a political opportunist and wanted to distinguish their Socialist faith more clearly from existing social conventions and values. Others thought Hyndman doctrinaire and impractical and hoped for a more flexible strategy and new opportunities for working-class industrial and political action. Morris, having reluctantly accepted the leadership of the

---

of the need for the "two revolts" to "join hands, or at least understand each other" (May Morris, *Morris*, I, 267). For a recent discussion of Morris' Socialism, which stresses the influence of Kropotkin, see James Hulse, *Revolutionists in London* (Oxford, 1970), pp. 77–110

[43] Henderson, ed., *Letters*, pp. 180–181, 226–229. Also see May Morris, *Morris*, II, 592–595; Friedrich Buenger, *Engels und die Britische Sozialische Bewegung* (Berlin, 1962), pp. 55–79.

League, attempted to mediate between the developing anarchist and reformist factions. For a time this divergence was contained, and the League grew. By 1886 it had enlisted a thousand members and embraced more than a score of branches, including small but vital groups in Glasgow, Bradford, Leeds, and Norwich.[44] The growing internal antagonism made a showdown inevitable. Morris, strongly suspicious of palliatives, whether pursued through trade union or political channels, sided with the more militant and increasingly anarchist wing. During 1888 and 1889 the anarchist element gained control of the League and its weekly, *Commonweal*, and then forced out the more moderate Morris. But during its brief and stormy life the League developed, largely due to Morris, a view of Socialist strategy and consciousness which deeply influenced the movement.

Morris insisted that the primary task of the League was education—the "making of Socialists." In his propaganda work Morris did not neglect economic questions; he insisted that the abolition of private property and the collectivization of the means of production, distribution, and exchange were fundamental goals. Nor did he ignore the problem of organization. He envisioned the creation of a body of men—many of them workers—with a good grasp of theory and capable of imparting to the masses an understanding of their exploited position and an awareness of their potential power. This body would also provide leadership during the revolutionary crisis. But Morris' view of education, or the task of building up a Socialist consciousness, indicated his persistence in moral and aesthetic preoccupations carried over from Ruskin. His Socialism may be distinguished sharply from the Marxism of Hyndman, both in its view of progress toward Socialism and its deep concern with the nature of the future society.

Most Marxists, including Engels and Hyndman, measured progress toward Socialism mainly in objective terms such as the growth of an organized, self-conscious working class or the developing economic crises within capitalism. But Morris judged the progress of the movement in terms of the purity and strength of its principles and the

---

[44] Thompson, *Morris,* pp. 488–489. This book provides the best account of the development of the League.

capacity of Socialists to exemplify these principles in their daily lives. "Let us remember," he wrote in 1886, "the religion of Socialism calls upon us to be better than other people since we owe ourselves to the society which we have accepted as the hope of the future." Dedicated to the task of nurturing a higher moral and social life, Morris resisted all forms of action which might endanger the purity of Socialist consciousness. As early as 1885 he had begun to worry about the possibility of the middle classes drawing the workers into their own ranks and infecting them with their "terrible moral degradation . . . their hypocrisy, their cowardice, their joylessness." Later, after the breakup of the League, he expressed his fears that the "tremendous organization of civilized commercial society" might play "the cat and mouse game with socialists, adopting quasi-socialistic machinery" to uphold "a society of inequality . . . in a somewhat shorn condition . . . but a safe one." The working classes might be "contented with some outward show of . . . real socialism" and be satisfied simply with an "increase of prosperity" because they did not "know what the pleasures of life might be if they treated their own capacities and the resources of nature reasonably." [45] And so Morris set out to guard the Socialist ideal against the tempting but fraudulent opportunities provided by existing economic and political institutions. For example, he opposed cooperation with the trade unionists, agreeing with Hyndman that they represented a privileged minority among the workers.

The purist Socialist consciousness of Morris was expressed most clearly in his attitude toward politics. As against those in the League who favored political action, Morris argued that there was "no necessity for a revolutionary party doing any 'dirty work' at all, or soiling ourselves with anything that would unfit us for being true citizens in the new order of things." Political activity would lower their "moral tone." To play the parliamentary game would implicate Socialists in the corrupt way of life they were seeking to supersede. At times in the late eighties he wondered whether the League had not been "too stiff" in its refusal to compromise. But he continued

[45] Commonweal, Aug. 28, 1886, July, 1885; "Communism," The Collected Works of William Morris, ed. May Morris, XXIII (London, 1910), 267–268.

to urge his companions back to their "first idea," the need to make "genuine, convinced Socialists." They must continue to abstain from politics.[46] Engels, observing the League's course, dismissed Morris as an "emotional socialist" and described the League as dominated by "muddle heads" and "faddists" who were too stupid to "concern themselves with the living movement." [47]

Morris still expressed the idealistic outlook which Marx had attempted to exorcise by means of the dialectic. Marx, following Ludwig Feuerbach, had viewed previous religious or ethical ideals as aspects of a "false consciousness," as compensations men had developed for a mean existence. A dialectical understanding of history overcame the divorce between ideals and reality by disclosing the true nature of social development. To Marx ethics was simply a form of knowledge; moral behavior corresponded to the "real" or "significant" trends in present society. But the dialectic was no more a part of Morris' outlook than it had been of Hyndman's. The latter had instead fallen back on conventional materialism and emphasized the rational or scientific bent in Marxism. Now, Morris, working out of a romantic tradition, reverted to the utopianism from which Marx believed he had rescued Socialists. In the divergence between Hyndman and Morris two sides of Marxism, welded together by means of the dialectic, broke apart and underwent independent developments. The idealism of Morris expressed itself mainly in an attempt to develop a more vivid picture of the Socialist future.

On one occasion Morris divided Socialists into the "analytical" and the "constructive" types. While the former delighted in the "perfection of some favorite theory," the latter, with whom Morris identified himself, "use our eyes more than our reasoning powers" and take pleasure in "guessing about the future." [48] As a Marxist, Morris recognized the dangers of such ideal constructions, and he

[46] Henderson, ed., *Letters,* pp. 262, 291–293, 304. Also see Laurence Thompson, *The Enthusiasts: A Biography of John and Katharine Bruce Glasier* (London, 1971), pp. 34–39.

[47] Engels to Sorge, April 29, Sept. 17, Nov. 29, 1886, *Karl Marx and Friedrich Engels: Letters to Americans,* ed. Leonard Mins (New York, 1942), pp. 156, 162, 165. Other letters are cited in Buenger, *Engels,* pp. 80ff.

[48] "The Society of the Future," May Morris, *Morris,* II, 453ff.

disclaimed any intention of presenting in his *News From Nowhere* a blueprint for the future Socialist society. But the vision offered in his utopian novel was the natural outcome of ideas and beliefs scattered throughout his essays and letters.[49] It also represented a culminating expression of the social romanticism he had drawn from Carlyle and Ruskin and the emergence of a form of Socialist consciousness which, after a series of mediations, would reach the lower classes in the years just ahead.

The most striking feature of "Nowhere" was the virtual disappearance of external restraint in human relationships. Having abolished private property and attained equality of material conditions through a revolutionary upheaval, the people of "Nowhere" had done away with prisons, criminal laws, regulations about marriage and divorce, indeed, the whole apparatus of government and politics in the old sense. The less tangible pressures of public opinion and moral convention were eliminated as well. Even the notion of duty, felt as constraint, ceased to burden the individual.[50] The new society found unity through man's natural urge toward "fellowship" and "association." Only a passing reference to the possible destructive effects of sexual passion marred the picture which Morris drew of a coming social harmony. "We should trend," he wrote in another context, "to the abolition of all government, and even of all regulations that were not merely habitual; and voluntary associations would become a necessary habit, and the only bond of society." In the future Socialist community men would be neighbors rather than citizens; human relationships would be those of "loved and lover, parent and child, friend and friend." [51]

This emphasis on the primary affections and the image of the loving family expressed a fundamental strain in Morris' outlook.

[49] The fullest statement appears in four letters written to the Reverend George Bainton in April and May of 1888. The social philosophy expressed here is very close to the picture of life in Morris' *News From Nowhere* (London, 1891). See Henderson, ed., *Letters*, pp. 282–291.

[50] At times Morris suggested that constraint would simply be reduced to a minimum rather than abolished.

[51] Henderson, ed., *Letters*, p. 288. Also see "True and False Society," in Morris, ed., *Collected Works*, XXIII, 237.

Indeed, to his friend William Butler Yeats, all that he wrote seemed "like the make believe of a child, who is remaking the world, not always in the same way, but always after his own heart . . . [and] out of unending pictures of happiness." A few years earlier Morris had "demanded" the "end of all asceticisms." In *News From Nowhere* he had elevated the spontaneous desires of the individual to the supreme place in life. Even morality took its place alongside work and art as the "pleasurable exercise of one's energies," as the natural activity of the healthy individual. The vitality of the new society would derive from an "art or work pleasure . . . springing up almost spontaneously, it seems, from a kind of instinct among the people." [52]

In the aesthetic utopia portrayed by Morris, objective social and economic forces also ceased to operate as significant restraints on the individual. Despite his Marxism, Morris could not fully reconcile himself to modern technology. He was less hostile to industrialization than Ruskin, but he shared the latter's sense of the antagonism between man and the machine. And he hoped that men would "forego some of the power over nature won by past ages in order to be more human and less mechanical." [53]

The Socialist vision of Morris expressed once more the archaism of Carlyle and Ruskin; he shared their nostalgia for earlier and simpler forms of community. He also carried much further the tendency, apparent in the thought of Ruskin, to exclude from men's consciousness acknowledgment of those forces in life, formerly categorized as the sinful or the tragic, which moderated the desires and hopes of men. Viewed from traditional philosophical and religious wisdom, Morris' vision was regressive and escapist, but he was also protesting on behalf of qualities of life which were menaced by the relentless drive of modern society toward economic rationalization. Through his resolute refusal to adjust to the demands of "modernization," Morris transmitted to the subsequent development

[52] Peter Faulkner, *William Morris and W. B. Yeats* (Dublin, 1962), p. 16; "The Society of the Future," in May Morris, *Morris,* II, 457; Cole, ed., *Selected Writings,* p. 300.

[53] "The Society of the Future," in May Morris, *Morris,* II, 461.

of British Socialism a concern for the quality of existence which possessed an enduring appeal. He was one of the first figures in the later history of Marxism who attempted to reinstate the humanistic impulses present in its origins.

Morris lost something of his intransigence after 1890 when he ceased to play a very active part in the movement. As Socialism began to take a more practical and political direction he conceded that it was "spreading on the only lines on which it could spread." Yet he could not, given his view of the good life, reconcile himself to the trend. Indeed, the change "towards unideal and humdrum 'gradual improvement' " reinforced his belief in a coming "general deadlock and breakup." Nor could he hide his disgust with the typical man of his day. "The humbug which floats to the top in all 'branches of intelligence,' " he wrote, was "such a damned greasy pot of scum." [54]

His refusal to accommodate the Socialist vision to existing human and social realities, as much as his elaboration of the vision itself, gives Morris significance in the developing life of the movement. More than any other figure he expressed a kind of idealism, strongly inclined toward anarchism and strongly hostile to conventional political activity, which worked deeply into popular Socialism. Carlyle and Ruskin had done much to nurture this spirit; Morris articulated it within the movement. Yet Morris himself had little direct impact on these sections of the lower classes that were turning toward Socialism. He was not an effective speaker or propagandist. "For street corners," a colleague wrote, "his style was a trifle profound." [55] But it was not primarily a matter of rhetoric. His central concerns— the problem of making producers creative and products genuinely useful and beautiful—simply did not correspond to the deeply felt needs of his working-class audiences. In developing some of the aesthetic possiblities of a new cultivated middle-class taste, Morris had passed well beyond the sensibilities of all but a few of the workers. Indeed, on a number of issues, including politics and religion,

[54] Henderson, ed., *Letters*, p. 321; *Commonweal*, Oct. 7, 1890.
[55] James Leatham, *William Morris: Master of Many Crafts* (London, 1899).

Morris and the League were even more antagonistic than the Federation to those who might otherwise have been their most promising recruits.[56] Viewed simply in terms of those moral and aesthetic values which Morris himself regarded as supremely important, he had fewer ties with the outlook of the working classes than did Carlyle or Ruskin.

Morris did gain a small personal following, not from the working classes, but from the indeterminate social strata just above or outside. Actually, the League had drawn a substantial part of its membership from the lower middle classes,[57] and Morris' real disciples were most often young men from this sector of society who had poetic temperament and aspirations. They included Fred Henderson, a clerk in Norwich; John Bruce Glasier, an architect's apprentice in Glasgow; James Leatham, a printer-journalist in Aberdeen; Joe Whittaker, a clerk in Wolverhampton; and Tom Maguire, a photographer and newspaper vendor in Leeds. These men and others, most notably Robert Blatchford, blended the aesthetic gospel of Morris with their own particular religious, moral, and social views and carried forward the work of linking the Socialist ideal with the immediate sentiments and interests of the working classes. In the process Morris' utopian bent was confirmed and strengthened; it was also translated, in the form of Ethical Socialism, into a more popular idiom.

The main line of the movement's growth may be clarified further, however, by looking briefly at two other important Socialist writers of the eighties. In their very different ways, Ernest Belfort Bax and Edward Carpenter were also attempting to translate Socialism into a new and comprehensive view of life. The relative failure of Bax and the relative success of Carpenter in communicating their ver-

[56] The League's correspondence indicates that its propaganda work was greatly hindered, especially in Scotland, by the claim made in the "Manifesto" that the religion of Socialism was the "only religion the League possesses" (Socialist League Correspondence and Papers, No. 1298/1, 1298/2, International Institute of Social History, Amsterdam).

[57] The Manchester branch consisted of 5 students, 1 accountant, 1 traveler, 1 draughtsman, 1 photographer, 1 foreign correspondent, 1 gardener, 2 warehousemen, 1 agent, 2 press, 1 cotton spinner (ibid.), No. 605. Correspondents to the League's headquarters most often described themselves as clerks.

sions of Socialism suggested the forms of thought and feeling on which the movement would largely depend in the years ahead.

Two Prophets of a Socialist World View: Ernest Belfort Bax and Edward Carpenter

Bax and Carpenter approached the task of nurturing a Socialist consciousness from sharply contrasting perspectives. Bax was a philosopher and Carpenter a poet. Yet beneath these different approaches lay a common desire to replace prevailing moral and religious conventions with the values they believed to be implicit in Socialism. Both were seeking to expand the meaning of Socialism to embrace all aspects of life.

In 1871 the struggle of the French Communards awakened Bax's sympathy for revolution and hastened his estrangement from a middle-class, Nonconformist religious background. In search of a new faith, he turned initially to the English Positivists and while he did not join the movement the Comtean idea of a "religion of humanity" became fundamental in his outlook.[58] He took a strong philosophical turn in the mid-seventies after he had gone to Germany to study music. Contact with German thought encouraged him to develop his own philosophical system, an embryonic form of which appeared in a short essay published in 1879, "The Word Religion." Here he attempted to appropriate the concept of the "religious" for purely humanistic ends. Following Comte, he fixed on the moral idea of humanity as the only ideal capable of serving as the object of the "religion of the future." Man's moral sense, as distinguished from his aesthetic or rational capacities, "supplied an end directly incentive to action." [59]

Bax thus renewed the struggle of Mill and others to displace the old religious sentiments with feelings and energies centered on a social ideal. The future religion would immortalize the "social man rather

---

[58] For biographical details see Ernest Belfort Bax, *Reminiscences and Reflections of a Mid and Late Victorian* (London, 1918). Bax's relationship to Positivism is discussed briefly in Royden Harrison, *Before the Socialists* (London, 1965), pp. 375ff.

[59] *Modern Thought,* May 1879, pp. 67–69.

than the individual man." But unlike the utilitarians and the Positivists, Bax did not dismiss metaphysical questions. Science did not exhaust the knowable. There was within man's consciousness a "feeling" of "something beyond," an intuition of "being" as distinguished from the "phenomena" or "experience" which dominated everyday existence. This notion of an elemental force beneath consciousness became pivotal to his philosophy of Socialism; it was also a sign of his continuing debt to German thought. Indeed, his philosophical position can best be seen as an extension of the German idealist tradition. It was expressed in scattered essays on German thinkers and most fully in his *Handbook to a History of Philosophy,* published in 1886.

In developing his own system of philosophy Bax drew mainly on Kant, Hegel, Arthur Schopenhauer, and the contemporary German thinker, Eduard von Hartmann, whom he knew personally. The idea of the "alogical," on which Bax's system rested, was inspired by von Hartmann's notion of the "unconscious." By means of the "alogical" Bax attempted to describe more adequately the "source" or "ultimate datum of consciousness" and the "point of contact" between "that which appears and that which is." He described the "alogical" in various ways—as "Being," or a "feltness through which Being disclosed itself in consciousness" and as the element of "chance" in the natural world. It was prior to thought but passed into the synthetic object of consciousness only through the mediation of thought. Although the spontaneous underlying force could not attain actuality without the act of thought, it dominated the resulting synthesis. Reason was ever the "handmaid of feeling." [60]

The metaphysical notion of the "alogical" was crucial to Bax's approach to Socialism. He viewed Marxism, in the context of German philosophy, as a case of arrested development. Marx, along with the other left-wing Hegelians, had recognized, according to Bax, the limi-

[60] Bax discusses the concept in an essay, "Arthur Schopenhauer," *Modern Thought,* Oct. 1880, p. 488. Also see the introduction in E. Belfort Bax, ed., *Selected Essays of Arthur Schopenhauer* (London, 1891), and the discussion in his *Handbook to a History of Philosophy* (London, 1886), pp. 398ff. He develops it more fully in *The Problem of Reality* (London, 1892), especially pp. 14, 90–92, 102.

tations of idealism and acknowledged the place of nonlogical or material elements in the "production of the experienced world." But Marx had attempted, mistakenly, to retain Hegel's dialectical method "apart from metaphysics." "Without metaphysics," Bax argued, the "dialectical method" was a "tree cut away from its roots." It possessed "no justification as an instrument of research." "Where is our ground for observing a determined order at all," Bax asked, if we don't recognize that "the unity of our experience and the rationality which we find in the universe . . . is deducible in the last resort from the primal unity of the consciousness?" Because they ignored the underlying metaphysical issues, Marx and Engels had become imprisoned in a "crude and dogmatic materialism." Nevertheless, Bax believed that Marx had discovered the "basal factor determining the constitution of society" in its "material and economic condition." [61] He accepted the Marxist analysis of economic development and the prognosis of a revolutionary transformation. Fundamental changes in human consciousness would await this transformation.

Bax presented a summary of Marxism for English readers in an article written in 1882. The piece earned him the gratitude and praise of Marx himself, though privately Marx expressed some reservations.[62] Bax had concentrated on the economic and social analyses within Marxism and did not raise metaphysical or ethical questions. But these questions, and the problem of consciousness, would largely occupy Bax in the years ahead as he set out to develop a philosophy for Socialists.

Bax placed his philosophy in a scheme of history which drew on Hegel, Comte, Thomas Spence, and Lewis Morgan, as well as Marx and Engels.[63] He viewed history as man's development from the un-

[61] Bax, *Handbook,* pp. 340–341; *Outlooks,* pp. 187–188; *Reminiscences,* p. 46; *The Religion of Socialism* (London, 1885), p. iv.

[62] "Karl Marx," *Modern Thought,* Dec. 1881, pp. 349–354; Marx to Sorge, Dec. 15, 1881, Dona Torr, ed., *Marx and Engels: Selected Correspondence,* p. 398.

[63] See Bax's essays "Universal History from a Socialist Standpoint," in *Religion of Socialism;* "The New Ethic," in *The Ethics of Socialism* (London, 1887); "The Economical Basis of History," in *Outlooks;* "The Materialist Doctrine of History," in *Outspoken Essays on Social Subjects* (London, 1897).

conscious social solidarity of primitive society through a period of private property, individualism, and class struggle, toward a conscious social solidarity in communism. Where Marx and Engels were preoccupied with economic change and attempted to lay bare the contradictions within objective economic and social forces, Bax was interested primarily in subjective states—in ideals, values, and attitudes. He differentiated historical periods in terms of their metaphysical and ethical outlooks and sought to uncover the tensions in man's inner life. The drama of history consisted of the evolution of man's consciousness.

According to Bax, just as the rise of Christianity represented a decisive moment in the development of man's consciousness, its breakdown prepared the way for the new Socialist outlook. Christian thinkers had recognized that "the empirical self implied more than it expressed" and postulated a supernatural realm in which man might find completion. Men had turned introspective and ascetic, seeking to purge themselves of natural desires. It was "to this moment or stage in the evolution of moral consciousness that the conceptions of sin and holiness, with the derivative ones of chastity and purity belong." Social obligations and the worth of this life were disparaged; the "earth" had been "drained of its ideal to feed heaven." In short, the "ethics of inwardness," as Bax called it, "severed the individual from society and nature and from the pleasures of the phenomenal world" and destroyed "natural desires and affections." This ethic led to a "complete withdrawal of the individual into himself," for it insisted that the "primal impulse to total regeneration and the realization of world progress must come from within." Bax believed, however, that Christianity was nearly exhausted in contemporary life, and he saw signs of the growth of a new ethic which, in its "highest potency," would become the "religion of Socialism." [64]

Bax was confident that the dialectical mode of understanding enabled him to penetrate beneath the "phenomena as presented to the common sense world" and "unlock the innermost secret of

[64] Bax, *Ethics of Socialism*, pp. 13, 51; *Handbook*, p. 402; *Ethics of Socialism*, p. 5.

every reality." Applied to man's own nature, a dialectical analysis indicated that the "true significance" of man's personality did not "lie in itself." Man was "merely a passing phase in something intrinsically more comprehensive than himself," a mere "incident" in a larger process. Bax foresaw the emergence of a higher or "super organic" consciousness:

May not the true significance of Ethics, of Duty, of the Ought, of Conscience, the conviction that the telos of the individual lies out of himself as such, consist in the fact that he is already tending toward absorption in a Consciousness which is his own indeed, but yet not his own, that this limited self consciousness of the animal body with the narrow range of its memory synthesis is simply subservient and contributory to a completer and more determinate Self Consciousness of the Social body as yet inchoate in Time? If this be so, the craving of the mystic for union with the Divine Consciousness in some transcendent sphere would be but the distorted expression of a truth perfectly consistent with the recognized lines of scientific materialism . . . that self conscious though he may be, the personality of the human animal is yet not the last word of Self Consciousness, but is in its nature subordinate to a higher Self Consciousness, his relation to which the individual human being dimly feels but cannot formulate in Thought.[65]

Bax's Socialist philosophy thus culminated in the vision of a restored harmony, not only of man with his fellows, but of his inner life as well. Consciousness in the old sense would disappear, absorbed in a higher consciousness or immediate communion with reality. In the perfect integration of the future, conscience, or traditional moral tension, would be eliminated, for the "alogical" itself would be "immediately presented as universal." Spontaneity rather than law would triumph. The "truth" as formulated in the "categories of scientific thought" would be absorbed in "truths expressed in the immediacy we call feeling," which were now realized "more or less imperfectly in the various forms of art." [66]

Bax's speculations about the future provided a kind of philosophical counterpart to the utopianism of Morris. In their different

[65] Bax, *Outlooks,* p. 187.
[66] Bax, *Problem of Reality,* pp. 96, 56–57, 130, 103.

ways the two men foresaw an escape from the tensions of ordinary consciousness and the achievement of a way of life free from conflict and anxiety. Bax, like Morris, devoted his main efforts within the movement to the task of enlightening Socialists as to their ethical or religious mission rather than to the political and economic struggles of the workers.

Bax was one of the pioneer Social Democrats and, in the early years, one of the most outspoken critics of Hyndman's policies. With Morris he believed that Hyndman's leadership endangered the integrity of the Socialist creed, and he played a major role in the formation of the Socialist League.[67] Bax and Morris wrote the League's "Manifesto," which concluded with an exhortation on behalf of the "religion of Socialism." Bax also worked closely with Morris in preparing the League's paper, *Commonweal,* and the two men collaborated in writing a book, *Socialism, Its Growth and Outcome.* As the League floundered in factional strife, however, Bax returned to the Federation, where he served on the executive for a number of years and, for a brief period, edited *Justice.*

In his work for the Socialist press and the propaganda platform, Bax was largely occupied in attacking middle-class conventions. Socialism was "the great modern protest against unreality . . . against the delusive shams which now masquerade as verities." He denounced the bourgeois family, for example, as "a complete sham," lacking in natural affection, and he virtually endorsed the idea of free love. He attacked the legal system as a by-product of capitalism and attributed most crimes, including those of passion, to the institution of private property. For Bax, the whole commercial system was a "lifeless bloodless vampire." incompatible with "moral relations." [68]

Bax was also concerned in his writing with clarifying the new Socialist consciousness which he saw emerging within the working classes. The Socialist ethic, he believed, was already implicit in the behavior of the workers:

---

[67] On the relationship between Bax and Morris see May Morris, *Morris,* II, 173ff, and Thompson, *Morris,* pp. 895–896.

[68] Bax, *Religion of Socialism,* pp. ix, 141, 85.

The whole life of the working class of today under the conditions of the great industries is a collective one. Personal holiness has never been [the working man's] ethical aim. He has tended to stress such virtues as integrity, generosity, sincerity, comradeship, rather than purity, piety, meekness, and self abnegation. In short, social and objective virtues, those immediately referable to social environment, rather than subjective ones.[69]

Yet Bax also distinguished the Socialist ethic from the immediate interests of the individual and his class. This marked a fundamental divergence from the characteristic Marxist view of class consciousness. What "makes a revolutionist," he wrote, is a "habit of mind" or "culture in its widest sense" which carries the individual "beyond the here and now of his particular interest." He contrasted Socialism and "class instinct."

Mere class instinct per se is necessarily anti social. . . . [It] can never give us Socialism. That is why the most degraded section of the proletariat are to a large extent useless for the cause of Socialism. Their lower class instincts are incapable of being purified of their grosser elements and transformed into that higher instinct which, though on the face of it has the impress of a class, is in its essence above and beyond class; which sees in the immediate principle of class mainly a means to the ultimate realization of a purely human society in which class has disappeared. With those who have attained to this instinct classhood or class interest has become identified with humanity or human interest.[70]

Yet Bax was forced to acknowledge the resistance which traditional attitudes and feelings presented to the growth of a truly Socialist consciousness. "How disheartening to the propagation of new truth," he wrote, "to find the overwhelming influence of emotional presuppositions attaching to old jingles and catchwords." He noted in particular the rise in England during the late eighties of "sentimental Socialists" who were not necessarily Christian but retained "essentially the introspective ethic of the Christian ethos." The attempt to attach Socialism to Christianity or to Christian sentiments, he argued, was "born of the morbid self consciousness of our

[69] Bax, *Ethics of Socialism*, pp. 16–17.
[70] Bax, *Religion of Socialism*, p. 55; *Ethics of Socialism*, p. 104.

Christian and middle class civilization run to seed." [71] It was a "bastard enthusiasm," with which there could be no compromise:

The devotion of all true Socialists today will be based on science and involve no cultus. The Socialist, whose social creed is his own religion, requires no travesty of Christian rites to aid him keeping his ideal before him. . . . In Socialism the separation of politics and religion has ceased to be, since their object is the same.[72]

Bax conceded that the addiction of a young movement to "mythic phrases" was unavoidable, but they must "prevent the process of crystallization as much as possible" and drive into its thought the "fresh air of intelligence." For Bax this meant constant insistence on the broader philosophical implications of Socialism. Within the Federation he distinguished himself by his strong hostility to any suggestion that Socialism was compatible with Christianity. When the issue arose in the columns of *Justice* or at the annual conferences, Bax rushed in to champion atheism and call on the members of the Federation to oppose strenuously "the Christian doctrine of the great personal renunciation of the lower man." [73]

Few Social Democrats accepted Bax's position. It was not that the majority necessarily differed with him about the relationship between the two systems of belief. Most members were simply more worried about the political liabilities resulting from open enmity to Christianity. Engels recognized Bax's defects: "For practical agitation poor Bax is most dangerous, being utterly inexperienced. . . . [He] throws the ideas of the study, quite raw as they are, into the meeting rooms, has the feeling that something must be done to set the ball rolling, and does not know what." [74]

Bax was not without influence in the movement. Each of his first two volumes of essays, *The Religion of Socialism* and *The Ethics of Socialism,* went through six editions. Ideas derived from his writings appeared occasionally in the propaganda of the Social Democrats. But, for obvious reasons, he made little impact on the most important

[71] Bax, *Ethics of Socialism,* p. 132; *Religion of Socialism,* p. 100.
[72] *Justice,* June 24, 1884.
[73] Bax, *Ethics of Socialism,* p. 133; *Justice,* Aug. 13, 1899.
[74] *Friedrich Engels–Paul and Laura LaFargue, Correspondence, 1868–1886,* ed. Emile Bottigelli (Paris, 1956–1959), I, 340.

Socialist writers and speakers. His philosophical ideas were too abstruse and his attacks on moral conventions too bold to appeal to most Socialists. Bax made few concessions to existing sensibilities, for he was convinced that prevailing attitudes had to be exorcised before a true Socialist consciousness could develop. Faithful to his own conception of that consciousness, he retained, in the words of Engels, a "hermit-like simplicity in the greatest city in the world." [75]

Bax diverged from strict Marxism because that theory did not satisfy his religious or metaphysical concerns. His notion of the "alogical" and his millennial-like vision of man's future harmony provided new meaning for the older religious categories. Despite his remoteness from the Socialist rank and file Bax's attempt to reorient Socialists anticipated the subsequent development of the popular movement, which was marked by a comparable appropriation of religious categories. However, the sharp opposition between Christianity and Socialism, on which Bax insisted, faded out; Socialist ideas were increasingly attached to Christian sentiments. This process was expressed most clearly in the writings of Carpenter.

No leader in the early Socialist movement provided so intimate an account of his entrance into the new cause as did Carpenter. Born in a wealthy middle-class family in Brighton, he later observed that he suffered almost from his first years from a lack of natural affection and from extreme alienation. His life was one of "silent concealment and loneliness," in which nature became more important to him than "any human attachment." [76] His sense of isolation helps to explain the paralyzing crisis Carpenter experienced as a young man.

Until he was past twenty-five Carpenter conformed successfully to middle-class norms and expectations. His educational progress was brilliant. He entered Cambridge in 1864 to study mathematics and quickly rose to the top of his class, won two major essay prizes, and was selected, even before graduation, for the clerical fellowship vacated earlier on grounds of conscience by Leslie Stephen. Despite the examining bishop's hesitancy over his views on the atonement, he was ordained in 1870. To gain parish experience he took a curacy

---

[75] *Ibid.*, 1887–1890, II, 60.
[76] See Carpenter's autobiography, *My Days and Dreams* (London, 1916), pp. 13–15, 28.

at St. Edwards Church, Cambridge, where a short time later F. D. Maurice became his vicar. The older man's spiritual force greatly impressed Carpenter, though he found Maurice's theology "baffling." [77] Something of Maurice's religious vision of love as the center of life may be found in Carpenter's later outlook.

At this time the future seemed to hold for Carpenter a secure and perhaps distinguished academic or clerical career. The outward successes, however, helped to bring his internal discord to a critical point. His difficulties were partly intellectual. Ideas from a variety of sources, including Giuseppi Mazzini, Comte, Walt Whitman, and W. K. Clifford, were undermining his orthodoxy. At his ordination he had been honest and the bishop tolerant, but the problem lay deeper than conscious belief. He found no aspect of his life satisfactory. The "everyday world" was becoming less and less bearable. It was not simply the "petty vulgarities" of the "little provincial congregation." University life, too, with its "cheap philosophizing and ornamental cleverness" and "endless book learning" seemed a "fraud and weariness." Nor could he find escape or reassurance in his inner life, complaining of the "nightmare horrors" which "haunt the hollow caverns of contemplation." [78]

His growing sense of "falsity and dislocation" was no doubt connected to the series of breakdowns and vague illnesses Carpenter suffered in the early seventies. After extended leaves from his clerical and academic duties he decided, in 1873, to start legal proceedings for his "defrocking," and he resigned his fellowship. He thus confronted, at the age of thirty, the task of finding anew his place in the world.

Carpenter's "crisis of identity" corresponds closely to a pattern of self-alienation common in the literature of modern psychoanalysis.[79] As his crisis grew more acute over the next few years, he displayed such characteristic symptoms as narcissism, indiscriminate

[77] *Ibid.*, pp. 55–58.

[78] *Ibid.*, pp. 52, 72; Carpenter to Charles Oates, Nov. 15, 1871, April 22, 1872, Edward Carpenter Correspondence and Papers, Sheffield Public Library, Sheffield.

[79] A pattern which fits Carpenter very closely is presented by Frederick A. Weiss, "Self-Alienation: Dynamics and Therapy," *American Journal of Psychoanalysis*, XI (Nov. 1961).

condemnation of all social and cultural forms, the sense of being controlled by hidden forces, extreme self-idealization, and homosexuality. Carpenter's poetic vision and his Socialism registered those traits in various ways.

For a time Carpenter contemplated a literary career. Then he turned to the work of university extension lecturing in hopes of recovering purpose by making "my life with the mass of the people and the manual workers." This nomadic lecturing life continued during the seventies, but the years were painful, marked by great loneliness. "Narcissus," the title poem of a volume of verse, probably symbolized his own condition. The effort to escape from the "mirror prison of the self" was a recurrent theme in his later writings. Yet he could conceive of breaking through the circle of self only in heroic, or (as in his poem-drama, "Moses," published in 1876) in messianic terms.[80] Gradually, however, he began to find new values and meanings. He had discovered the writings of Walt Whitman with a "leap of joy" for the poet offered "a treatment of sex which accorded with my own sentiments." He had, Carpenter wrote to Whitman in 1874, given him a ground for the love of man.[81] But not until the early eighties did Carpenter begin to fashion a new way of life. Using part of a six-thousand-pound legacy, he purchased several acres near Sheffield and set out, with a working-class acquaintance and his wife, to produce enough food and a marketable surplus to support a simple existence. He observed later that he had been "driven" back to the land by "unaccounted impulses and instincts." The fields and the open sky seemed to Carpenter his "natural habitat." He had now come to accept his homosexuality as "a most intimate and organic part" of his nature. And with the discovery that men of "like temperament . . . were abundant in all directions," the "world of the heart became as rich in that which it needed as before it had seemed fruitless and barren." [82]

Meanwhile, the death of Carpenter's mother in 1881 had suddenly

[80] Carpenter, *Days and Dreams,* pp. 77, 30; *Narcissus and Other Poems* (London, 1873).

[81] There is a copy of the letter in the Alfred Mattison Papers, Brotherton Library, Leeds.

[82] Carpenter, *Days and Dreams,* pp. 114, 105. See Carpenter's letters Jan. 16, 1890, and Dec. 12, 1887, Carpenter Correspondence.

released ideas and feelings hitherto repressed. He found himself in "touch with a mood of exaltation and inspiration—a kind of super-consciousness"—which brought a new harmony of outlook.[83] The "illumination," as he called it, gave birth to *Towards Democracy,* a long Whitmanesque work which, in four installments (1882, 1885, 1889, and 1902), reached over five hundred pages. *Towards Democracy* was Carpenter's central statement about life; it provided a poetic and mythic form for his Socialism.

Carpenter discovered Socialism in 1883 through reading Hyndman's *England for All.* "The instant I read *England for All*," he recalled, "the mass of floating impressions, sentiments, ideals, etc., in my mind fell into shape and I had a clear line of social reconstruction before me." Socialism also provided an "excellent text for an attack upon the existing competitive system and a good means of rousing the slumbering consciences . . . of the rich." Carpenter took over only those elements in Marxism which were congenial to his own outlook. He accepted the Marxist theory of surplus value or exploitation as the best "working hypothesis," but insisted that a new social order would not rest on self-interest as did the old but on "justice and fair play." Socialism would spring from and demand as its basis a new "sentiment of humanity." [84] This moralistic attitude toward life pervaded *Towards Democracy* and the two volumes of essays, *Civilization: Its Cause and Cure* and *England's Ideal,* in which Carpenter developed further his main ideas.

In his writings and lectures before Socialist groups in the eighties Carpenter presented both a bitter indictment of contemporary civilization and a vision of man's liberation from the repressions of civilization. "I conceive," he wrote in *Towards Democracy,* "a millennium . . . a time when men all over the earth . . . shall attain freedom and joy." The liberation was primarily sexual. "Sex still goes first, and hands, eyes, mind, brain, follow; from the midst of belly and thighs radiate the knowledge of self, religion and immortality." Yet Carpenter celebrated this coming emancipation in traditional religious terminology and imagery. "Being filled with love, having completed

---

[83] Carpenter, *Days and Dreams,* p. 106.
[84] *Ibid.,* pp. 114–115; Carpenter, *England's Ideal* (London, 1887), pp. 58–59.

our pilgrimage," he wrote, "life shall pass into peace and joy eternal."
He promised the appearance of the "son of man." Men would be
freed from all "secret terrors, stress, disfigurement, death itself,"
and each would become "a sovereign lord over the world." [85]

Carpenter, like Bax, supported his vision with a scheme of history
which owed much to Marxism and to the work of Lewis Morgan.
Mankind had moved from the "naive insouciance of the pagan and
primitive world" through the "strange sense of inward strife and discord" called "civilization," toward a future unity and harmony under
communism.[86] The introduction of private property explained the
"fall" into "civilization," which, for Carpenter, was a "disease." It
meant a loss of wholeness. Most important, religion and sex ceased
to be united. The divorce of spiritual reality and bodily fulfillment
gave rise to a "sense of sin" and shame. The loss of man's primitive
harmony through the growth of the property system led to the formation of governments, external controls, and spurious gratifications:

The individual loses all memory and tradition of his heavenly guide and
counter part. His nobler passions fail for want of a leader to whom to
dedicate themselves; his identity and his intellect serve but to minister to
his little swarming desires. This is the era of anarchy, the democracy of
Carlyle; the rule of the rabble and mob law; caucuses and cackle, competition and universal greed, breaking out in cancerous tyrannies and
plutocracies, a mere chaos and confusion of society.[87]

Yet the "nightmare of civilization" was a necessary part of man's
growth. The purpose of the "long exile from the earlier paradise"
was self-knowledge. Through separation and individuality man
learned his true powers as well as his "freedom and blessedness."
Man could realize the perfect life and the "resurrection" only by
suffering "divorce from it." Having "descended into Hell," mankind

---

[85] Carpenter, *Towards Democracy* (3rd ed., London, 1892), pp. 9, 22, 258,
35.

[86] These ideas were developed in the title essay of *Civilization: Its Cause and
Cure* (London, 1889). The essay was first presented as a lecture before the
Fabian Society in 1886, where it was strongly attacked by Sidney Webb and
George Bernard Shaw. See Carpenter, *Days and Dreams,* p. 202.

[87] Carpenter, *Civilization,* p. 32.

began to mount "deliberately and unconsciously back again towards the unity which he has lost." Carpenter described this return as a slow process of "exfoliation," an "inner force . . . ever urging" nature on to new forms. The concept of "exfoliation" served Carpenter much as the notion of the "alogical" served Bax; it freed him from the circle of mechanical necessity or physical laws and made qualitative change possible. It held the promise of the "perfect man," who "at last made manifest . . . the purpose of creation." [88]

Perfection, or the "soul's return to paradise," meant for Carpenter the overcoming of self-consciousness, the greatest burden man carried and the source of "nine tenths of the pain of life." Man would lose his old sense of individuality and attain a "cosmical or universal" consciousness. For Carpenter, as for Morris and Bax, "morality" would disappear and a genuine community be realized. In the life of the future there was neither "effort or strain"; mutual help was "spontaneous and instinctive." Having regained his oneness with the cosmos and his fellow man, the individual could enter at last into a harmonious relationship with his own body. The "long vain fight of man against Nature" would be over. "No desire or indulgence" would be forbidden; love and desire could converge. Mankind would also recover its old objects of worship:

The old Nature Religion . . . will come back. . . . Man will feel his unity with the animals, with the mountains and the streams, with the earth itself. . . . . Long before Christianity existed the sexual and the astronomical were the main forces of religion. . . . Men instinctively felt and worshipped the great life coming to them through sex, the great life coming to them through the deeps of heaven. They deified both.[89]

This primitivist bent in Carpenter found various expressions. He praised "savagery and wild woods" and insisted that a "fresh influx of savagery" was necessary from time to time to renew the course of human progress. Men should escape, so far as possible, from houses

---

[88] Carpenter, *England's Ideal,* p. 130; *Civilization,* pp. 21ff, 33, 143.

[89] Carpenter, *Civilization,* pp. 24, 156; *Towards Democracy,* p. 254; *Civilization,* pp. 45–47.

and even clothes; nudity and sun bathing were essential features of the new life.

At times Carpenter struck an apocalyptic note, referring to the "wreck of cities and civilizations" which might lie ahead. But he did not welcome violent revolution or show much interest in direct political action. The "Socialist or communal life," toward which "both the masses and the thinkers of the advanced nations" were "consciously feeling their way" would be a society of "infinite helpfulness and sympathy as between children of a common mother." All men would do the work they wished to do, what was "obviously before them to do." [90] Here then was the vision Carpenter presented to the Socialists.

Carpenter was not active in the Socialist movement at first though he helped Hyndman launch his paper, *Justice,* with a contribution of three hundred pounds. Late in 1885, however, Morris drew Carpenter into the Socialist League, and early the next year a Sheffield branch was formed. At this time Carpenter shared Morris' hope that the various Socialist groups would "form a network over the land" and "constitute the new society within the framework of the old." Morris, with his "ideal of a sensible, free human brotherhood," seemed to Carpenter to represent the "new society more effectively and vitally than anyone else." Morris, in turn, told Carpenter that he was greatly attracted to his way of life, though privately he also expressed the view that it was "cowardly to desert." [91]

Through his lecturing Carpenter developed close ties with some Socialist groups in the Midlands and the North. His influence was most significant in Bristol, which held one of the most vital Socialist societies in the late eighties. Like its parent organization, the London Social Democratic Federation, Bristol Socialism developed out of political radicalism and Secularism. In 1886, however, members of the group became independent from Hyndman's organization. They found in Carpenter a "true counselor" and began to view their

[90] Carpenter, *Towards Democracy,* pp. 260, 41–42.

[91] Carpenter, *Days and Dreams,* pp. 125, 216; Henderson, ed., *Letters,* p. 223. After a lecture in Glasgow, Morris told a comrade that he thought Carpenter was the "most conceited man in England" (Macleod, *Morris without Mackail,* p. 11).

Socialism primarily as a "new sentiment of humanity and a higher morality." [92] Several of the Bristol Socialists carried their version of Carpenter's message directly into the popular propaganda of the early nineties. One was Katharine Conway, who lectured widely for the Socialist movement. Later she acknowledged her debt to Carpenter: "I came under Carpenter's influence as a morbid High Church-woman with vague humanitarian impulses and the lead he gave me was literally from darkness and bondage out into life and liberty. No one ever did so much for me—for he gave me Jesus Christ's teaching in its wholeness and truth for the first time." [93] As Miss Conway's remarks suggest, Carpenter encouraged some Socialists to transfer Christian sentiment and imagery to the new cause. His strongly moralistic outlook, still saturated with religious feeling, gave Carpenter access to minds which Hyndman or Morris or Bax could not touch. Robert Blatchford, the most effective of the new popularizers of Socialism in the nineties, conveyed something of the difference between Bax and Carpenter in a letter to the latter. He had just read *Civilization: Its Cause and Cure*. "It has given me a lot of light . . . [and] helped me to understand myself. . . . I have been trying to read Belfort Bax but I don't like him. He is uncharitable, cynical, not true. . . . Cynicism revolts me." Yet few Socialists could accept Carpenter's whole vision. Thus, when Carpenter sent Blatchford a volume by a German primitivist and asked him to write about sexual matters, the popular Socialist journalist declined. "I am radical but . . . the whole subject is 'nasty' to me. Be charitable. I can't help it." [94]

Carpenter, like so many of the most effective Socialist propagandists in the years just ahead, appealed particularly to young men and women who had recently broken away from organized religion. "His *Towards Democracy* was our Bible," one of them wrote, "We

[92] See Samson Bryher, *An Account of the Labour and Socialist Movement in Bristol* (Bristol, 1931), Part I, pp. 21–24.

[93] Quoted in Tom Shaw, *Edward Carpenter* (London, 1922), p. 7. Also see Gilbert Beith, ed., *Edward Carpenter: An Appreciation* (London, 1931), pp. 182–188.

[94] Blatchford to Carpenter, Dec. 27, 1893, Jan. 11, 1894, Carpenter Correspondence.

read it at those moments when we wanted to retire from the excitement of our Socialist work and in quietude seek the calm and power that alone gives sustaining strength. We no longer believed in dogmatic theology. Edward Carpenter gave us the spiritual food we still needed." [95]

Carpenter contributed much to the current of millennial feeling which entered popular Socialism. But the new, ethically charged Socialism of the early nineties did not bear the distinctive impress of Carpenter or any identifiable individual. It arose spontaneously out of the interaction of Socialist propagandists with the working classes of the northern industrial counties. Before turning to that development, however, the next chapter examines, in the growth of Fabianism, another way in which Marxist ideas were assimilated and transformed during the eighties.

[95] Fenner Brockway, "A Memory of Edward Carpenter," *New Leader,* July 5, 1929. For a fuller treatment of Carpenter see Stanley Pierson, "Edward Carpenter, Prophet of a Socialist Millennium," *Victorian Studies,* XIII (March 1970), 301–318.

5
The Fabians

Fabian Socialism emerged out of a "long and clarifying experience" during which all that was "superfluous and non-essential" was thrown aside, observed one of its leaders, Hubert Bland.[1] The Fabians came to view as superfluous and nonessential those hopes for a radical change in the quality of existence which drew figures like Morris, Bax, and Carpenter to the movement. The Fabians carried forward the work in which Hyndman was engaged before his Marxism stiffened into dogmatism—the adaptation of Socialism to the native utilitarian modes of thought. In its Fabian form Socialist consciousness was purged not only of fundamental philosophical concerns about man and society, but dispensed with Hyndman's doctrinaire attitudes toward economic and historical development. Fabian Socialism tended to contract to the kind of legislative and administrative problems which had largely occupied Bentham.

The creators of Fabianism were educated young men of diverse middle-class backgrounds. Most of them had come to London from the provinces and were beginning careers in such professions as the civil service, journalism, and education. Most were single and suffered in varying degrees from a sense of social dislocation and religious uncertainty. They were peculiarly sensitive to the major problems of late Victorian life, ranging from the most intimate questions of belief and conduct to the broader economic and political issues of the day. They readily entered the small study and discussion groups dedicated to philosophical, religious, social, or economic inquiry which

[1] "The Faith I Hold," *Essays by Hubert Bland,* ed. Edith Nesbit Bland (London, 1914), p. 228.

were numerous in the London of these years. One such group gathered around the philosopher-prophet Thomas Davidson in the fall of 1882; it was here that the first stage in the process of Fabian clarification took place.

Thomas Davidson and the Fellowship of the New Life

Several of the prominent founders of the Fabian Society had become active in the Progressive Association, organized in 1882 by J. C. Foulger. Foulger (whom Shaw later referred to as the "genuine original Fabian"), was editor, publisher, and printer of *Modern Thought,* a monthly journal for advanced ideas. The Sunday evening meetings of the Association drew together young men and women of diverse political outlooks ranging from the older political radicalism of Foulger himself to the newer radicalism of the land nationalizers and the Social Democrats. But the Progressive Association was more concerned with ethics than with politics. It hoped to "bring about the moral awakening which is itself the occasion of all political and social improvement." [2] The Association's meetings contained something of the atmosphere of the church or chapel. There were hymns —freed from all obvious theological reference—followed by a lecture and a question period.

The other early leaders of the Association were Havelock Ellis, Frank Podmore, William Clarke, and Percival Chubb. Each in his own way exemplified the quest, characteristic of many young men of the middle classes in these years, for new meaning in life. Ellis was a medical student who had earlier undergone a "conversion" out of Christianity through reading James Hinton's *Life in Nature.* To Ellis, Hinton's thought provided a way of reconciling the "soulless . . . scientific concept of an evolutionary world" with the "divine vision of life and beauty" formerly provided by religion.[3] Moreover, Hinton's conviction that polygamy and sexual freedom would bring a new age of happiness had helped to turn Ellis toward the investigation of sexual

[2] George Bernard Shaw, *Letters,* ed. Dan Laurence (New York, 1967), p. 351. The Progressive Association is described in Isaac Goldberg, *Havelock Ellis* (London, 1926), pp. 96–98.

[3] Havelock Ellis, *Life* (Boston, 1939), p. 16.

behavior. In time this interest would draw him away from a medical career into a solitary exploration of questions long smothered by Victorian conventions.

Podmore held a degree in science from Oxford and was employed in the Post Office. He had already begun the study of abnormal psychological phenomena, spiritualism, mesmerism, and telepathy, which occupied him much of his life. His critical, disciplined intelligence and his determination to subordinate "spiritual" phenomena to the canons of scientific method tended to separate him from his early associates. He was fearful of "binding" himself in "a moment of enthusiasm" and convinced that in religious matters men "must be content to be learners for a long time to come." [4]

Clarke was a journalist. A few years earlier, while studying at Cambridge, he had helped to organize a Unitarian church. Now, having moved beyond organized religion, he wavered between "complete skepticism" and a belief in the possibility of "a great moral change." Convinced that contemporary civilization was "founded on injustice and selfishness" and "crumbling to pieces," Clarke was impatient with science and formal philosophy and agreed with William Wordsworth that men who "regulated their lives by a few strong instincts and plain rules" had done more for mankind than "all the pride of intellect and thought." [5] He also found solace and inspiration in the writings of Emerson, on whom he lectured from time to time.

Chubb, at twenty-one the youngest of the group, had come from the North Country, where his father had been a struggling and largely unsuccessful craftsman. After three years in a merchant's office, Chubb had become a clerk at the Local Government Board but suffered deeply from its "routine and spirit of worldliness." He dreamed of making a "new start" abroad and getting "away from the matter of factness that clings to things here." Chubb's yearning for a life "more congenial to one's higher tastes and aspirations" had drawn him to a nomadic scholar-philosopher, Thomas Davidson,

---

[4] Frank Podmore to Thomas Davidson, Dec. 31, 1883, Thomas Davidson Papers, Yale University Library, New Haven, Conn.

[5] William Clarke to Thomas Davidson, June 12, 1882, Jan. 23, 1883, *ibid.*

whose teachings held not only the promise of self-perfection but the hope of a "Social Utopia." When Davidson arrived in London for a visit in the fall of 1882, Chubb gathered a small group, including Ellis, Podmore, Clarke, and three others, H. H. Champion, Edward Pease, and Hubert Bland, to listen to the sage.[6]

Davidson had grown up in rural Scotland and studied at Kings College, Aberdeen, before adopting the life of a wandering teacher. From the Presbyterianism of his youth he had passed through the "German sentimental school," Comte, and Spencer, before finding in Aristotle the assurance of "something higher than discursive distracting reason." Convinced that man possessed a faculty for seeing God directly, Davidson also began to seek ways of implementing his faith philosophically and institutionally. Although he was repelled by the doctrines of the Catholic church, its "organized life" seemed to him to cultivate the highest spiritual existence. But he discovered in the early nineteenth-century Catholic thinker, Antonio Rosmini-Serbati, philosophical support for his belief that man could apprehend the divine. For two years he devoted himself to the study and translation of Rosmini's writings at the Rosminian Order at Domodossola in Italy. The Order also inspired Davidson to develop his own design for a new community and to seek to "do for the natural freedom guided life of the future what the church undertook to do for the authority awed life of the past." He envisioned a "small devoted band of men and women, of fearless character, clear philosophical insight, and mighty spiritual love, living a divine life in their relations to each other." They would be interested in "all social movements" and "help to give them a spiritual turn." [7]

To the small group that gathered to listen to him in London in the autumn of 1882, Davidson brought both a metaphysical message and a plan for a new community. He was attempting to free them from "that terrible monism from which hardly any English thinker

[6] Percival Chubb to Thomas Davidson, April 1, 1882, *ibid.*

[7] *Memorials of Thomas Davidson,* ed. William Knight (New York, 1907), pp. 15ff; Joseph Blau, "Rosmini, Domodossola and Thomas Davidson"; Albert Lataner, "Introduction to Davidson's Autobiographical Sketch," *Journal of the History of Ideas,* XVIII (1957), 523–536.

escapes." Life, he insisted, must rest on an "abiding reality . . . behind the physical and sensuous phenomena." Davidson appealed directly, as he told Ellis, to "unanalyzed sentiment and unrecognized tradition, without helm or compass." Indeed it seemed to him futile to "work with men, however good, who have lost the religious sentiment." [8]

Davidson's efforts, over the next year or so, to propagate a new metaphysic on the basis of the old religious sentiments encountered considerable opposition. Clarke denied that the "solution of an intellectual puzzle" was necessary for "an unselfish, noble, human life." "Life's problems" consisted mainly of developing love and "helpful attitudes towards one's fellow creatures." This strong moralistic outlook, so characteristic of young men of the middle classes at this time, came out even more strongly in the resistance of Ellis:

> You and I are not aiming at the same things. You want to change people's metaphysical opinions. I want to make people's relations to each other true. . . . And I say with Hinton that this may be done by the acceptance of a true moral law and the falling off of traditional and rigid laws. . . . For everyone to accept the same metaphysic would . . . mean spiritual and intellectual death.[9]

Even Chubb, who came closest to being Davidson's disciple, could not accept his solutions to "the fundamental problems of life" and promised instead support for realizing a "moral ideal." Davidson had failed, therefore, to gain genuine converts to his fundamental philosophical beliefs. In 1883 he moved to New York to carry on his mission in what he referred to as the "unexhausted West." [10]

But while Davidson's metaphysical ideas found little response, his notion of a new community or "Fellowship" did. Late in October of 1883 the group, now expanded to about thirty, met to discuss a set of principles and rules provided by Davidson and aimed at "intellectual clarity, moral purity, and an ethic of love and charity." Having abandoned its initial idea of starting a new colony abroad, the

[8] Quoted by Knight, ed., *Davidson,* pp. 15ff.

[9] Clarke to Davidson, Jan. 23, 1883; Havelock Ellis to Davidson, Oct. 4, 1883, Davidson Papers.

[10] Chubb to Davidson, Jan. 3, 1883, *ibid.;* Knight, ed., *Davidson,* p. 7.

group decided that a "club," would have "instrumental and transitional value." Already, however, Chubb detected a "loss of ideality" and a "more practical note." "My pitch for striving after greater self perfection," he wrote Davidson, "didn't get very far." [11]

Chubb attributed the lowering of moral tone partly to the presence of Pease and Podmore. "I can't help but feel," he wrote Davidson, "that people like Pease and Podmore are not of the right fibre." They are "good fellows" but "without depth," "careless of philosophy," and "typical moderns" in that they tend "downward rather than upward." They were, he concluded, "too timid" to make themselves the "living embodiment of a new spiritual gospel." But Chubb was also disturbed by the influence of Bland and Champion, both of whom were members of Hyndman's Democratic Federation. Champion, in particular, seemed to Chubb to be overly concerned with the "economic aspect" of reform; his association with Hyndman and other agitators inevitably meant a loss of "inwardness." By December, Chubb and others had determined to make a "fresh start with passionate apostles." [12] The parting was friendly. Chubb and his associates carried on as the "Fellowship of the New Life," while another group, led by Podmore and Bland, organized the Fabian Society along new lines. The title indicated the determination of the Fabians to proceed cautiously, through study, to formulate a program for the "reconstruction of society." Several members of the Fellowship, including Chubb, participated in the Fabian Society as well.

The Fellowship of the New Life did not thrive, though it lasted until 1898. Its small membership, led for a time by Clarke and Chubb, discussed ethical and utopian writings and considered the possibility of communal experiments as protests "against the unreality and meanness of life." [13] In the years ahead they drew close to other ethical reformers, including Carpenter, the leaders of the

[11] Chubb to Davidson, Oct. 25, 1883, Davidson Papers.

[12] *Ibid.,* Nov. 1883, Dec. 15, 1883.

[13] The Fellowship is described in W. H. G. Armytage, *Heavens Below* (Toronto, 1961), pp. 227–241; Chubb to Davidson, May 11, 1884, Davidson Papers.

Ethical Culture movement, and the English followers of Leo Tolstoy. Meanwhile, the Fabians were slowly developing a new theory and a new strategy for Socialists.

Fabian Beginnings and Sidney Webb

To Davidson, viewing events in London from New York in 1884, the Fabians seemed to be departing much more sharply from his teachings than was the Fellowship.[14] The Fabian leaders did not agree; Podmore was quick to assure him that "we look upon you as our founder." [15] The Fabians did turn away from Davidson's philosophical system and from his emphasis on personal regeneration as the key to the good society. But they nurtured far more effectively than did the Fellowship, the powers of "pure intelligence" and the Socratic method, on which the teacher also insisted.[16] Bland, who was the dominant figure in the Society at this time, later acknowledged the importance of Davidson's "conviction that the human mind is capable of solving all problems and the human will of overthrowing all obstacles." He attributed to Davidson's influence other qualities of mind which became characteristic of the Fabian Society—"its dislike of exaggeration, its contempt for the gaseous and the flatulent, its suspicion of pretentious formulae . . . above all the critical attitude of its corporate mind." [17]

Bland's role in the Society suggests the initial strength of Social Democratic ideas and a more practical political bent. But Bland's outlook was complex and included the conflict which was already splitting the Federation. His Socialism was a recent conquest, wrested

[14] In an address to the New York Fellowship of the New Life, Davidson observed that the Fabians were "less spiritual in tendency" (Latener, "Autobiographical Sketch," p. 535).

[15] Podmore to Davidson, Jan. 16, 1884, Davidson Papers.

[16] Morris Cohen, one of Davidson's American students, quotes from a letter from Davidson: "The true teacher . . . strives merely to help his pupils to insight of their own. . . . Be willing that your pupils should contradict you, and come to conclusions entirely different than yours, even on points that seem essential" (cited by Leonora Cohen Rosenfeld, "Morris R. Cohen, The Teacher," *Journal of the History of Ideas,* XVIII [Oct. 1957], 553).

[17] Bland, ed., *Essays,* p. 225.

out of a deep pessimism bordering on despair. Having failed in business, Bland had turned to journalism. For a time, however, James Thomson's "The City of Dreadful Night" seemed to him "an evangel of the Real Truth of Things." In Schopenhauer he discovered both a philosophical justification for this dark view of life and a "temporary escape in aesthetic contemplation." Then he learned that William Morris was a Socialist, and he knew that "whatever else Socialism might be it would not be ugly." At first Morris encouraged Bland to "shut oneself up as it were in a little mansion of one's own and with a few eclectic friends to think scornfully of the world outside."

We felt that we had the misfortune to be born in a stupid, vulgar, grimy age . . . and so we turned away from it . . . disgusted with the present, apprehensive of the future, we naturally were amorous of the past. I think on the whole we preferred the thirteenth century to any other century. . . . We called ourselves the elect . . . Mr. William Morris was our laureate; his work our standard.

But Hyndman and his "exhilarating atmosphere of confidence" brought a fuller commitment to Socialism: "The Marxist system, as expounded by Hyndman, with its air of pontifical infallibility, with its prophetic note of fatefulness, with its pose of scientific exactitude, with its confident appeal to history, is of all others best fitted to impose upon and impress the plastic mind of the uninstructed inquirer." [18]

As Bland's development suggests, the Fabian Society continued to hold non-utilitarian aspirations. For several years it accommodated varying approaches to Socialism, ranging from Marxist collectivism to anarchism.[19] During the mid-eighties its members mingled on easy terms with the Social Democrats and with the adherents of the Socialist League. In 1886, when the Fabians decided to publish a

[18] *Ibid.*, pp. 214, 223.
[19] In March 1884 the Society listened to a lecture on "The Two Socialisms" by one of its more idealistic female members. See Edward R. Pease, *History of the Fabian Society* (London, 1916), p. 37.

tract on Socialism, they asked Engels, "as a universally accepted authority on scientific Socialism," to contribute an essay.[20]

A distinctly Fabian point of view emerged slowly through the efforts of Bland and four gifted newcomers, George Bernard Shaw, Sidney Webb, Graham Wallas, and Sydney Olivier. All four became active during 1884 and 1885. Although not influenced directly by Davidson, they accentuated the initial Fabian bent toward rational inquiry. They also carried much further the process begun by Hyndman, through which Marxist ideas were assimilated to the utilitarian tradition in British social thought.

When he joined the Fabian Society in May 1884, Shaw was an unsuccessful novelist and a struggling journalist. For five years he had frequented the various debating and discussion societies of London, sharpening his mind, wit, and powers of public address. A lecture by Henry George in 1882 had turned him from "barren agnostic controversy to economics," and during 1883 he discovered Hyndman and Marxism. Marx, Shaw recalled, transformed his "revolt against bourgeois morals" from an "instinctive" into "a reasoned scientific conviction"; he became "a man with some business in the world." [21] Shaw's novel, *An Unsocial Socialist,* written during 1884, reflected a recent reading of the French edition of *Capital.* The ethical indignation so apparent in the novel was controlled by a view of the economic and historical sources of exploitation drawn from Marx.

Shaw was on the verge of joining Hyndman's organization when he instead entered the Fabian Society. "What has kept me off and finally determined me not to join the Federation," he told one of its members, was Hyndman's "impatience" and his failure to see the "importance of educating the party." Shaw was also suspicious of Hyndman's form of collectivism: "I am at heart an Anarchist and Free Competition man, opposed to the present system more because I believe competition in it to be the reverse of free than because I believe

[20] E. R. Pease to Friedrich Engels, Jan. 26, 1886, Friedrich Engels Correspondence, International Institute of Social History, Amsterdam.
[21] George Bernard Shaw, *Sixteen Self Sketches* (New York, 1949), p. 96. For an examination of Shaw's "crisis of identity" see Erik Erikson, *Identity, Youth and Crisis* (New York, 1968), pp. 142–150.

it to be in itself more mischievous than any other principle." [22] Shaw's addition was a major event to the Society. He brought not only exceptional qualities of mind but a flair for publicity which would win for the Fabians a wide, if often undeserved, reputation in the years ahead. Shaw also recruited, directly or indirectly, Wallas, Olivier, and most important, Webb.

Olivier and Wallas, both sons of clergymen, had become friends at Oxford. Wallas was teaching at Highgate School in London in 1883, but before the year was out he had lost his position because he was unwilling to attend communion. After his dismissal he turned to university extension lecturing. Wallas carried into the Fabian Society a strong concern for educational work, a great capacity for research, and a deepening commitment to a strictly secular approach to life. Olivier, who held a post in the Colonial Office, had also rejected orthodox religion. He was attending the meetings of the Positivist leader, Dr. Richard Congreve. Yet, as Olivier confided to his fiancée at this time, he was full of desire to investigate all forms of religious thought and feeling and to discover the "common element." [23] Such a concern, though largely extruded from his Fabianism, would help to account for Olivier's dissenting role at crucial points in the development of the Society. It was Webb, however, who exercised the most important influence on the growth of Fabianism. His personal development holds one key to the emergence of a distinctly Fabian form of Socialist consciousness.

Webb, more than any other early Socialist leader, was a child of London; he loved the city, accepted fully its mode of life, and was wholly lacking in the nostalgia for rural or simpler forms of community which pervaded the Socialist movement.[24] He was born near Leicester Square where his mother ran a hairdresser's shop. His father,

[22] Shaw to Andreas Scheu, Oct. 26, 1889, Andreas Scheu Papers, International Institute of Social History, Amsterdam.

[23] Margaret Olivier, *Sydney Olivier: Letters and Selected Writings* (London, 1948), p. 63.

[24] For biographical details see Mary Hamilton, *Sidney and Beatrice Webb* (London, 1934), pp. 10ff. Also see the summary of Royden Harrison's talk on Webb's early life in the *Bulletin for the Study of Labour History*, XVII (Autumn 1968), 15–18.

an accountant and keen radical, had been active in politics. Though the family was sufficiently prosperous to send its two sons abroad to study languages, its fortunes worsened when Sidney was sixteen, and he took a job as a clerk. Meanwhile, he continued his education at London University in evening classes, eventually receiving a degree. In 1878 he sat for the Civil Service examinations and, having scored extraordinarily high, secured a place in the War Office. After further successes in competitive examinations, Webb entered the Colonial Office, where he remained until his marriage to Beatrice Potter in 1892.

Webb's life during the early eighties remains obscure. Shaw met him first in 1879 at the Zetetical Society, a club for the discussion of political and social questions, and later described Webb's manner:

He knew all about the subject of the debate; knew more than anybody present; had read everything that had ever been written on the subject; and remembered all the facts that bore upon it. He used notes, read them, ticked them off one by one and threw them away, and finished with a coolness and clearness that to me, in my then tremblish state, seemed miraculous.[25]

But the Webb who joined the Fabians in May of 1885 was, for all his surface composure, an insecure, sensitive, and often brooding person, struggling like so many of his contemporaries with problems of personal belief and values. A recent bitter disappointment in love threw a dark shadow over these years. The thought of suicide, though not the "impulse to suicide," he confided to Wallas in 1885, "has never been totally absent from my mind for years." Webb was also a confirmed atheist, "unsettled" in ethical questions, and "for at least seven years . . . a pessimist by profession." He felt that life was in the main run by "blind and unconscious forces." [26]

Webb probably exaggerated his pessimism. Certainly it did not prevent him from taking an increasingly active role in the young

[25] Shaw, *Self Sketches*, p. 107.
[26] Webb to Wallas, Aug. 6, 17, 1885, Passfield Papers, British Library of Political and Economic Science, London. Webb's initial talks before the Fabian Society are discussed in A. M. McBriar, *Fabian Socialism and English Politics,* 1884–1918 (Cambridge, 1962), p. 14.

Fabian Society. He was, moreover, developing new attitudes toward life. Webb's changing outlook was of decisive importance in the process through which the Fabians transformed the meaning of Socialism.

There was a striking parallel between Webb's development in these years and that of the young Mill. Significantly, Webb was devoted to the Mill of the *Autobiography*, for he, too, had passed through a mental crisis and then found spiritual succor in romantic literature. Carlyle's *Sartor Resartus* was, as late as 1890, the book to which Webb turned most readily in times of inner disquiet. And his remedy for personal anxieties tended to be the Carlylean solution of work, "to accept as duty whatever may come to be done." [27]

Webb also found help for his mental state in a novel by Edward Bellamy, *Dr. Heidenhoff's Process*. In this novel Bellamy created a fictional precursor of the modern psychoanalyst, for "Dr. Heidenhoff" used a technique of "cerebral hygiene" to exorcise tormenting thoughts and memories from consciousness.[28] Bellamy was attempting to deal with the religious anxieties which, he believed, weighed oppressively on Western man. Webb was fascinated by the book and, in a letter written six years later, could still cite the relevant passages from it. The point of view developed in the novel corresponded closely to that which characterized Webb's Socialism—a comparative indifference to fundamental ethical and metaphysical questions in favor of a pragmatic concern with pressing social problems and a strong disposition to subordinate the individual personality to the needs of the social whole.

Webb's mature outlook was not, however, simply a personal conquest of mind and will. Again, as with Mill, it was fortified and

[27] Graham Wallas, "Meeting with Sidney Webb" (notes), Graham Wallas Correspondence and Papers, British Library of Political and Economic Science, London; Webb to Beatrice Potter, June 29, 1890, Passfield Papers. In a letter to Beatrice in June 1890, Webb confessed half jokingly that he had turned to *Sartor Resartus* for "confirmation before taking your advice" (Passfield Papers).

[28] Five years after reading the book Webb recommended the section on "cerebral hygiene" in a letter to Beatrice Potter, Oct. 11, 1890, *ibid.* Bellamy's ideas in *Dr Heidenhoff's Process* are examined by Arthur E. Morgan, *The Philosophy of Edward Bellamy* (New York, 1945), pp. 5–21, 35–68.

preserved by a woman's love. Webb even suggested at one point to Beatrice Potter that her decision to marry him had saved him from going under "mentally and morally." In his letters to her Webb indicated his sense of the hazards of a strictly rational or utilitarian approach to life. He wrote of his "dread of the horrible intellectual coldness which unconsciously grows on a student," and he acknowledged the "enormous risks to character and personality" in his dedication to social research. Certainly his life in these years was fixed within narrow limits.

I do not number the hours of work because I do nothing else. I see no friends save in the work. I have not been to a theater or concert or picture gallery in London for years. I have holidays but save for these I am at work from morning to bedtime. It is a cramped and joyless life but I see no chance of changing it.

Even after Webb had assumed the leading role in the Fabian Society, he continued to be troubled by a deep sense of insecurity. As late as 1890 he expressed the "sickening fear that I am really, somehow, a fraud." He retained, too, a strong distrust of thoroughgoing rationalism. His narrow conception of the scope of Fabian activity rested on somewhat skeptical and conservative attitudes toward life. "How little we really know," he wrote, "and how imperfectly we can weigh that which we think we know." Webb was suspicious of "preconceived visions of one's work in life." Lacking general certainty, men should "recognize instinct and feeling as of some claim on motives, as being indeed that organically registered expression of the past experience of the race, notifying to us the 'general line' of the human nature of the world." Webb believed that "great thoughts come from the heart." Yet he feared sentimentalism and was skeptical toward absolute principles in moral or religious behavior. The figure of Jesus, even apart from the "sentimental" version of "today," held little attraction for him: "He ought to have taken it fighting to some extent. The beauty of sacrifice as sacrifice does not adequately appeal to me. There ought to be a reasonable calculation of means to ends, and attempt at adaptation to the environment."

Through his marriage Webb found a relationship which was at once intellectually rich and emotionally satisfying. Existential issues ceased, so far as one can see, to disturb him; he could dedicate himself with extraordinary concentration to the task of social reform. Indeed, he came close to achieving his self-proclaimed goal—"never to act alone or for myself" but "to feel at every moment that I am acting as a member of a committee and for that committee" on behalf of larger human ends.[29]

During the mid-eighties Webb had discovered, in his association with Shaw, Wallas, and Olivier, a kind of relationship which came close to his ideal of public service. The work of the four men, as Webb described it to Beatrice, was a "pretty piece of intellectual communism," marked by "trust in each other, willingness to obey each other, and subordinate ourselves to the group."[30] The association began early in 1885, outside the Fabian Society in a small discussion circle in Hampstead, organized to study the work of Karl Marx.

The Hampstead Group: From Marxism to Fabianism

The "Hampstead Marx Circle" originated, according to Shaw, in a growing sense of intellectual inadequacy among some Fabians. "The mischief was not that our generalizations were unsound but that we had no detailed knowledge of the content of them. We had borrowed them ready made as articles of faith and when opponents like Charles Bradlaugh asked us for details we sneered at the demand without being in the least able to comply with it."[31] The starting point of the discussions was the first volume of *Capital*, in the French edition. Belfort Bax chaired the initial meeting early in 1885, and the sessions continued fortnightly through the year. Webb was an enthusiastic participant and in August, when he began to teach Shaw to read German, the two started the second volume of *Capital,* getting through "two pages in two hours." At the end of the year Shaw found

---

[29] Webb to Beatrice Potter, April 6, Jan. 19, 1891, Aug. 26, June 29, 1890; Webb to Miss Davidson (fiancée of Pease), Dec. 12, 1888, Passfield Papers.

[30] Webb to Beatrice Potter, Aug. 26, 1890, *ibid.*

[31] G. B. Shaw, *The Fabian Society: Its Early History* (London, 1892), p. 16.

it necessary to have his copy of *Capital* rebound. "We expected," Wallas recalled, "to agree with Marx." [32]

Yet disagreements with Marx began early. Even before the discussions commenced Henry Wicksteed had attacked Marx's theory of value from the standpoint of the marginal utility theory developed by the English economist, W. S. Jevons. [33] This position was advanced within the Hampstead discussion circle by F. Y. Edgeworth, and attention soon centered on Marx's conception of value. Criticism from Webb, even more than Jevon's ideas, broke down the group's confidence in Marx. Webb drew on David Ricardo and Mill and questioned the logic by means of which Marx had developed the idea of labor as the sole determinant of the value of a commodity. Webb pointed out that Marx's reasoning specifically ignored the Ricardian theory of rent, with its argument that differences of soil fertility were crucial in determining the value which the commodity, in this case land, might command on the market. The recognition of rent as a value not reducible to individual human labor had already been crucial in the development of the ideas of Henry George. A generalized theory of rent, constructed by the Fabians from the thought of Ricardo, Mill, and George, became, according to Webb, "the very cornerstone of collective economy." Elaboration of the theory took several years and led to the differentation of three "surplus rents" or "monopolies"—land, capital, and ability or special skills. These three rents, which displaced Marx's "surplus value," were viewed by the Fabians as socially created and hence subject to expropriation by society for the good of the whole. [34]

Bax left the Hampstead circle early, leaving Shaw as the main

[32] Webb to Wallas, Aug. 17, 1885, Passfield Papers; G. B. Shaw, "Diaries," Dec. 3, 1885, British Library of Political and Economic Sciences, London. Graham Wallas, "Socialism and the Fabian Society," *Men and Ideas,* ed. May Wallas (London, 1940), p. 103.

[33] *Today,* Oct. 1884.

[34] The fullest discussion of the development of Fabian economic thought is in McBriar, *Fabian Socialism,* pp. 29–42. Also see D. M. Ricci, "Fabian Socialism: A Theory of Rent as Exploitation," *Journal of British Studies,* IX (1969), 105–121.

defender of Marx. Although Shaw's Marxism had been shaken by an encounter with Wicksteed, he remained unconvinced by Webb's reasoning. His search for a more satisfactory explanation of value led him to join another discussion group, organized by men who were not Socialists at all but interested primarily in economic issues. They discussed economics along purely abstract lines, free from the pressing social questions which tended to intrude into the Socialist meetings. Here Shaw and Wallas finally discarded the Marxist theory of value in favor of the Jevonian view that the value of a commodity was determined by the quantity available or by the utility of the final unit worth producing. The theory of marginal utility assumed a central place, alongside the expanded theory of rent, in Fabian thinking about economic life.[35]

Shaw claimed that these changes in economic theory did not cause "essential damage to Marx's superstructure." [36] He meant that Marx's picture of social exploitation, as well as the promise of decisive social change, remained more or less intact. "Read Jevons and the rest for your economics," he wrote in 1887, and "read Marx for the history of their working in the past and the conditions of their application in the present. And never mind the metaphysics." Given the Fabian interpretation of Marxism, which was much like Hyndman's, there was some truth to Shaw's view. Despite the abandonment of Marx's theory of surplus value, even Webb continued to see the "class war" and the "struggle to secure the surplus or 'economic rent' as the key to the confused history of all European progress." [37]

However, the ideas of the Hampstead Fabians altered profoundly the meaning of exploitation, the class struggle, and, indeed, of So-

[35] Webb assured Alfred Marshall in 1889 that they agreed "absolutely in economics" and observed, "I am accepted by the Socialists as one of them" (Webb to Marshall, Feb. 28, 1889, Passfield Papers).

[36] See Shaw's long review of *Capital,* in *National Reformer,* Oct. 7, 14, 21, 1887; reprinted in R. W. Ellis, ed., *Bernard Shaw and Karl Marx: A Symposium* (New York, 1930).

[37] Sidney Webb, *English Progress towards Social Democracy* (London, 1888), pp. 4–5.

cialist reconstruction itself. Their economic ideas did not open up fruitful lines of theoretical analysis,[38] but they began to view Socialist growth as much more closely related to the existing structure of society. "Instead of looking at 'capitalism' and 'exploitation' as a single fact to be destroyed by the shock tactics of class war and revolution," Wallas recalled, the Fabians came to see economic advantages and deprivations as "matters of more or less." [39] The sharp distinctions which Marx had drawn between the propertied and the propertyless, and his emphasis on the class struggle, tended to fade out. Socialism was viewed not as the creation of an organized and class-conscious proletariat, but rather as the outcome of the progressive enlightenment of society at large. Led by Webb, the Hampstead Fabians resumed the task undertaken by Hyndman until his outlook and that of the Federation hardened; Webb too was seeking to adapt Marxism to English circumstances and ward off violent political change.

Webb disclosed the shifting basis of Socialist apologetics in his influential Fabian tract, *Facts for Socialists,* published early in 1887. Here, without clearly abandoning the Marxist conception of surplus value, he appealed chiefly to "recognized authorities and statistics" and to the "doctrines of political Economy." He thus began to build the case for Socialism out of native traditions of economic thought and social experience. Socialism was not, according to this view, primarily the possession of the working classes, however augmented by middle-class converts, but rather the self-reforming activity of the total community. It meant "the control by the community of the means of production for public advantage instead of private property" and "the absorbtion of rent and interest by the community collectively." [40]

Webb believed that the "area of private exploitation" had been steadily lessening in English life. He was confident that Socialism represented simply a "more complete recognition and the conscious

[38] On this point see McBriar, *Fabian Socialism,* pp. 42–47.
[39] Wallas, *Men and Ideas,* p. 104.
[40] Sidney Webb, *Facts for Socialists* (London, 1887), p. 15; *English Progress towards Social Democracy,* p. 4.

adoption" of principles already present in the "social organism." Along with several other leading Fabians, Webb turned increasingly to history for insight into the possibilities of Socialist growth. His sense of the "rolling tide . . . of Democratic Collectivism," of the way in which "social evolution" proceeded "without our knowledge, even against our will," suggested a determinism drawn from Marx. He referred later to an "unconscious socialism" working out in ways unrecognized. Nevertheless, he held that the "common intelligence of the natural leaders of the community" could understand the "rising force, . . . give it reasonable expression, and, within limits even direct its course." [41] Thus, while the Social Democrats emphasized the necessity of inculcating into the working classes a distinct consciousness of Marxist theory, Webb viewed Socialism as the enlightened consciousness of society as a whole. It found expression not through the material strivings of the working classes but through the rational capacity of political and administrative leaders.

While Webb attempted to free Socialism from the strong economic determinism and class orientation of Hyndman's Marxism, he also sought to eliminate or radically play down the emphasis on ethical or aesthetic motives found in Morris, Carpenter, and others. But his rejection of ethical idealism as a decisive force in Socialism met considerable resistance from some of his Hampstead colleagues. Almost from the outset members of the circle had been interested in the problem of ethics and volition, for they became convinced that Marxism taught a "narrow and mechanistic reference of all human actions to economic motives" and that it viewed the social revolution as an "automatic process." [42] Olivier, in particular, had challenged Marxism on ethical grounds. He criticized Hyndman's *Historical Basis of Socialism* for its failure to appreciate the necessity of a "moral revolution" accompanying the development of Socialism. In an article published in 1886 he distinguished a "larger" and essentially ethical Socialism from Marxism and attacked the propagandists of the Federation and the Socialist League for basing their appeal on the "perverse" and "reactionary" principle of ma-

[41] *English Progress towards Social Democracy,* pp. 13, 15.
[42] Wallas, *Men and Ideas,* p. 103.

terial self-interest. Since, according to Jevons, "values exist only in society in terms of the desires and needs of the purchasers," Olivier argued that Marxists had failed to see the primary need for "a revolution in economic motive." The antithesis of Socialism was not capitalism, but "individualism" or "egotism," which could only be overcome by a new "social religion" based on love.[43] The argument reflected Olivier's debt to Comte's Positivism. But his attempt to identify Socialism with an inner moral revolution was supported in varying degrees by Pease, Wallas, and Chubb.[44]

Webb firmly opposed these efforts. He discussed the problem of motives, or the means toward Socialism, in a tract published in 1888. After dismissing trade unionism and cooperatives as reliable vehicles for Socialism (because they did not involve a "fundamental change in property relations"), he considered the appeal to moral force:

There remains the ideal of the rapid approach of Christlike unselfishness. Of this hope let us speak with all the respect so ancient a dream deserves. If it were realized it would, indeed, involve an upset of present property arrangements, compared with which Socialism is a mere trifle; yet science must perforce declare that the expectation of any but the slowest real improvement in general moral habit is absolutely without warrant. Forms of egoism may change and moral habits vary; but, constituted as we are, it seems inevitable for healthy personal development that an at best instructed and unconscious egoism should predominate the individual. It is the business of the community not to lead into temp-

---

[43] "Perverse Socialism," *Today*, Aug., Sept. 1886, in which Olivier grafted ethical values onto the theory of Jevons. The latter would not have appreciated this. He was trying to make economic theory a matter of pure mathematics. Insofar as he considered ethical values, Jevons relied on utilitarian premises. The object of economics was "to maximize happiness by purchasing pleasure, as it were, at the lowest cost of pain" (W. S. Jevons, *The Theory of Political Economy* [2nd ed., London, 1879], p. 23).

[44] Pease called for a reinterpretation of the New Testament for purposes of modern economic life in a paper delivered before the Fabians and published as "Ethics and Socialism," *Practical Socialist*, Jan. 1886. Chubb argued his case for greater ethical idealism in "The Two Alternatives," *Today*, Sept. 1887. Wallas emphasized the importance of "social duty." See Pease, *History*, p. 65. Later he emphasized the role of "common social feeling," *Sunday Chronicle*, Dec. 7, 1890. He believed this motive power was increasing, but denied that it was identified with Socialism.

tation this healthy natural feeling but so to develop social institutions that individual egoism is necessarily directed to promote only the well-being of all.

Here then, was utilitarianism in the spirit of those Benthamites who had put aside the larger dream of a fully rational order, accepted prevailing moral conventions, and concentrated on the immediate possibilities for reform within existing institutions. The Fabian Society adopted this outlook slowly over the next few years and confirmed it in Tract 70, published in 1896. That tract limited the Fabian concern to those "ills of human society . . . produced by defective organization of industry and by a radically bad distribution of wealth." In the process the Fabians largely detached Socialism from the more radical criticisms of social and cultural life which inspired, in varying measures, the Marxists and their more ethically oriented successors.[45]

Webb's views did not win easy acceptance within the Fabian Society; it continued during 1887 and 1888 to serve as a meeting place for varied conceptions of Socialism and Socialist strategy. Its meetings were addressed by members of the Federation and the Socialist League as well as more independent Socialists like Carpenter. The Fabian openness reflected desire for an intellectual give and take which was impossible amid the polemical exchanges of the outdoor propaganda meeting. Few Fabians had, in fact, much taste for popular agitation.[46] Annie Besant was an exception. Her experience in Secularist propaganda, together with her printing facilities, disposed her toward a more direct appeal to the people. She and Shaw were active in the free speech demonstrations in London during 1887. But while her role here and her leadership of the "Match Girls' strike" in 1888 gained some support from Fabian leaders, the Society as a whole avoided deep involvement. Meanwhile the Fabians were developing their own reform strategy.

[45] Webb, English Progress, p. 10; The Fabian Society, *Report on Fabian Policy* (London, 1896).

[46] For a discussion of the social composition of the Fabians, see Eric Hobsbawm, "The Fabians Reconsidered," *Labouring Men* (London, 1964), pp. 255–259. Hobsbawm's Ph.D. dissertation, "Fabianism and the Fabians, 1889–1914," Cambridge University, 1950, is a valuable study of the Society.

The strategy emerged after a series of moves and countermoves within the Society beginning early in 1886. At the urging of Mrs. Besant and Bland a committee had been appointed to explore the possibilities for direct political action by the Fabians. Both Bland and Mrs. Besant retained a strongly Marxist view of class exploitation and regarded a working-class political party as the natural consequence. Their attempt to push the Society in this direction hastened the process of ideological clarification already under way, for it provoked a debate between the collectivists and the anarchists over the merits of political action. Members of the Federation and the Socialist League took part in the discussions. At the crucial meeting in December 1886 a group of Social Democrats supported the politically oriented Fabians while a contingent led by Morris opposed parliamentary action. The vote demonstrated, however, that the anarchists possessed little strength in the Society. A "manifesto" issued two months later by the triumphant political wing pledged the Fabians to take an "active part in all general and local elections" and looked to an eventual "Socialist party in Parliament." [47]

The triumph of Bland and Mrs. Besant was short-lived. Their efforts to launch the Fabians on a course of direct political action dispersed the anarchists but did not lead toward a new party. The influence of the Hampstead group was now growing; Webb and Shaw were on the executive and Olivier and Wallas joined them within a year or so. In June 1887, when the Society adopted a minimal basis for membership, the statement of aims reflected the growing influence of Webb.

Webb did not favor the idea of a new Socialist party. "The chief work at present," he believed, was to "change the principles on which the politicians and the voters act in social matters." [48] Like most leading Fabians, Webb had been a political radical and still looked to the Liberal party as the most promising vehicle for Social-

[47] *The Practical Socialist,* Feb. 1887. The best source for information about the Society during 1886 and 1887 is Mrs. Besant's monthly journal, *Our Corner.* A report of the key meeting on political policy appeared in *The Practical Socialist,* Oct. 1886.

[48] Webb to Sir H. B. Bacon, Aug. 1888, Passfield Papers.

ist reforms. But he also recognized an important new field for Socialist propaganda and activity in local politics. In his tracts, *Facts for Londoners*, published in 1889, and in the later *London Programme*, Webb attempted to connect his own ideas of social development with the municipal reform ideas of the London radicals. By 1888 Mrs. Besant and two other Fabians were sitting on the London School Board, and the Fabians were eyeing the newly created London County Council as an even more promising sphere for their work. Direct participation on the Council had to await the election of 1892, when Webb and five other Fabians were returned. But during the late eighties the Fabians developed close ties with the London radicals and began cooperation which, under the auspices of the Progressive party, would bring far-reaching reforms in London life. The Society also found in this way a model for its subsequent efforts to influence national politics through the Liberal party.

The strategy of "permeation," as the policy of working alternatively or simultaneously through several political organizations came to be called, was the logical outcome of Webb's Socialism. It denied the need for radical change in the consciousness of people at large and rejected as well the need for strong assertion of working-class power. It assumed that Socialists could rely on the fund of common sense and good will in society generally and achieve Socialism through gradual modifications of existing institutions. These attitudes found their fullest expression in the *Fabian Essays*.

Delivered as a series of carefully planned lectures in the autumn of 1888 and published the following year, the *Essays* indicated clearly the Fabian contraction of Socialist consciousness. The Socialism of the *Essays* was, as Olivier described it, "primarily a property form . . . an industrial system for the supply of the material requisites of human social existence." Olivier denied that there was a "specific ethic or morality of Socialism" in a metaphysical sense and rejected the "impressive dialectic pageant" and the "right of appeal to that theologic habit of mind common to Socialists." The morality of Socialism consisted simply of "those actions and habits" which tended to "preserve the existence of society and the cohesion and convenience of its members." Socialists could appeal to the "canons of moral judgement accepted generally," confident that, whatever their various metaphysical justifications, "moral ideas appropriate to Socialism were permeating the whole of modern society." [49]

The Fabian analysis of the existing property system was presented by Shaw in the opening essay of the volume. It was a worthy expression of Shaw's great polemical powers. First he attempted to demonstrate the nature of capitalistic exploitation by employing the Fabian theory of rent. Then, drawing on Ruskin's notion of "illth" and the Jevonian view of exchange value, Shaw denounced what the "genteel economists" called "effective demand" as "no longer utility but the cravings of lust, folly, vanity, gluttony and madness" on the part of the rich. This strong tone of moral indignation carried over into Shaw's discussion of the plight of the working classes, which reflected his reading of Marx's treatment of the proletariat in *Capital*. Shaw conducted his critique of capitalism in both moralistic and economic terms. There was, he insisted, a happy correspondence between economic science and "our hearts," which had so long rebelled against the teachings of "proprietary respectability." Yet, Shaw also argued that "no exercise in abstract economics" was "to be trusted unless it can be experimentally verified by tracing its expression in history." [50] At the center of Fabian Socialism lay this appeal to history and to a new form of economic determinism. It was developed most fully in the second essay, written by Webb.

Webb divided the nineteenth century into three overlapping stages —the destruction of a precapitalistic "social nexus" by industrialism, an ensuing period of social disintegration and "anarchistic spiritual isolation," and finally a period of striving after a new social nexus and a "true society" or "community." "The mainstream which has borne European society towards Socialism" was ostensibly the "irresistible progress of Democracy." But economic forces lay behind the growth of democracy. In terms reminiscent of Marx, Webb described the steam engine as a "Frankenstein" monster, which the

[49] George Bernard Shaw, ed., *Fabian Essays* (London, 1948), pp. 96–100, 119.
[50] *Ibid.*, pp. 21, 23, 27.

landlords and capitalists "had better not have raised; for with it comes inevitably urban democracy." And like Marx, Webb criticized the early Socialists for taking "no account of blind social forces which they could not control, and which went on inexorably working out social salvation in ways unsuspected by the Utopians." [51]

What Webb referred to as the "irresistible glide into collectivist Socialism" was elaborated by William Clarke, who combined a Marxist analysis of capitalistic development with his own knowledge of the growth of industrial monopoly in America. The economic processes, he wrote, were proceeding "practically independent of our individual desires and prejudices" and, by "changing the conditions of material production," effecting "a revolution of our modern life." [52] The nature of that revolution was presented in two essays by Wallas and Mrs. Besant on property and industry under Socialism. Both writers foresaw a gradual extension of the control of the state or local government boards over economic life.

The two concluding essays, by Shaw and Bland, discussed the problem of strategy. For Shaw the steps through which private property would be extinguished were simply "applications of principles" and "extensions of practices" already found in English development. But Bland's essay was much more radical and, in fact destroyed the unity of the volume. For while he shared the emphases of the other essayists on economic determinism and gradualism, Bland took sharp exception to two of Webb's main ideas. Bland was much less optimistic about social progress than the other Fabians and retained more of the Marxist emphasis on the role of class interest, power, and conflict. Only "material self interest," he wrote, would "furnish a motive strong enough to shatter monopoly." Nor did he share Webb's belief in an alliance with radicals and Liberals. The English political system appeared to Bland to be dominated by a single capitalistic party; the old distinction between Whig and Tory had long ceased to symbolize "real inward and spiritual facts." Socialist strategy, therefore, demanded the "formation of a definitely Socialist party . . . pledged to the communalization of all the

[51] *Ibid.*, pp. 31–35.
[52] *Ibid.*, p. 58.

means of production and exhange." Only then would the House of Commons begin to reflect the "real condition of the nation outside" and permit a "well defined confrontation of the rich and the poor." [53]

The *Fabian Essays* presented a new view of Socialist consciousness. Its sources were diverse and included ideas drawn from Marx, Hegel, Comte, Charles Darwin, Herbert Spencer, Mill, and Ruskin. But it rested on a form of utilitarianism which, having abandoned all claim to being a comprehensive philosophy of life, simply addressed itself to the possibilities for improvement within existing institutions and moral conventions. The utilitarianism of the Fabians was, as Clarke described it, "a useful provisional hypothesis for the rough and superficial work of ordinary reformers." The viability of Fabianism, however, remained to be demonstrated. Indeed, within a year after the publication of the *Essays*, the Society seemed to Shaw to be "on the eve of disruption." [54] The difficulties arose over two issues—the proper scope of Socialist concern and the role of the Fabians in the political system.

Fabians in the Early Nineties

The framework of Fabian activity, fashioned largely by Webb, soon proved too narrow for two of the essayists. Even before the publication of the volume, Mrs. Besant had abandoned the Fabian Society in order to work with the Social Democrats. Their "heroic" outlook, Shaw observed, was more congenial to her temperament. She was, moreover, increasingly interested in Theosophy and decided, in 1890, to leave "politics for the inner life." Socialism, like Secularism earlier, had failed to satisfy her. Clarke also found the work of the Society too restrictive. In 1890 he complained to Shaw that the Fabians had "no ultimate aims, or, if they did, they were not his." [55] Clarke remained a member of the Society for several

---

[53] *Ibid.*, pp. 186, 204, 192, 202.

[54] H. Burrows and J. A. Hobson, *William Clarke: A Collection of His Writings* (London, 1908), p. 202; Shaw to Wallas, Dec. 16, 1890, Wallas Papers.

[55] Arthur Nethercot, *The First Five Lives of Annie Besant* (Chicago, 1960), p. 275; Webb to Beatrice Potter, Oct. 11, 1890, Passfield Papers; Clarke quoted by Shaw in a letter to Wallas, Dec. 16, 1890, Wallas Papers.

years, but increasingly concentrated on what seemed to him the main problem of the age—the development of a new spiritual basis for democracy. He was convinced that science, or "mere analysis" with its "withering blast" could not serve as this basis; he looked to art, to the German idealist tradition, and to the writings of Emerson for fresh inspiration. At the end of the decade Clarke told Webb that they were "separated widely" in their ideas and expressed regret for "giving so many of the best years of my life . . . to questions which are barren to me." [56]

Wallas and Olivier remained content to work within the limits set by the *Essays*. As their subsequent roles in the Society indicated, however, the two men were searching in different ways for new connections between those public and private spheres of life which Webb had separated. Bland, in contrast, was the strongest supporter of Webb's conception of Socialism. This was somewhat paradoxical in view of his dissenting position within the *Essays*, but Bland's insistence on a rigid divorce between public and private concerns was probably related to the striking contrast between his own rather disorderly personal life and the extreme propriety and fastidiousness of his public bearing.[57]

Shaw's situation was more complicated. He accepted Webb's view that visionary schemes of social reconstruction lay outside the province of the Fabians. But his passionate antibourgeois attitudes and his deep admiration for Morris made it impossible for him to lay aside the hope for radical changes in man's moral, aesthetic, and religious outlook. In Henrik Ibsen he had discovered a prophet bent on freeing mankind from what Shaw viewed as the special curse of his time—its excessive moralism and idealization of life. Shaw's *Quintessence of Ibsenism*, first presented in lectures for the Society in 1890, argued that existing moral ideals must be demolished for men to progress. While the cultured classes still "wallowed" in a

[56] See William Clarke, "The Limits of Collectivism," *Contemporary Review* LXIII (Feb. 1893), 263–278, and other essays in Burrows and Hobson, *William Clarke;* Clarke to Webb, Nov. 21, 1899, Passfield Papers.

[57] Bland's illegitimate children are discussed in Doris L. Moore, *Edith Nesbit* (London, 1933). H. G. Wells has an interesting description of the Bland household in his *Experiment in Autobiography* (London, 1934), pp. 513ff.

"sentimental religion of love," Shaw wrote, Ibsen "repudiates duties, tramples on ideals, profanes what was sacred, sanctifies what was infamous . . . always letting in light and air to hasten the putrefaction of decaying matter." The attack on current morality was, Shaw declared, a "symptom of the revival of religion, not of its extinction." Shaw's sense of the ethical demands of the age ran counter to his commitments as a Fabian and produced continuing tension within his Socialist activity in the years ahead; it was reflected in a growing tendency for Shaw the Fabian to be separated from Shaw the artist-prophet. Nevertheless, while Shaw accepted the Fabian contraction of Socialism, his aesthetic explorations and particularly his "glorification of the individual will" were already a source of distress for Webb.[58]

In matters of personal faith the Fabian essayists ranged across the spectrum of the ethical and metaphysical beliefs of the late Victorians. Mrs. Besant turned to the mysticism of the East, Bland went back to the Catholic church, Clarke adopted a form of ethical-aesthetic idealism, Wallas resumed the quest for a utilitarian or scientific humanism, and Olivier later formulated his own notion of a "cosmic emotion" or "mystical experience." Shaw and Webb met the problem of personal belief in strikingly different ways. Without abandoning fundamental moral concern Shaw began to explore in his drama the possibilities of the liberated ego, while Webb exemplified his belief that the self should be immersed in the needs and functions of society. The "perfect and fitting development of each individual," he had written in his Fabian essay, "is not necessarily the utmost and highest cultivation of his own personality, but the filling, in the best possible way, of his humble function in the great social machine." [59]

However restive individual Fabians may have been with the framework of the Society, it had delineated a common ground of

[58] G. B. Shaw, *The Quintessence of Ibsen* (3rd ed.; London, 1913), pp. 57, 152; Webb to Beatrice Potter, Sept. 18, 1891, Passfield Papers.

[59] See Olivier's exchange of letters with William James reprinted in Olivier, *Sydney Olivier*, pp. 124–126; *Fabian Essays*, p. 54.

action and one which could foster close friendships. Shaw recognized the terms on which the Fabians worked together:

We are all persons of tolerably strong individuality and very diverse temperaments and take that along with the fact that no one of us is strong enough to impose his will on the rest or weak enough to allow himself to be overridden you will I think allow me to claim our escape from the quarrels which rent asunder both the Federation and the League as proof that our method stands the test of experience in the matter of keeping our forces together.[60]

The main threat to Fabian unity during the early nineties came from disagreements about the political role of the Society. The publication of the *Essays* had introduced their ideas to a wide audience. Moreover, in 1890 they had launched the first of a series of lecturing campaigns in the North, which gave them new contact with the industrial working classes. Most of the lectures were given by Webb, Wallas, Shaw, and, the most active speaker of all, W. S. DeMattos. They addressed cooperative societies, trade unions, and political clubs of Liberal or independent working-class outlook, as well as Socialist groups. For the most part the lectures dealt with immediate practical issues. The Fabians were being drawn, Webb observed, into a "long rolling fight all over the country." He welcomed the "chance of translating the crude abstractions of the doctrinaire Socialists into the proposals of practical politics." The prospect fascinated Webb: "How can Mill fear that life will become uninteresting? To play on these millions of minds, to watch them slowly respond to an unseen stimulus, to guide their aspirations without their knowledge—all this, whether in high capacities or in humble, is a big and endless game of chess, of ever extraordinary excitement." And in a rare display of moral fervor Webb added, "Sanctify by altruism and emotion, and you get the raw material of the New Religion." [61]

The wider dissemination of its ideas and the growth of provincial societies, drawn largely from the working class, also renewed the

---

[60] Shaw, *Fabian Society*, p. 24.
[61] Webb to Beatrice Potter, April 30, Aug. 26, 1890, Passfield Papers.

hopes of those London Fabians who sought a Socialist political party. Working-class leaders in the North were increasingly dissatisfied with the older political parties and, partly under the influence of Socialist ideas, were scouting the possibility of an independent labor party. This development contributed to a growing opposition among the London Fabians to the Society's close alliance with the Liberals.

By 1890 even Shaw had concluded that it was time to "burn our boats" and repudiate Gladstone and the Liberal party in "express terms." "Holding our tongues, lest we discover . . . our disunion," he told Wallas, simply left Hyndman as the "only man on his legs."

We must fall back on the Worker's Political Program to show that we also said so all along; and it is a definite Social Democratic Party, prepared to act with the Radical party as far as that party pursues its historic mission of overthrowing capitalist liberalism that is the intent of the working classes.[62]

Meanwhile Bland, already a strong advocate of an independent party, was attacking the policies of the "inner ring," led by Webb, and mobilizing support for a new political strategy. During 1891, Webb began to fear that the Society would be "ruined." "The new men who have not been 'under influence' long," he wrote, "have risen up and want to throw the whole movement into the labor party." "Wallas and I," he added, "are losing influence because we are suspected of too much attachment to the Liberal party." [63]

At a critical meeting in December 1891, Webb vigorously defended the "educational spirit of the Fabians." His views still had considerable support, most notably among "the nebulous mass of Fabians," as Shaw scornfully described them, who were "practical liberals." [64] But Webb now skillfully sought to dissociate Fabian Socialism from all existing parties and interest groups, Liberal and labor alike. He criticized the idea of an independent labor party in Parliament, "selling its votes like the Irish, as a mean, degrading

[62] Shaw to Wallas, Dec. 16, 1890, Wallas Papers.
[63] Bland to Wallas, May 7, 1890, *ibid.;* Webb to Beatrice Potter, Dec. 11, 12, 1891, Passfield Papers.
[64] Shaw to Wallas, Dec. 16, 1890, Wallas Papers.

political policy." Fabians, he argued, should not pursue "class interests but the welfare of the whole community." He even raised the prospect of a new "independent collective party" emerging in the near future. In such a party the Fabians "ought to play a great though unobtrusive part" through careful study of the issues.[65] Webb thus attempted to restate the idea of permeation in a way which, without directly offending the Liberals in the Society, made some concessions to the growing desire among Socialists for an independent party.

Webb and his supporters checked for a while the surge of Fabian interest in a new party. During the following summer, as the parliamentary elections neared, he expressed satisfaction at their success in "eliminating third candidates" and working for the more progressive Liberals and radicals. "Our proper policy," he repeated, "is to educate the constituencies without upsetting the coach by running Labor candidates." But in his determination to guard the Fabian mission and protect their increasingly fruitful political alliance with the Liberals and radicals in London, Webb had not reckoned with the working classes in the North. Shaw recognized that the "permeation racket" simply would not succeed in areas such as Lancashire, where the workers were mainly Tories. More important, he saw in the movement for working-class political independence a new opportunity for Fabian influence. They should, he argued, "wedge" themselves "into the heaviest crush" of the movement.[66] This was pretty much what Shaw attempted to do as the Fabian delegate to the founding conference of the Independent Labour party early in 1893.[67] But by this time the Fabians as a body had lost the chance to influence strongly the formation of the new party. Generally unsympathetic to the political aspirations of the

[65] Notes of Webb's talk are in the Passfield Papers.

[66] Webb to Beatrice Potter, summer 1892; Shaw to Webb, Aug. 12, 22, 1892, Passfield Papers.

[67] Shaw was still in an equivocal position, however. His work at the Bradford conference is discussesd in Henry Pelling, *The Origins of the Labour Party* (London, 1954). Also see Joseph Burgess, *Will Lloyd George Replace Ramsay MacDonald?* (Ilford, 1926), pp. 151ff.

working-class Socialists in the North, the London Fabians watched helplessly as virtually all their provincial societies reorganized as branches of the Independent Labour party.[68]

Not until September 1893, in the face of the rapid growth of the new party and the unwillingness of the Liberals to develop a strong program of social reform, did Webb change his views. A Fabian manifesto, "To Your Tents, O Israel," published in October, attacked the Liberal party for its failure to push welfare legislation and called on labor to put as many third candidates into the field as possible. Liberals inside the Fabian Society were dismayed. Fabianism had changed, H. V. Nevinson told Shaw, and "I, who remain a Fabian," decline to "turn a somersault as you have done" and "wreck our influence with the Radicals." [69] Yet, little more than a year later, disappointed with the outcome of their cooperation with the Independent Labour Party, the Fabians reverted to the policy of permeation. Over the next twenty years they wavered between the alternatives of permeation and a Socialist or labor party.

If Webb's view of Socialist strategy met considerable opposition during the early nineties, he did advance his idea of the educational mission of the Society. The main energies of the Fabians in these years were directed toward developing a more rational understanding of social, economic, and political problems by means of lectures, tracts, and the book boxes which they sent out to local Socialist and labor groups. For a time it apppeared as if the Fabians might concentrate on developing a more rational Socialist consciousness among the lower classes. Indeed, to some extent they were attempting to counter the influence of those Socialists who were carrying forward the ethical and utopian message of Morris. Socialists of this kind, Webb argued, had "forgotten their Karl Marx" and failed to recognize that the "steam engine, factory, and mine have come to stay."

We must make up our mind between contrary ideals. If our aim is the transformation of England into a Social Democracy we must frankly

[68] Several letters in the Passfield Papers indicate that the London Fabians were not happy about this development.

[69] H. V. Nevinson to Shaw, Oct. 20, 1893, Passfield Papers.

accept the changes brought about by the Industrial Revolution, the factory system, the massing of populations in great cities, the elaborate differentiation and complication of modern civilization, the subordination of the worker to the citizen and of the individual to the community. We must rid ourselves resolutely of those schemes and projects of bygone Socialism which have now passed out of date, as well as from the specious devices of Individualism in a new dress (i.e., utopian colonies). All these I class together as Spurious Collectivism making, in my view not for social progress, but for reaction.[70]

The lectures, the tracts, and the efforts to check the romantic impulses in popular Socialism were not in Webb's view the most important part of the Society's educational work. He was more concerned with the "solid work of costly [and] not showy character going on behind" the public propaganda. Webb discerned a "dangerous . . . want of precision" in Socialist thinking. The "greatest need," he wrote in 1894, was men and women with "brains," who would through serious study "work out the detailed application of collectivist principles to the actual problems of modern life." [71] A short time later, when the Fabians received a legacy of ten thousand pounds from Henry Hutchinson, a member in Derby, Webb recognized an opportunity to give institutional form to the deeper need for serious study.

The details of the founding of the London School of Economics have been related by Margaret Cole,[72] but no episode in the history of the Fabian Society reveals so clearly Webb's force of mind and will. Shaw, who wanted the money used for Socialist propaganda, was outraged by Webb's plans and believed him guilty of a malversation of funds. In the face of Webb's desire for a school dedicated to pure or "abstract research," Shaw insisted that the "Collectivist flag must be waved." [73] But here, as in most of the disputes between the two men, Webb prevailed; when the smoke of controversy cleared, the school had been set up along the lines he desired.

[70] Sidney Webb, *Socialism, True and False* (London, 1894), p. 10.
[71] Webb to Pease, July 8, 1896, Aug. 25, 1895, Passfield Papers.
[72] Margaret Cole, *The Story of Fabian Socialism* (London, 1961), pp. 67ff.
[73] Shaw to Beatrice Webb, July 1, 1895, Passfield Papers. A long passage from the letter appears in Cole, *Fabian Socialism,* p. 71.

By 1895, largely under the guidance of Webb, the Fabians had developed their distinctive view of the Socialists' work. The extent to which they had limited the range of Socialist concern was apparent in Tract 70, published the following year. The Fabians, a key sentence read, had "no distinctive opinions on the Marriage Question, Religion, Art, abstract Economics, historic Evolution, Currency or any other subject than its own special business of practical Democracy and Socialism." [74] Even the economic ideas and the view of history expressed in the *Fabian Essays* were denied an official place in the Society's basis. And if the phrase "practical Democracy and Socialism" held a number of ambiguities it meant that the Fabians were primarily concerned with the immediate reforms which could be effected by legislative and administrative changes. Here was a framework, though at times a precarious one, for the subsequent development of the Society.

The Fabian reinterpretation of Socialism entailed both gains and losses. Insofar as the Fabians extruded basic philosophical concerns from their Socialism they freed themselves from the kind of ethical and religious disputes which arose periodically in the other sections of the movement. The limitation of the scope of Socialism also fostered the openness of discussion which became characteristic of the Fabian Society; the Fabians largely avoided the tendency, found in so much of Socialism, to become imprisoned in dogmas and slogans.

The losses resulting from the Fabian contraction of Socialist consciousness were, however, of major significance. Insofar as they discounted the Marxist emphasis on social conflict and power relations, the Fabians cut themselves off from the growing awareness of class and sectional interests which was arousing the working classes, particularly in the North, to new political activity. And to the extent that they played down the role of moral and religious feelings the Fabians tended to divorce themselves from the aspirations that were drawing so many idealistic young men and women to the movement. Separated from the growing class consciousness of the workers, the Fabians lost much of the social realism found in Marxism; sep-

[74] Tract 70, *Report on Fabian Policy* (London, 1896), p. 1.

arated from popular moral and religious sentiments, Fabian Socialism lost much of its power to move individuals to make sacrifices
for the new cause far beyond the immediate horizons of what Webb
called an "instructed egoism." Indeed, in so limiting their field of
action and propaganda the Fabian Society disqualified itself from
the guiding role which some of its members wished to play in the
movement.

Meanwhile, the two forms of British Marxism which Hyndman
and Morris had articulated were undergoing further development.
The utopian Socialism of Morris was being translated into a more
popular "Ethical Socialism." At the same time Hyndman's emphasis on class interests and working-class political power was finding
new and more practical modes of expression. The growth of these
utopian and realistic forms of Socialism will be examined in the
two following chapters.

6
Ethical Socialism

In a lecture to the London Fabian Society in 1907, Sam Hobson contrasted two types of Socialism in the early movement, the "Ethical" and the "Economic." [1] This important distinction separates the main line of British Socialist growth from the Marxist and Fabian sections, for while the popular Socialism of the early nineties owed much to the Marxists and the Fabians, many of its characteristic ideas and its special vitality were derived from different sources.

Ethical Socialism possessed little intellectual coherence. Its spokesmen emphasized a few basic ideas centering on the notion of the collectivization of wealth or the public ownership of the means of production, distribution, and exchange. But they addressed themselves mainly to moral and religious sentiments, preaching Socialism as a new way of life inspired by a higher social ethic. They did not ignore practical political and economic reforms; indeed it may be asked how much their moral and religious rhetoric simply served conventional class or sectional interests. However, during the early nineties Socialism found a British idiom, a matter both of feeling and terminology, and evoked a response far beyond anything achieved by the Social Democratic Federation, the Socialist League, or the Fabian Society.

The chief inspiration for Ethical Socialism came from Morris, and its emergence was due to several strongly poetic young men who

[1] *Fabian News,* Dec. 1907. Also see the discussion in G. D. H. Cole, *History of Socialist Thought,* (London, 1953–1960), III: *The Second International, 1889–1914,* Part II, 136–144.

had been attracted by the romantic and aesthetic ideals of the League's leader. As the League disintegrated in the late eighties these men were stranded, and while they kept their Socialist faith they tended to move away from the Marxism that had given it a theoretical, if tenuous, meaning. Their Socialism took on the more immediate impress of their personal hopes and sentiments. It tended to lose much of the objective theoretical significance it still possessed within the League and became a highly subjective, even expressionistic, creed. This process can be followed in the life of one of the most dedicated among the disciples of Morris, John Bruce Glasier.

John Bruce Glasier and the Poetic Impulse in British Socialism

Glasier has not received close attention in accounts of the movement but no figure exemplified so clearly the emergence and growth of Ethical Socialism.[2] Just as he expressed in his early years many of the hopes and values of the new Socialism, so too his later years revealed its vicissitudes and disappointments. Moreover, Glasier brought from his Scottish background qualities of inspiration which contributed significantly to the early development of the movement.

As a youth Glasier had aspired to be a Presbyterian minister, but at the age of seventeen he read Darwin, T. H. Huxley, and John Tyndall and lost his belief in revealed religion. A poem, "The Oracles of Night," written several years later, recorded the "agony of doubt" through which he passed:

> Twas in the Joy of thy companionship
> That oft times in my youthful questionings
> I strayed alone among the silent hills
> And hidden glens to meditate on themes
> That racked my heart-sick brain without respite,
> While doubt lurked as a devil in my soul,
> And Reason's light was as the flame of hell.
> Until at last worn almost to a spectral thing,
> I gave my soul to Reason, fearing still

[2] Laurence Thompson's *The Enthusiasts: A Biography of John and Katharine Bruce Glasier* (London, 1971), which appeared after this study was completed, does much to remedy the neglect of Glasier and his wife. Also see the biographical sketch by J. W. Wallace, *Socialist Review,* XVII (Oct. 1920).

> Lest I had sinned the sin of sins, for ever
> Closing upon myself the Kingdom's gates.[3]

Glasier joined the Glasgow Secular Society, then became active in the cause of land reform, and, in 1884, helped to found the Glasgow branch of the Social Democratic Federation. The next year he followed Morris into the Socialist League and became one of his confidants. Glasier chose architecture for a vocation, but his concern for social reform checked, and in time overwhelmed, his professional interests. During the mid-eighties he became the "chief apostle" for Socialism in Scotland, conducting propaganda work in Glasgow as well as in the towns and mining areas nearby. His message, like that of Morris, had little to do with economic gains or the "machinery of politics." He offered instead a "picture of a grand and gracious social order, of beautiful streets and gardens—the redemption of life from the multifarious blights of commercialism, moral, mental and physical." [4]

A friend of these years later described Glasier as a "barricades man," and, indeed, his early contributions to *Commonweal* stood out for their militant spirit and scorn of compromise in an organization not given to moderation. He directed his most scathing remarks at the clergy, who, he insisted, "served the cause admirably as enemies" but "would spoil it as friends." [5] Glasier retained much of the religious outlook of his youth. "Jesus of Nazareth," a poem written in 1886 but not published until after his death, indicated the continuing strength of older attitudes and feelings:

> Thou wert the agitator of thy day,
> Assailing wrongs that had grown fat and gray. . . .
>
> O Christ! Thy spirit does not dwell in these

[3] John Bruce Glasier, *On the Road to Liberty: Poems and Ballads* (London, 1920), pp. 15–22.

[4] James Leatham, *Glasgow in the Limelight* (Turriff, 1923), pp. 33–40, describes Glasier's early propaganda work. Also see William Martin Haddow, *My Seventy Years* (London, 1943), p. 167.

[5] *Commonweal,* Sept. 8, 1888. See Leatham's reminiscences, "Sixty Years of World Mending," which appeared in installments in *The Gateway,* XXVIII (April 1940–June 1944).

the modern scribes and priests and pharisees
the usurers that crowd the market place
Who would to Pilate drag thee quick wert thou
Again within their grasp, and bind thy brow
With triple thorns, and spit upon thy face:
And crying "Lawbreaker" and "Communist"
Scoff, scourge, and crucify again the Christ.

No, not with these does thy pure spirit bide . . .
But rather as of old, with the despised,
With those who would a fairer temple raise
To thee of gratitude and love and praise
Than ever yet has been beneath the skies
By building up of human happiness.

With these O Christ, art thou! with these we claim
Thy martyrdom, thy precepts and thy name,
Thy healing hand, thy blessing, thy redress.
Ours is the resurrection and thy reign.
Thy Kingdom spreading wide from man to man,
Thy peace, thy fellowship, thy gentleness.
From thrones, dominions, priesthoods and all the powers,
We claim thee—we unbind thee—Christ is ours! [6]

Glasier loved poetry, but he came to see its writing as a "kind of temptation," which "kept him working at night in a fierce emotional mood and left him exhausted" and unable to do propaganda work. So finally he "thrust it away once and for all." [7]

Within the Socialist League, Glasier had supported Morris' emphasis on educational work and opposition to those who favored a parliamentary political strategy. Glasier's own bent was strongly anarchist, but it lacked serious theoretical justification. With the disappearance of the discipline provided by the League, Glasier's Socialism became purely moral and subjective. The genuine Socialist, he argued, was not one who held certain views about the objective development of social and economic life, but one who was a "truly

[6] Glasier, *Road to Liberty*, pp. 32–35.
[7] *Ibid.*, Preface; see also Thompson, *Enthusiasts*, pp. 24–27.

socialized being." When his anarchist friends in Sheffield, inspired in part by Carpenter, addressed a "Manifesto" to criminals on the ground that their crimes were a "form of social revolt," Glasier objected. "No, my boy," he wrote, "criminals commit crime *conscious* that they are doing wrong. I rather recognize as comrades all people who act bravely and usefully for what they honestly think is for the good of society even though their acts may be in my opinion wrong. That, I think, is the true test of socialized instinct." [8] Glasier's insistence on the right motives, regardless of objective ideas or actions, became more and more characteristic of his Socialism.

By 1892, Glasier could state more clearly his developing view of the Socialist's faith. "It is well to remember," he wrote, "that we have no divine revelation as to what we ought or ought not to do." The important thing was to make sure that "the people have the true aim of Socialism vividly before their eyes and its true feeling in their hearts." If that was assured, "[we] need trouble ourselves little as to what methods are adopted today or adopted tomorrow." The chief task was to overcome "self regarding impulses."

False methods only arise when we act as men having too little faith in Socialism, and too much faith and concern for ourselves. . . . The question of whether we shall stand behind the barricades or stand on the steps at street corners or political platforms will be no question of policy with us; we shall, in which ever way we act, do so simply because we could not, without feeling that we are traitors or fools, act otherwise . . . even if it comes to a sanguinary struggle. That our ideal may so overpower our individual self seeking, and exalt us above any of the loathesome social inducements of our time, is the most precious blessing that the heroic efforts of our comrades in the past and the genius of our cause can give them.[9]

Having subordinated strategy and doctrine to quality of faith, Glasier felt free to identify himself with almost any expression of Socialism he judged to be sincere. He still viewed Fabianism as an impossible alternative. But in 1891 he opened the platform of the

[8] Glasier to James Brown, Feb. 26, 1891, Glasier Correspondence, Archives of the Independent Labour Party, Bristol.

[9] *Hammersmith Socialist Record*, July 1892.

Glasgow Socialist Society, which he headed, to speakers representing diverse forms of Socialism. There was, he had begun to feel, "a great need for charitable thinking" in the movement. He praised the former Social Democrat John Burns, despite his collaboration with the Liberals, and commended Robert Blatchford, the popular Socialist writer, even though he was an "avowed parliamentary man." By January 1893, Carpenter could suggest to Glasier that they were "the only two who worked with all factions of the movement." Later in that year Glasier joined the new Independent Labour party, a body with which he would be closely identified the rest of his life. He had concluded that the party's "trend towards opportunism is not of a very deep rooted character." The great majority of the members were "sincere Socialists, anxious to do their best to hasten the day of the Social revolution." [10]

Glasier expressed his creed most fully in a paper, *The Religion of Socialism*, published in the spring of 1893. He defined religion as "the highest faith and purpose of life" and argued that Socialism could be viewed as "an all sufficing religion of itself—so far as concerns the doings and relations of men and women in the visible world." He disassociated Socialism from specific metaphysical or supernatural beliefs, but admitted that there was "much truth" in the frequent assertion that its advocates had been "mostly unbelievers." The power of Christianity was "fast fading in the land," and new influences were at work to humanize the "prevailing system of class privilege and commercialism." They owed "their virtue to the elements of Socialism" which they contained.[11]

Glasier's Socialism had slight economic or political content and little intellectual coherence. The "reason and social intuition of the people" would provide the authority for Socialism; its moral code "would consist of the restraints and coordinations of individual doings adopted because of their self-evident advantage to one and all."

[10] Glasier to James Brown, Feb. 8, 1891, Feb. 2, 1892; Edward Carpenter to Glasier, Jan. 1, 1893, Glasier Correspondence; *Hammersmith Socialist Record,* July 1892.

[11] Katharine St. John Conway and John Bruce Glasier, *The Religion of Socialism: Two Aspects* (Manchester, 1894), pp. 11, 15.

But this utilitarian note was exceptional, for the "religion of Social-ism" also had its "martyrs." The Russian Nihilists, the Chicago anarchists, and the Paris Communards "fought, suffered and died" in the "hope of making a heaven for you and me and all mankind upon earth." [12] Indeed, to Glasier the most important sources of the Socialist vision were the poets—Morris, Carpenter, Whitman, and others. In an essay written in later years he summarized their con-tributions to the movement:

The poet, released from the limitations of the common mold of thought, communicates to his fellows the revelations of the freer vision which he enjoys. His fellows are thus enabled to share in his liberty and see with his eyes. While rarely giving of its best to the politics and happenings of the hour, poetry has been the chief source from which down the ages popular sentiment and political movements have derived whatever ideal-ism or spiritual vehemence they have possessed. Poetry sings and speaks to the heart, knowing how to reach its deeper and more lasting chords.[13]

Glasier's own gift for raising "popular sentiment" to a higher level of "spiritual vehemence" made him one of the most effective So-cialist propagandists in the nineties. He carried into his work some-thing of the style of the vagabond poet, hence the description written shortly after his death in 1920: "Free and unconventional in dress and manner, a disreputable hat crowning his shaggy locks, a picturesque flowing cloak for wet weather . . . he bravely trudged from village to town, carrying song and sunshine wherever he went and proclaiming his message for all who had ears to hear." [14]

The belief that poetic inspiration gave "truer views of life" and provided the "maps of the country toward which human progress is turned" was an important element in Ethical Socialism. It found ex-pression in a number of other young men in the provinces. In the West Riding of Yorkshire, which provided the most fertile soil for Ethical Socialism, the most important of the Socialist pioneers was

[12] *Ibid.*, p. 16.

[13] Glasier's introduction to his edition of the Socialist poetry of Morris, *Socialism in Song* (London, 1919), pp. xii–xiv.

[14] Wilfrid Whitley, *J. Bruce Glasier: A Memorial* (London, 1920), p. 9.

Tom Maguire of Leeds.[15] Maguire's life exemplified a pattern of development common to many early Socialists of the North. At the age of seventeen he had discarded his religious faith, and in the face of bitter antagonism from his Irish Catholic compatriots, joined the Secularist cause. He then discovered the Marxism of the Federation and before long followed Morris into the League. Maguire's small band of Socialists consisted chiefly of workingmen, and even before the League broke up they had taken up the cause of the unskilled workers in the area. Maguire and his companions provided the leadership for the growth of the new unions, particularly among the gasworkers, which took place in the West Riding during 1889 and 1890. They also entered early into the campaign to create a new working-class party.

Maguire's poems, many of which first appeared in *Commonweal,* frequently were sentimental, but they exhibited strong moral compassion for the stunted lives of the lower classes. He wrote of "soul and senses grown numb in meaningless toil," the opiate of "novellette reading," maidens who "sate the lust" of "factory Minotaurs," the "living Christ hourly sacrificed," and finally, of "socialism coming." To a Fabian, reviewing his small volume of verse, Maguire seemed "the enthusiastic young man from the hills . . . uninfluenced by London cynicism . . . ever inspired by the 'pure passionate cause' rather than by an academic regard for Marx or Jevons." His poems conveyed "the essence of that earnest pseudo-religious spirit, which is characteristic of the Labour movement in the North of England." [16]

Maguire's Socialism retained, in its strong sense of the class struggle and its concern for working-class organization, something of its Marxist source. But here, too, as for Morris and Glasier, Socialism meant above all transformed lives. "People call themselves Socialists," he complained, but they are really "just ordinary men with

[15] See Edward Thompson, "Homage to Tom Maguire," in *Essays in Labour History, in Memory of G. D. H. Cole,* ed. Asa Briggs and John Saville (London, 1960). Also see Carpenter, ed., *Tom Maguire: A Remembrance* (Manchester, 1895).

[16] Tom Maguire, *Machine Room Chants,* ed. David Lowe, London, 1895); *Fabian News,* Jan. 1896.

Socialist opinions hung round; they haven't got it inside of them." [17]
The tension, dimly felt by Maguire, between Socialism as a new
religious faith and Socialism as a practical program for advancing
working-class interests, helped to bring disillusionment and an early
death in 1896.

Another provincial leader was Fred Henderson of Norwich, a
disciple of Morris who wrote poems combining a strong emotional
attachment to Jesus with a hatred of the "useless faith that tricks
the people into prayer." His verse also told of the young man from
the provinces encountering the modern city. Its "soulless crowds,"
"plunder of commerce," "dying faith," all seemed a "world forsaken
of truth." Yet for those who were willing to fight there were "golden
days to come." Other poets developed the idea, so common in Socialist writings, of a new heaven or kingdom of God. A volume of verses
published by the Wolverhampton Socialist leader Joseph Whittaker
had as its central poem "The Storming of Heaven." It related
God's dethronement and the transformation of earth into "a new
heaven" of "stately homes," "gorgeous towns and streets," a "wealth
of noble gardens and delicate love retreats." Whittaker also envisioned a future where "strenuous toil is worship." Even when a
Socialist poet acknowledged Marxist inspiration, moral feelings dominated the economic or historical message. The Social Democrat
Francis Adams, best known for his *Songs of the Army of the Night,*
wrote a poem, "To Karl Marx," in which he expressed gratitude,
"not for the thought that burns as keen and clear . . . but for the
heart of love divine and bright." Marx appeared to Adams as a
"worker, thinker, poet, and seer." [18]

The work of Glasier, Maguire, Henderson, Whittaker, and others
suggested how a new popular Socialist consciousness was emerging
out of a disintegrating Marxism. To some extent, as with Maguire,

[17] See Bessie Ford's preface to Carpenter, ed., *Tom Maguire,* p. vi.
[18] *Commonweal,* Oct. 9, 1886,; Fred Henderson, *Echoes of the Coming Day*
(London, 1887); Fred Henderson, *"By the Sea" and Other Poems* (London,
1892); Joseph Whittaker, *In Divers Tones* (Manchester, 1894); Francis Adams,
Songs of the Army of the Night (London, 1894), p. 98. Adams' work is discussed in the *Progressive Review,* June 1897, and Henry Salt, *Company I've
Kept* (London, 1930), pp. 70–76.

the new Socialism gave fresh purpose and form to the practical struggles of the workers. It was mainly ethical and utopian, and though it still derived much inspiration from Marx, it also tapped the springs of motivation provided by inherited moral and religious sentiment. This blend of utopian aspiration and popular moral sentiment underlay the enormous appeal of Robert Blatchford and his *Merrie England*.

"Nunquam" and *Merrie England*

In the summer of 1890 a correspondent for *Commonweal,* the organ of the nearly extinct Socialist League, reported that the role of "Socialist Messiah" in the North of England had for over a year been "nobly played" by "Nunquam" of the *Sunday Chronicle*. He added, somewhat condescendingly, that Nunquam's Socialism was "sentimental" rather than "practical." Before long the Social Democratic weekly, *Justice,* also acknowledged Nunquam's "extraordinary affect on thousands and tens of thousands who could be reached in no other way." [19] Through the nineties, Robert Blatchford, the man behind the nom de plume, was by far the most effective recruiter for Socialism in England.

Blatchford had grown up in a working-class district of Halifax, where, between the ages of fourteen and twenty, he worked as an apprentice in a brush-making factory. Like many other ambitious and talented working-class youths of the North, Blatchford was encouraged along the path of self-improvement by a Congregational chapel. But at the age of twenty he impetuously left home to "tramp" and, a few weeks later, after experiencing the life of the down and out in London, found refuge in the army. Six years in the army were crucial to Blatchford's development, for, while much of the moral cast of the chapel remained, military life greatly broadened his sympathies and his army experience stimulated his artistic and literary interests.[20]

[19] *Commonweal,* June 28, 1890; *Justice,* March 9, 1892.
[20] Blatchford's mother was the daughter of a theatrical composer of Italian descent, and his father, who died in 1853 when he was two, was a strolling comedian. Laurence Thompson's *Robert Blatchford* (London, 1951) provides

Leaving the army in 1877, Blatchford hoped to become an artist. He lacked the means for professional training and had a family to support after 1880, so turned to journalism. He taught himself to write by intensive study of the Old Testament and the writings of John Bunyan, Cobbett, and Carlyle. In time he secured a job on a London sporting paper, *Bell's Life.* Carlyle's great impact on Blatchford in the mid-eighties helps to explain his growing dissatisfaction with his work as a writer of light and easily digested reading material. In terms of the Carlylean image of the "hero as man of letters," his work seemed trivial. To his closest friend and fellow journalist, A. M. Thompson, he confessed that their writing was "mere froth, empty sounds, mechanical wit and flippant jokes. Utterly worthless, no purpose in them, nothing new. . . . It is a waste of time," he concluded "for a sensible earnest man to read anything that we write." [21]

Blatchford moved to Manchester in 1887 to write for the *Sunday Chronicle,* one of the most successful of the papers recently created to appeal to the newly literate masses. Here his popularity grew rapidly. His column, "As I Lay Thynkynge," both entertained and informed his readers as he shared with them his personal experiences, the authors he had discovered, or his musings on life generally. Blatchford's style gave him ready passage into the minds of the new reading public. He was simple, direct, and vigorous; his tone was as personal as a letter, and he elicited a steady stream of correspondence. He avoided complexity and enhanced his readability by the frequent use of dialogue. Only slight demands were made on the reasoning powers of his audience.[22]

Blatchford's style was fashioned by long self-discipline, but it also expressed an outlook close to the working-class milieu from which

---

the best account of his life. See also A. Neil Lyons, *Robert Blatchford* (London, 1910), pp. 21–22; and Robert Blatchford, *My Eighty Years* (London, 1931), p. 100.

[21] Blatchford to Thompson, Oct. 11, 1885, Robert Blatchford–A. M. Thompson Correspondence, Manchester Public Libraries, Manchester.

[22] Discussions of the reading habits of the lower classes, which suggest the nature of Blatchford's appeal, may be found in Richard Hoggart's *The Uses of Literacy,* Penguin Edition (Harmondsworth, 1957), especially pp. 79–94.

he had come. "As soon as I enter the realm of abstract thought," he once observed, "I become paralyzed and incapable of finding my way about." [23] His need for a "solid foothold in fact" probably enhanced his appeal to working-class readers whose lives were usually set in a densely practical existence. But as a popular columnist Blatchford was concerned primarily with the immediate facts of consciousness and addressed himself chiefly to the moral sentiments.

Early in his journalistic career Blatchford had displayed a strong tendency to preach, conceding at one point that "a jolly good parson was lost to the church when I went to the soldiers." He was most disturbed over the cramped lives of the lower classes, particularly their arrested cultural development. In his columns he attempted to introduce readers to the world of secular culture, but also punctuated his writings with jibes at middle-class mores and institutions. A favorite target was the utilitarian concept of self-interest, which Blatchford regarded as the cornerstone of existing society. "Millism," as he labeled the prevailing social outlook, was simply "a scramble after wealth." It led logically to the "conversion of beautiful England into a great ugly, foetid, horrible, overgrown Manchester and Salford." He drew on Ruskin and Plato to support the claim that a more just and virtuous social order was possible. [24]

Organized religion, which, with art, was the "supposed agent for the spread of virtue and cultivation," also came under repeated attack. Blatchford's religious views had been reduced to a simple New Testament ethic of love. "Religion," he wrote, "exists for the sake of virtue . . . a fact that has been somewhat obscured by the clouds of theology." When a minister objected to the sale of the *Sunday Chronicle* on Sabbatarian grounds, Blatchford declared: "We expect the enmity of the Church. . . . Parsons and ourselves are natural antagonists. We preach virtue, charity and humanity. They preach religion. The two are diametrically opposed to one

[23] Blatchford to Edward Carpenter, Dec. 27, 1893, Edward Carpenter Correspondence and Papers, Sheffield Public Library, Sheffield.

[24] Blatchford to Thompson, Sept. 1885, Blatchford Correspondence; *Sunday Chronicle,* March 10, 1889.

another." By the end of 1889 Blatchford frequently devoted his column to religious controversy and was attacked for purveying a new "popular agnosticism." [25]

Blatchford became a Socialist in 1889 while in a state of moral indignation over the living conditions he had encountered during a tour of the Manchester slums.[26] A pamphlet by Hyndman and Morris proved to be "the very thing I had been looking for." Blatchford's Socialism owed most to Morris, although he also drew important elements from Peter Kropotkin and the Fabians. As early as October 1889 he called on the working men to "form a party of their own—a Labour Party." [27]

During 1889 and 1890 Blatchford's fame as a Socialist writer grew, and he became active in the efforts toward economic and political action among the working classes in Lancashire and Yorkshire. He investigated industrial disputes, served as the first president of the Manchester Fabian Society, and in the summer of 1891 consented to stand for Parliament in Bradford under the auspices of the local labor men.[28] He also helped to organize the Manchester Independent Labour Party, one of the first of the local parties that came together in 1893 to form the national Independent Labour Party.

[25] *Sunday Chronicle,* March 10, Feb. 3, March 3, 1889. Blatchford discussed his religious views in a long letter to Thompson in 1885, most of which is reprinted in Thompson, *Blatchford,* pp. 41–47. Blatchford was especially fond of the assertion "The best religion is to do good." The attack came from a Catholic magazine. Blatchford's reply appears in *Sunday Chronicle,* Dec. 1, 1889.

[26] Blatchford devoted all his space during May and June 1889 to an exposure of living conditions in the Manchester slums.

[27] *Sunday Chronicle,* Oct. 20, 1889. H. M. Hyndman *et al., How I Became a Socialist,* (London, 1894), pp. 64–67, has an account by Blatchford. The pamphlet was H. M. Hyndman and William Morris, *A Summary of the Principles of Socialism* (London, 1884).

[28] Blatchford remained an active candidate for six months but withdrew before the election due to the work connected with founding the *Clarion.* He held a low view of politics, confiding to Thompson at the time of his withdrawal: "I despise the arts of politicians, and I could never stoop to them" (quoted by Thompson, *Blatchford,* p. 85). Earlier Blatchford had told his *Chronicle* readers not to "waste" their "best men" on Parliament but to save them for "better

Blatchford left the *Chronicle* after a quarrel with the owner in October 1891.[29] Early in December, with several colleagues whom he had drawn away from the *Chronicle,* he published the first issue of a new weekly paper, the *Clarion.* The founders hoped to take much of the *Chronicle*'s mass readership, but they fell far short of this goal. The circulation of the *Clarion,* hurt no doubt by the omission of the racing notes and scandal carried by the *Chronicle,* soon leveled out at around thirty thousand. Though this was somewhat disappointing, the depth of the *Clarion*'s hold on its readers was extraordinary; it soon found expression in a variety of local associations. Blatchford and his staff began to create, to use a term they borrowed from Morris, a new "fellowship." [30]

The *Clarion*'s popularity and the network of clubs and societies that sprang up around it were symptomatic of heightened self-consciousness in the lower classes. Increased educational facilities, extension of the suffrage, the decline of organized religion, and changes in the nature of social and economic organization all helped to make older forms of life less binding. Many young men and, less frequently, young women of the working classes were gaining new views of life's possibilities from different sources. For a few the theatre "opened the doors to a wider outlook and taught such manners and customs as were current" in the larger world. Usually books were decisive. A single volume like Ernest Renan's *Life of Jesus* might drastically alter one's outlook. "That little book has helped shape my life. . . . I went home that night with new sentences ringing

---

work." They should send "honest and intelligent men" who would be entirely instruments of (their) will" (*Sunday Chronicle,* Feb. 23, 1890).

[29] According to Thompson, Blatchford's rift with the *Chronicle*'s publisher, Edward Hulton, sprang both from his growing involvement in the Socialist movement and from his neglect of newspaper work to help produce a comic opera (Thompson, *Blatchford,* pp. 67–81).

[30] First came the Cinderella societies, which originated during the *Chronicle* days and provided food and entertainment for underprivileged children. In the mid-nineties a network of Clarion clubs sprang up to carry on such activities as cycling, hiking, handicrafts, nature study, singing, and other hobbies. The "Clarionettes," as they called themselves, were especially fond of a statement in *The Dream of John Ball:* "Fellowship is Life, lack of Fellowship is death."

like clashing bells within my consciousness and read long after my usual late hour. . . . I vaguely envisioned the necessity of an earthquake in social conditions," wrote J. L. Clynes. In the growth of the new self-consciousness the writings of Carlyle and Ruskin were often the most important single influences. They encouraged, as one Socialist recalled, both a questioning of social institutions and values and a fresh "search for meaning in life." By the late eighties, however, many working men were going beyond Ruskin and Carlyle. Not only were they turning to the English Socialist writers, but they were finding new inspiration in the American Socialists particularly Lawrence Gronlund and Edward Bellamy.[31]

The *Clarion* appealed directly to the new self-consciousness. It offered new ethical goals to those who had ceased to find guidance in church or chapel. "The *Clarion* has done for me what nothing else would do," one correspondent reported, "it has expanded my sympathies, enlarged my charities, and brought me from narrow and bigoted individualism to a conception of my duty to God and man." Another reader, telling of his conversion to Socialism, declared that the *Clarion* "is now to me the breath of life. In it are my hopes and aspirations." [32] Such responses indicate a strong sense of the release of new moral energies. It underlay Blatchford's confident assertion in 1894: "I could, I think, if I went steadily to work, with all my strength and no other aim before me, in about seven years batter the whole economic and ethical system of this rotten country to pieces and utterly change the current of English life." [33]

The *Clarion's* appeal, like the associations which sprang up among its readers, was nearly as wide as life itself. Its pages contained capsules of human interest, tragic as well as comic, along with biting reminders of economic and social injustice. Middle-class con-

---

[31] Joseph Burgess, *A Potential Poet* (Ilford, 1927), p. 130; J. L. Clynes, *Life* (London, 1937, I, 38; Percy Redfern, *Journey to Understanding* (London, 1946), p. 99; Peter Marshall, "A British Sensation," in Sylvia Bowman, ed., *Edward Bellamy Abroad* (New York, 1962).

[32] *Clarion*, Dec 2, 1893, Jan. 16, 1895.

[33] Quoted by Thompson, *Blatchford*, p. 124.

ventions were subjected to constant satirical treatment by such columnists as "Whiffly Puncto," "Dangle," and "The Bounder"; a tone of the masses versus the classes informed its columns. But the dominant message was of emancipation, cultural as well as social. There were short stories and poetry, reviews of books and plays, making up a diverse cultural fare which drew the reader into a wider realm of imagination. The *Clarion* writers were strongly antipuritan and tended at times toward a hedonistic affirmation of the pleasures of this world. Some of the *Clarion* clubs became centers of a new form of lower-class bohemianism.

The soul of the *Clarion* was Blatchford. For "thousands of men and women in Lancashire factories" he was a "literary father and mother." For many still "untouched politically," as a leading journalist later observed, "the limpid clarity" of his articles also "had the effect of a revelation." Blatchford was recasting the ideas developed by the Socialists during the eighties into more vivid and concrete terms:

[He] translated our yearnings and imaginings into wondrous words . . . [He] could show a half timer in a cotton factory how to be a definite Socialist. Before I was twelve years old I had thoroughly grasped the fundamental principles of Socialism. The whole thing seemed so obvious and so easily comprehensible that I was amazed that anyone could doubt its essential rightness and righteousness.[34]

Blatchford's simple prose cut through the baffling complexities of existing social arrangements and revealed to his readers a social world made and managed by men and women like themselves and susceptible to almost infinite improvement. Most important, Blatchford began to develop a picture of a happier and more just society. He portrayed the Socialist future in *Merrie England*.

Later described as "the most effective piece of popular Socialist

[34] Annie Kenney, *Memories of a Militant* (London, 1923), p. 23; John Paton, *Proletarian Pilgrimage* (London, 1935), p. 96; Roland Kenney, *Westering* (London, 1939), pp. 23–25. John A. Hammerton, *Books and Myself* (London, 1944), declared that it was "impossible to gauge the impact of his mind on my generation."

propaganda ever written," [35] *Merrie England* first appeared in installments in the *Clarion* during 1893. When two editions at a shilling a copy quickly sold out, the *Clarion* board of directors decided to print a hundred thousand copies in a penny edition. Within a few years the total sales in Great Britian and abroad approached two million. In England thousands of Socialists peddled the book from door to door or on the streets.[36]

Merrie England was addressed to "John Smith of Oldham," a mythical "shrewd, hardheaded, practical man," who, as Blatchford declared, could recognize "the facts," use "cold reason," and exercise the "English love of fair play." [37] The second half of the two-part book dealt with common arguments against Socialism and devoted most attention to refuting the charge that the Socialists, after abolishing the incentives of competition and self-interest, would have to resort to coercion to keep society functioning. The great appeal of *Merrie England* lay in the first half where Blatchford described the future Socialist society. He carried over much of the utopian vision of Morris, along with elements drawn from his life in the army. But to the support of the vision Blatchford brought to bear theoretical and statistical material developed by the Fabians. He presented a highly inconsistent blend of the utilitarian and romantic traditions in English social thought.

Blatchford's Socialist ideal was well suited to those who were "mentally hungry and awake." It centered on a life marked by "frugality of body and opulence of mind." The "material needs of life," he argued, were "few and easily supplied" while the "range of spirtual and intellectual pleasures and capacities" was "practically boundless." Under Socialism the "monotonous, mechanical" toil of the factory worker would become more like the free, creative, and pur-

[35] Cole, *Socialist Thought,* III, Part I, p. 166.

[36] For example, John Brotherton of the Leeds ILP took pony and cart and paraded the streets selling it. Within a few weeks he had disposed of five thousand copies (Alfred Mattison Diaries, May 1934, Leeds Public Library, Leeds).

[37] Robert Blatchford, *Merrie England* (London, 1894), p. 1. Citations refer to the American "Social Democracy" edition (Chicago, 1897).

poseful activity of the artist. A sense of craftsmanship would be recovered.[38]

Blatchford despised the factory system and repudiated the idea that Britain should serve as the workshop of the world. He would cut imperial ties and end large-scale foreign trade. "Merrie England" would be decentralized, broken up into self-sufficing towns or communes as cooperation replaced competition.

I would have the towns rebuilt with wide streets, with detached houses, with gardens and fountains and avenues of trees. . . . I would make the houses loftier and larger, and clear them of all useless furniture. . . . I would have public parks, public theatres, refreshment. I would have all our children fed and clothed and educated at the cost of the State. I would have them all trained in athletics and to arms. I would have public halls of science. I would have the people become their own artists, actors, musicians, soldiers, and police. Then, by degrees I would make all these things free. So that clothing, lodging, fuel, food, amusement, intercourse, education and all the requirements for a perfect human life would be produced and distributed and enjoyed by the people without the use of money.

The drudgery of the working-class household would disappear.

We set up one laundry, with all the best machinery; we set up one drying field; we set up one great kitchen, one general dining hall, and one pleasant tea garden. Then we buy all the provisions and other things in large quantities, and we appoint certain wives as cooks and laundresses, or, as is the case with many military duties, we let the wives take the duties in turn. Don't you see how much better and how much cheaper the meals would be? Don't you see how much easier the lives of our women would be? Don't you see how much more comfortable our homes would be? Don't you see how much more social and friendly we should become? [39]

In Merrie England, as in "Nowhere," coercive techniques virtually disappeared, for Blatchford believed that "men instinctively prefer light to dark, love to hate, and good to evil." Law, for "the great mass of the people," was "almost a dead letter anyway" since

---

[38] Redfern, *Journey,* p. 20; Blatchford, *Merrie England,* pp. 26, 81.
[39] Blatchford, *Merrie England, pp.* 15–16, 25–26, 30.

"honest men need no laws—except to defend them from rascals." [40] Governing the transformed society presented no great difficulty, for the "science of government . . . was no more mysterious" than the "ordinary affairs of domestic and everyday life. The men who have virtue and sense to rule their families, to manage their business, to master their professions, their arts and crafts, are quite capable of managing the affairs of state." [41]

Blatchford looked to existing political methods to bring about the change, though he foresaw a transitional state of "practical Socialism," or a Socialism marked by state ownership and regulation of economic life. To this end Blatchford urged the working classes to form a Socialist political party. But the primary task was to get "the people to understand and desire Socialism." "Give us a Socialist people," he wrote, "and Socialism will establish itself." Again, as with Morris, the concern with morally transformed lives took precedence over all objective considerations of economic development or political organization. In place of the Marxist conception of a class-conscious proletariat, Blatchford substituted the ethical-religious category of a righteous people. Hence the simple alternative he placed before his readers:

The question of Socialism is the most important and imperative question of the age. It will divide, is now dividing, society into two camps. In which camp will you elect to stand? On the one side there are individualism and competition—leading to a "great trade" and great miseries. On the other side is justice, without which can come no good, from which can come no evil. On the one hand are ranged all the sages, all the saints, all the martyrs, all the noble manhood and pure womanhood of the world; on the other hand are the tyrant, the robber, the manslayer, the libertine, the usurer, the slave driver, the drunkard, and the sweater. Choose your party then, my friend, and let us get to fighting.[42]

Blatchford did not recommend the use of physical force, but he believed that the Socialist movement should take on the character of a religious crusade. "If Socialism is to live and conquer," he de-

[40] *Ibid.,* pp. 93, 153.
[41] Quoted by Thompson, *Blatchford,* p. 113.
[42] Blatchford, *Merrie England,* pp 79–83, 181, 89.

clared in 1896, "it must be a religion. If Socialists are to prove themselves equal to the task assigned them they must have faith, a real faith, a new faith." [43]

After the turn of the century Blatchford attempted to give a new metaphysical foundation to Socialism and sought a form of consciousness informed by scientific truth, but in the earlier years he trusted in the more or less spontaneous growth of altruistic feeling. Although he had left the chapel behind, he appealed mainly to lower-class moral sensibilities which were still, particularly in the northern industrial counties, largely formed by Nonconformist religion.

Nowhere was this fusion of Socialist ideas and religious sentiment more apparent than in the West Riding of Yorkshire. The Nonconformist chapels of the West Riding, particularly the Congregationalist and the Methodist chapels, exerted a strong though diminishing influence on the lower classes. As the new social creed found local spokesmen they rapidly translated it into the ethically centered gospel which was becoming characteristic of the theologically liberal sections of Nonconformity. Indeed, a Huddersfield Socialist, Ramsden Balmforth, advanced the view that the renewal of religious feeling within the Socialist movement was the most significant tendency of the time. Balmforth, a clerk in the local cooperative society and an active Unitarian, developed his ideas in a series of articles published in the *Westminster Review* during 1892.[44] Socialism, he argued, was the outcome of the teachings of the early Christians, Owen, Carlyle, and Ruskin; it represented the modern expression of the movement toward a higher humanity. The decay of religion meant that morality had to be rescued from the "shiftings of theological doctrine" and based firmly on the facts of human experience. For Balmforth, Socialism held the promise of a "New Refor-

[43] *Clarion*, April 25, 1896. Also see his essay "The New Religion," in *The New Party*, ed. Andrew Reid (London, 1894).

[44] The series under the pseudonym Laon Ramsay, was "The Sanctions of Morality in Their Relation to Religious Life," *Westminster Review*, Nov. 1892, Feb. 1893. It was published in book form as *The New Reformation* (London, 1893).

mation" which would enrich not only man's personal existence but his social and economic life as well.

Some of the Socialist pioneers in the West Riding retained their ties with organized religion. Thus Fred Jowett of Bradford, who joined the Socialist League in the late eighties, remained active in a Congregational chapel until 1892. Usually, however, the Socialist convert broke with organized religion when he entered the movement. Edward Hartley, for example, had been a Sunday School teacher in a Methodist chapel before discovering a more compelling gospel in Socialism.[45] Even though the West Riding Socialists drew on the area's strong Secularist tradition, they still employed the rhetoric of the chapel for propaganda purposes. Thus, George Minty, a Secularist speaker until he was converted to Socialism, appealed directly to the religious sentiments. "The essence of religion," he told one working-class audience, was "doing good," and he contrasted the "perverted religion of the chapels" with the "divine revelation contained in the labor movement." But whatever their immediate background the Socialists of the West Riding usually acknowledged the influence of Carlyle and Ruskin, of Morris or Carpenter, and they cast their social creed in quasi-religious terms. Their lectures bore such titles as "The Religion of Labor," "The Religion of Socialism," and "Socialism and Christianity." [46]

Outside the West Riding, Ethical Socialism lost some of its force. Yet the special blend of utopianism and moral feelings, expressed most effectively by Blatchford, could be found throughout Great Britain in these years. Its most devoted apostles were often men and women of the middle classes who, for various reasons, had become estranged from their social background. This was the case

[45] See Fred Jowett, *What Made Me a Socialist* (Manchester, 1925, p. 5. Hartley described his conversion in a pamphlet, *Rounds With Socialists* (London, 1914), and in *Forward,* July 6, 1906. Alf Mattison was another Methodist who broke with the chapel when he joined the movement. See Mattison Diaries, Sept. 24, 1933. Another example was Charles Pearson, a Socialist candidate for the Bradford City Council. See *Labour Echo* (Bradford), Oct. 13, 1894.

[46] *Bradford Labour Journal,* Oct. 14, 1892. For lecture titles see especially the *Bradford Labour Journal* and the *Workman's Times* during this period.

with four remarkable middle-class women, who became perhaps the most inspired spokesmen for Ethical Socialism.

Socialism and the "New Women"

There were obvious affinities between the Socialist cause and the rising expectations of women in late Victorian society. Increasingly sensitive to the contradictions between the liberal values of freedom and equality and the restrictions imposed on women by social conventions, some of the "new women" discovered that in the Socialist movement "equality was taken for granted," that the "full emancipation of the woman was implicit" in its program. The Socialist movement was, moreover, poor in trained speakers and organizers. To young, well-educated middle-class women, particularly those who were entering such fields as teaching and social welfare, the movement offered "a new platform, public office, every kind of opportunity to the rarest novice." The alliance seemed inevitable. "The Reveille of the proletariat then is the Reveille of women. Their emancipation must be simultaneous. Each, in freeing themselves [sic] must free the other. At the bottom of all their efforts lies the same aim: self realization, a full and conscious life of personal and social activity." [47]

But if the women drawn to Socialism were impelled in part by feminist motives, they also shared to the full the aspirations of the movement. The four women examined in this section—Margaret McMillan, Katharine St. John Conway, Enid Stacy, and Carolyn Martyn—revealed the intensity of the commitment which Ethical Socialism might obtain.

Margaret McMillan and her sister Rachel had been jolted out of their comfortable middle-class existence in Scotland by W. T. Stead's pamphlet, *The Maiden Tribute of Modern Babylon,* published in 1886. This pamphlet, dealing with the problem of prostitution, convinced the two sisters that the pulpits, with their perennial discussions of theological questions, were "silent on actual problems of good and evil." A year later Rachel visited Edinburgh where a friend, John Gilray, was a leader in the local Socialist League. She

[47] Margaret McMillan, *The Life of Rachel McMillan* (London, 1927), p. 27; *Labour Annual* (Manchester, 1895), p. 138.

described her impressions of the Socialists in a letter to Margaret: "I instinctively felt they were good people, and now I believe they are the true disciples and followers of Christ. . . . Socialism makes every noble expectation and hope realizable and opens up a sunlit track one can joyfully look along. . . . Ignorance is the curse of the world." Soon afterward Margaret secured a copy of *Capital* and began "to study it as a new Bible." [48]

Moving to London in 1888, Margaret entered into the new reform activity. She wrote for the *Christian Socialist,* lectured, sold Socialist literature during the great dock strike of 1889, and participated in a project to rehabilitate slum girls in the East End. She became acquainted with the whole range of Socialist opinion in London, extending from the anarchism of Kropotkin and Louise Michel, through the contrasting positions of Hyndman and Morris, to the Fabians. Initially she identified with the anarchists, but by 1892 she had moved to a more gradualist, parliamentary political outlook. In her articles and lectures for Socialism, she continued to appeal mainly to motives of love, which had ceased to have any connection with organized religion. In a popular novel, *Samson,* written in these years, she expressed what one reviewer saw as a "vague almost mystic desire for a deeper faith as the basis of Socialism." [49] For a time at least Theosophy seemed to provide such a basis.

With the rapid surge of Socialism in the North during 1892 and 1893, Margaret decided to work full time for the movement in Bradford while her sister Rachel remained in London as a sanitary inspector to help provide financial support. Later Margaret recalled the excitement and the diversity of the young movement:

And now the life of the working classes was no longer a secret or a thing remote or a creation of the imagination. It was a close and thrilling

[48] McMillan, *Rachel McMillan,* pp. 27, 40; *Labour Leader,* July 11, 1912.

[49] McMillan, *Rachel McMillan,* pp. 38ff, *Labour Leader,* June 8, 1895. Her changing outlook is discussed in a letter from B. M. Fraser to Glasier, Oct. 2, 1892, Glasier Correspondence. See her article, "Love Thy Neighbor as Thyself," *Christian Weekly,* Oct. 14, 1893. She discusses Theosophy in a letter to Glasier, Aug. 2, 1892, Glasier Correspondence.

reality. . . . The movement grew rapidly. . . . Many who left the chapel and some who remained in it joined the new party. We had friends in the Whitmanites at Bolton, in the Secularists at Leicester, and also in the Spiritualist groups in various towns and villages. . . . And the party quickly got a new literature of its own suited to the needs of the North Country people.[50]

In 1894, Margaret was elected to the Bradford School Board as an independent labor candidate, and during the years ahead she gained national attention for her pioneering work on behalf of under-privileged children.

Katharine St. John Conway was a student in classics at Newnham College, Cambridge, in 1889 when she felt compelled to protest against the existing social order. She had never "read a line of orthodox political economy" but, having come under the influence of Ruskin, she pinned a resolution on the college bulletin board challenging the "so called laws of political economy [as] only man made arrangements of a fallen race." They should be "fought to the death by all true believers in progress." [51] A year later in Bristol, where she had gone to teach, she joined the local Socialist society.

Miss Conway had grown up in Walthamstow, where her father was a Congregational minister noted for his liberal theological views. After leaving home she adopted the High Church form of Anglican-ism, and it was during a worship service in All Souls in Bristol that she met the Socialists. The encounter was dramatic. She often described it with great effect from the lecture platform:

It was in one of the most noble and wealthy churches of the land . . . at that moment when we are taught in symbolic form that Christ will appear in the midst of the people in answer to the prayers of the priests, when the music of the great organ burst out in joyous welcome . . . and the thurible sends out its streams of sweetly odorous incense, and the mind which believes literally in the actual presence of God, as I did in those days, is lifted out of all that is earthly and loses itself in realisa-tion of the sublime—then it was that there came suddenly the shock of

[50] McMillan, *Rachel McMillan*, p. 81.
[51] *Labour Leader*, July 18, 1912. For further biographical details see Thomp-son, *Enthusiasts*, pp. 58–78.

a great crash and jangle, the organ seemed to have broken down, the sublimity of the moment passed away like a lightning flash and we heard the noise of a brass band and a rabble at the door of the church. The door opened and into the church . . . came the cotton lassies. . . . It was my first sight of such misery and as they came into the church their wan white faces and haggard looks formed such a vivid contrast to all else in the magnificent edifice that I shall never forget it. . . . I saw from that moment that for too long we had been taught a religion which led us to believe that our brothers and sisters might be going as fast as they could to hell and that we might with perfect comfort and happiness travel to heaven and leave them to their fate.[52]

Shocked by the plight of the female cotton operatives, out on strike in the middle of the winter, and troubled by the seemingly indifferent splendor of the church, Miss Conway joined the Socialists who were leading the strike. A short time later her name was taken by the police at a "prohibited meeting," and she lost her teaching position. But the Socialist movement was growing and its platforms and press were open to the new convert. Over the next few years she lectured for various Socialist organizations, wrote for its press, and helped to organize new Socialist groups. Like other Ethical Socialists she found her most enthusiastic audiences in Lancashire and the West Riding of Yorkshire. In Bradford, she recalled, the women "were as keenly alive to the ideals of Socialism and as ready to make sacrifices for the cause as any man." [53]

Miss Conway's Socialism, which owed most to the writings of Morris and Carpenter, was saturated with religious meaning and imagery. The world, she insisted, was "governed by religions, molded by the objects of its worship, determined by its divinities." She denounced the old distinction between the sacred and the secular and the concern with saving one's own soul alone. For a Socialist "all life was sacred." The new party would rest on a "religious belief in the eternal progress towards the perfection of the 'great entity' of Humanity. . . . Slowly the Divine Man will win the world for Himself or to Himself. Slowly the Holy Spirit of Democracy will

[52] Quoted in *Bradford Labour Journal*, Sept. 30, 1892.
[53] *Labour Leader*, April 9, 1892.

work in the minds of men. Slowly the Kingdom of Heaven comes. . . . To worship God is to worship man." [54]

Like many Ethical Socialists, Miss Conway frequently employed Biblical materials in her exposition. Thus in her pamphlet, *The Religion of Socialism,* she adapted the New Testament parable of the rich young ruler. Jesus in the story was replaced by a "patriarchal figure with plentiful long flowing white hair and beard," whom "no class claims for their own." He taught that "Life is One. . . . And of God the source of life, this only do I believe: that he intends to perfection, all men to His own image . . . and there can be no fulness of life for any one man without the fulness of life for all. In the words of the Christian religion, 'no man can be saved alone.' " The old teacher described how in the past "the few seized the wealth" and imposed an "evil teaching" of "divine ordinance." But now, with "the widening of men's hearts and minds through the greater knowledge of themselves," doubts about the "righteousness of the present manner of life, and the clear mockery of the religion that countenances it" were "spreading like fire in a stubble field." A new order was coming with the "fullest life of all the people as its object, abundant leisure, with peaceful old age." [55]

Miss Conway's appeal was highly emotional and often sentimental. She was one of the most effective of the new Socialist propagandists, often enhancing her platform appeal by gay and unconventional dress. She gained great popularity among the working classes of the North and when, in 1893, the new political party was formed she was the only woman placed on its administrative council. Later that year she married Bruce Glasier and the two dedicated their union to the advance of Socialism.

Enid Stacy also entered the movement in Bristol where she had been a student of Miss Conway. She shared her teacher's initial devotion to Ruskin and the High Church position. Although the cotton strike helped to convert her to Socialism she had already concluded that society and the church regarded her as an "inferior being." After accepting Socialism, Miss Stacy passed from "extreme sacerdo-

---

[54] *Workman's Times,* Nov. 26, 1892, April 1, 1893.
[55] Conway and Glasier, *Religion of Socialism,* pp. 4, 5, 7–8.

talism to extreme secularism." On occasion, as in her best remembered series of lectures, "Modern Shams," Miss Stacy condemned indiscriminately all aspects of contemporary life. "This is an age of shams," she declared, "social, matrimonial, religious and political. . . . When we look around the religious world it is impossible to point out where the shams begin . . . for the whole of modern religion is a deliberate lie from beginning to end." [56]

Miss Stacy traveled almost constantly during the early nineties and was in wide demand as a speaker. Her audiences in the North frequently numbered in the thousands. She played an important role in the early growth of the Independent Labour Party and served on the party's council for two years.

The strong feminist outlook which accompanied her Socialism grew even stronger in the years ahead. But her hostility to the church moderated, largely through her growing friendship with an Oxford Socialist and Anglican clergyman, P. E. T. Widdrington. At the time of their courtship he was interested particularly in reconciling the thought of Carpenter and Whitman with Christian teaching.[57] After their marriage in 1896 the Widdringtons moved to Newcastle to work with the leading Anglican Socialist of the North, Canon W. E. Moll. From this center Mrs. Widdrington continued to lecture extensively for the movement until her sudden death in 1903.

A friend of Carolyn Martyn compared her fate to that of a "flower, which, being thrown into a vortex, helps us to see its force." [58] It was a rather cruel but illuminating metaphor, for perhaps no other figure in these early years was so completely dedicated to the movement or so willing to pay the price exacted by such dedication.

Miss Martyn grew up in a conservative middle-class family in Lincoln before taking a teaching post in London during the late eighties. Following dismissal from two positions because she was not a sufficiently strong disciplinarian, she became interested in social

[56] *Stockport Times,* Nov. 3, 1893. See the memoir by Katharine Glasier, *Enid Stacy* (Littleborough, 1903).

[57] P. E. T. Widdrington to Enid Stacy, Aug. 3, 1895, P. E. T. Widdrington–Enid Stacy Correspondence, Maurice Reckitt, London.

[58] Isabella Fyvie Mayo, *Recollections* (London, 1910), p. 229.

reform. She joined the Guild of St. Matthew and set out to discover Christian solutions to social problems. But she soon gave up the ritualistic Anglicanism of her youth and began to work closely with Bruce Wallace, a Congregational minister who had founded a theologically and socially advanced "Brotherhood Church." Miss Martyn also served as subeditor on his newspaper, the *Christian Weekly*. The "life and doctrines" of Wallace, she felt, were "nearest in my experience to the ideal that is Jesus Christ." [59]

In 1891 Miss Martyn joined the Fabian Society and began to lecture widely before working-class audiences. She did not address herself to the issues which occupied most Fabian lecturers. She spoke rather on such themes as the "gospel of brotherhood," "the sociology of the New Testament," and the "social teaching of Jesus." God, she felt, had "given her a message for every place where the way was open for her to go." To a group in Glasgow she explained her mission:

[It was] to raise to spiritual life and develop the religious instincts not only of those who are utterly discontented with existing forms of religion and have broken their connection, but also of all those who are interested in social questions and feel the necessity of religion in its truest and best sense, permeating all the relations of man's life. [60]

To small, struggling Socialist groups in various parts of England and Scotland Miss Martyn brought an inspirational power which few workers in the cause could match. In Leek, for example, where the Socialists had been "a handfull . . . a discussion group around the fire," she came and spoke before "seven or eight hundred people" in an open-air meeting. [61] Leek became for a time a vital center of Socialist propaganda. Elsewhere groups could trace the growth of new zeal to one of her visits.

Miss Martyn hesitated before taking part in the economic and political struggles of the lower classes. The working-class drive for a new political party initially offended her sense of moral and re-

[59] Lena Wallis, *Life and Letters of Carolyn Martyn* (London, 1898), p. 88.
[60] *Ibid.*, pp. 91, 88.
[61] *Labour Prophet*, Nov. 1897.

ligious commitment because it seemed to appeal primarily to material interests. During 1894, however, she joined the Independent Labour Party and a short time later confessed to a friend, "I have had my pentecost and all life is touched with a new meaning." Over the next two years she was almost constantly on the road, speaking and organizing for the new party, lecturing for the Fabians, and organizing trade-unions. In July 1895 she wrote to a friend from Sowerby Bridge in the North that she had had "six meetings each day, then ten, then eleven, after that I lost count." [62] Joseph Whittaker, a close friend, and other Socialists pleaded with her—in vain—to slow down lest her health be ruined by the incessant demands of the movement. In the spring of 1896, while organizing the female jute workers in Dundee, she died of pneumonia contracted in a state of physical exhaustion.

The lives of Margaret McMillan, Katharine Conway, Enid Stacy, and Carolyn Martyn illustrate the moral fervor of the new Socialism, but their enthusiasm began with slight intellectual substance. For the theoretical and practical meaning of Socialism they turned mainly to the Fabians. Each of them lectured under the auspices of the Fabian Society at various times during the nineties. Webb consciously attempted to build a structure of Fabian ideas on top of their basically ethical and utopian aspirations. His letter to Katharine Conway suggested some of the difficulties in the way:

But why should any criticism of Socialist schemes make you feel uncertain, even for a moment, about Socialist principles? . . . The only thing that prevents our converting the intelligent among our *well meaning* opponents is our general unwillingness—as Socialists—fairly and calmly to appreciate their difficulties. And the more I study the problems of England's industrial organization, the more I am persuaded of the need of thorough personal study by all Socialists, of the *facts* of modern industry rather than the *aspirations* of Socialists. Things are as they are, and the result will be as it will. So why should we wish to be deceived? Once we have got our faith we should, I think, do better to spend our nights and days over books like Charles Booth's than over William

[62] Wallis, *Martyn,* pp. 89, 43.

Morris—who is for the unconverted, not for those who have already found "salvation." [63]

Miss Conway's Socialism did not prove adaptable to Fabian purposes, and even Miss McMillan, despite her practical work in Bradford, was later seen as too "sentimental" for the work of the Society.[64] The Fabians were more successful with Miss Stacy and Miss Martyn; both women lectured extensively for the Society and accepted subsidies from it in order to undertake formal academic study of economic and social problems.

The emergence of Ethical Socialism presented a serious challenge to the older bodies. While the Fabian leaders were seeking, with some success, to harness the new enthusiasm to their principles and strategy, they also attempted to combat the utopian spirit growing up within the movement. The Social Democrats, too, were generally hostile; to them Ethical Socialism appeared to be a dangerous deviation from the path leading to a true Socialist consciousness. The response of the Marxists of the Federation to the "problem of sentiment" illustrates the growth of the new form of Socialism from still another perspective.

Social Democrats and the Problem of Sentiment

By the late eighties propagandists for the Social Democratic Federation had begun to complain about the "want of power among the workers to grasp abstract ideas" and "imagine new possibilities." One observer, noting their "cussedness," gave thanks that the progress of Socialism did not depend on the "acceptance of our ideas among the workers," for "sick indeed would be the heart of the socialist reformer." Herbert Burrows, however, was already warning the Federation's members that they tended "too much toward realism and too little toward idealism"; they were emphasizing the "administrative" side of Socialism at the expense of the "prophetic work of making Social Democrats." Burrows attacked those Socialists who re-

---

[63] Sidney Webb to Katharine Conway, May 3, 1892, Glasier Correspondence.
[64] Edward Pease to Joseph Fels, March 26, 1909, Fabian Society Correspondence, Fabian Society, London.

garded "self interest and nothing more" as the foundation of the new order.[65]

In 1890, H. W. Lee, secretary of the Federation, called for a reappraisal of its propaganda techniques. It was, he wrote, absurd to base "a serious movement . . . on mere abstract phrases" and fail to acknowledge "the value of sentiment to our cause." H. W. Hobart agreed. The movement, he declared, "depends a great deal on sentiment for the increase of members. In this respect it very much resembles the method of inculcation of religious ideas into the mind of the masses." He told his readers to "convert them by sentiment if possible, even if ninety-nine out of a hundred go back the moment the excitement has worn off [but] . . . never omit to say that socialism is based on science." Some months later Hunter Watts, a member of the executive, made an even stronger appeal to shift the emphasis of propaganda:

Devotion, the spirit of self abnegation, self sacrifice, the high moral virtues, which are unique factors in human progress, which Socialism is called to guide into a new epoch, these qualities are deficient in realist Socialism. The great mass of men is never stirred merely on grounds of personal interest—moral influence and still more sentimental influence alone have that power—realists and idealists are both welcome in our ranks.

But Harry Quelch, editor of *Justice,* strongly opposed Federation members who wished to modify the strict rationalism of its Marxism. Those who were giving Socialism an ethical turn, he argued, suffered from an "attack of sentimentality" and endangered the "fundamental principles" of the movement. "Mere sentiment," according to Quelch, was "absolute impotence" when "arrayed against hard facts." [66] During the nineties, as the Independent Labour Party, inspired in part by Ethical Socialism, became a political rival, their attacks on the "curse of sentiment" grew more intense.

The problem of sentiment was complicated, however. The Federation shared in the surge of Socialist enthusiasm in the early nineties,

[65] *Justice,* July 27, April 21, 1889, July 26, 1890.
[66] *Ibid.,* Sept. 6, 1890, Feb. 7, 1891, Nov. 19, 1892, Sept. 13, 1886, March 11, Dec. 23 1893.

and many of its new recruits, particularly in Lancashire, drew their ideas from Blatchford. The *Clarion* took its place alongside *Justice* on the stands at many of the Federation's branches, which also heard ethically oriented speakers such as Carolyn Martyn and Enid Stacy. In 1894, for example, the strong Burnley branch reported that Miss Stacy was attracting crowds of three or four thousand, their "largest audience in history." [67]

A number of the Social Democratic leaders were willing to alter the tone of their propaganda in order to reach the moral and religious feelings of the working classes in the North. In Herbert Burrows the Federation possessed a speaker who never allowed his Marxism to inhibit an essentially moralistic appeal. He constantly "pressed the point" in his talks that "the physical was the least part of man and that a social order based merely on the physical was bound to fail." Indeed, Burrows had supplemented his Marxism with Theosophy because the two creeds seemed to him to provide both a "scientific and philosophical basis" for man's consciousness.[68] Other strongly ethical propagandists within the ranks of the Social Democrats included William Diack of the Aberdeen branch, who produced several pamphlets dealing with Socialism as a new "gospel of love." He also argued that "religious reformers" were as important as "social reformers," for it was "still true that the beginning of reform is within." [69]

James Leatham, who had been strongly influenced by Morris and Bax, argued that the Social Democrats urgently needed a new system of ethics:

We Socialists have assumed a responsibility in connection with morals of which we do not always seem conscious. We have drawn the sword against the recognized teachers of the people. . . . But have we supplied the place of those whose authority we have so rudely shaken? We are asking people to recast their habits of thought and discard the individualistic

[67] *Workman's Times* Aug. 12, 1893.

[68] *Labour Leader,* Nov. 21, 1891.

[69] Diack's pamphlets included *Better Days for Working People, The Good Time Coming,* and *The Moral Effects of Socialism.* The last begins with a long quotation from Carpenter.

ideal . . . and we must show our better ideal working out to finer issues in our conduct and character. . . . I want to see Socialism making its adherents quite obviously and unmistakeably better men and women than those who are still without the gate.[70]

Leatham deplored the tendency for Socialists to fall back on the teachings of Jesus Christ and attempted, in a series of articles in *Justice*, to point the way toward a new Socialist morality. He started out with the assumption that the "belief in God" and the "idea of creation" had to be abandoned and went on to examine such questions as honesty, courage, sex, and diligence in the light of "reason and experience." [71] His argument, which owed something to Bax, was essentially utilitarian.

Most Social Democrats tended, despite their political militance and economic heterodoxy, to accept the moral standards of the middle class. Hyndman, whose personal life was beyond reproach, worried lest Socialists lose those qualities which made for an upright character in their struggle against the existing order. Indeed, in his early associate, Edward Aveling, social iconoclasm seemed to be accompanied by a complete loss of moral decency.[72] But Aveling was exceptional. Even Quelch, a working man and probably the most dogmatic of the Federation's Marxists, rested his Socialist creed on an almost puritanical moral foundation. His short stories portrayed Socialist heroes and martyrs who exemplified such virtues as faithfulness in marriage, sacrificial love for others, pride in poverty, industriousness and honesty in one's work, and devotion to one's country.[73]

However bound they may have been to conventional moral values, the Social Democrats continued to reject the appeal to sentiment in

---

[70] *Justice,* Nov. 23, 1895.

[71] The articles were later published as *Socialism and Character* (Manchester, 1896). Also see Leatham's pamphlet, *Was Jesus Christ a Socialist?* (Aberdeen, 1891.

[72] There is a perceptive discussion of Aveling's character in Salt, *Company,* pp. 80ff. Also see Shaw's portrayal of Aveling as "Dubedat" in *The Doctor's Dilemma* and the treatment in Chushichi Tsuzuki, *The Life of Eleanor Marx, 1855–1898* (Oxford, 1967), especially pp. 328–335.

[73] Harry Quelch, *Literary Remains* (London, 1912).

favor of the need to instill into the working classes a theoretical understanding of objective social developments. In their propaganda work they addressed themselves mainly to the rational comprehension of their audiences, and in their branch meetings they encouraged the study of Marxist doctrine. The Federation's appeal was not wholly ineffective. Although it failed to match the growth of the new Independent Labour Party, its membership grew rapidly in the early nineties, particularly in London and Lancashire. Its Marxism continued to represent a serious option for British Socialists and to exercise an important influence on the course of the movement.

By the early nineties the leadership of the movement had clearly passed to non-Marxist, ethical Socialists. Combined with this highly idealistic and utopian form of Socialism, however, were strongly practical drives. The Marxism of the eighties had also encouraged a few Socialists to identify themselves more closely with the immediate economic and political struggles of the workers. Inspired in large measure by the Marxist emphasis on class interests and the need for political power, these Socialists had broken away from the Federation and the League in order to develop a new strategy. The strategy of the Marxist "realists" would provide, along with the utopian enthusiasm of the Ethical Socialists, the basis of the Independent Labour Party.

7

The Realists

By 1887 the failure of the Social Democratic Federation and the Socialist League to win a substantial following among the working classes had produced a growing restiveness among some of the most active members. Convinced as Marxists that the organized power of the workers was a prerequisite for progress toward Socialism, they broke with the official policies of the two Marxist bodies in order to participate more directly in the practical struggles of the working classes. Two of these defectors were particularly significant in exploring a new Socialist strategy. One was H. H. Champion, a close associate of Hyndman's; the other was J. L. Mahon, the League's most effective recruiter in the provinces. Champion and Mahon set out independently to organize the workers, not on the basis of conscious Socialist theory or principles, but in terms of customary working-class attitudes and modes of common action. This departure from the Marxist strategy in Britain was encouraged by Engels. Champion and Mahon also won over several of the most important leaders of the London workers, including John Burns and Tom Mann, and gained support from a number of Socialists in the provinces who had been isolated by the breakup of the League.

In this way British Socialism came much closer to the immediate interests of the lower classes. But the new stress on obvious, tangible benefits for the workers and the more opportunistic attitude toward political action also furthered the disintegration of Marxist theory. The realistic elements in Marxism—its emphasis on the inevitability of social conflict and on the necessity for working-class organization—were freed from the doctrinal and visionary concerns of Hyndman and Morris respectively. A Marxism reduced to its realistic elements might lose its Socialist content. Yet it provided a practical strategy for the new Ethical Socialism of the North. The manner in which the realistic and utopian impulses came back together is illustrated in the development of Keir Hardie. The political implementation of this dual strain in British Socialism is examined in the early growth of the Independent Labour Party.

Marxism and the Working Classes: H. H. Champion, Friedrich Engels, and J. L. Mahon

Among the young men gathered around Thomas Davidson in the fall of 1882, Champion had been most skeptical of the moral idealism which Chubb and others hoped to make the "master impulse of our movement." His mind was, according to Chubb, ruled "too much . . . by the economic aspect of the undertaking." Champion was more intent on "doing than being." [1]

Training as well as temperament inclined Champion toward the role of activist.[2] Born in the upper classes, he had embarked on a military career before reading in the literature of social reform aroused an interest in economic and political problems. In 1882, at the age of twenty-three, he left the army, invested two thousand pounds in Foulger's Modern Press, and began to publish Socialist propaganda. He also joined the young Democratic Federation and remained loyal to Hyndman as his friends in the Fellowship, the Fabian Society, and the Socialist League successively opened new lines of reform activity.

Champion was the first secretary of the Federation and one of Hyndman's strongest supporters during the mid-eighties. Initially more sanguine than Hyndman about the possibility of radical social change, he played a leading role in organizing the demonstrations of the unemployed in London during 1886 and 1887. These events impressed Champion with the strength of the existing order and the

[1] Chubb to Davidson, Dec. 15, Nov. 17, 1883, Thomas Davidson Papers, Yale University Library, New Haven, Conn.

[2] Champion's work is discussed in H. M. Pelling, "H. H. Champion: Pioneer of Labour Representation," *Cambridge Journal,* VI (Jan. 1953), 222–238.

meager power resources of the lower classes. He grew discouraged over the "fatal lack of character in the advocates of the Socialist idea" and the "opportunities wasted by personal jealousies and ineptitudes." [3] Champion decided to explore an alternative strategy.

In May 1887 he started a monthly paper, *Common Sense*. The title, with its implied criticism of other Socialist groups, announced his intention of concentrating on "measures that can be put into effect now." He used the paper to publicize social and economic evils and even offered prizes for practical suggestions on how to "ameliorate the conditions of the British working classes." [4] Increasingly, however, Champion emphasized the need for the working classes to organize for independent political action.

Champion remained a member of the Federation despite charges of intrigue and "selling out," but in September 1887 he justified his new work in a lengthy critique of Hyndman's organization. He pointed to the enormous disparity between its ambition of "overthrowing class domination" and "reconstructing the social system" on the one hand and its membership of some seven hundred on the other. He maintained that its propaganda was too abstract; he condemned the tendency for some Social Democrats to appeal to physical force and deplored their "imputation of bad motives" to all who disagreed with them. Later Champion blamed Hyndman for his vacillating leadership. Too weak to "steer the ship" himself, the Federation's leader was unwilling to permit "steadier nerves to direct its course." [5] Champion urged Socialists to show the working classes how their own activity could "translate itself into progress for the realization of Socialism." He invoked the "Marx and Engels of the Communist Manifesto" and the Social Democratic parties on the continent to support his claim that the British workers could use existing political institutions to "conquer the fortress of political power."

I hold . . . so long as we are allowed full freedom to convert our minority into a majority by argument, we are not justified in appealing to the last

[3] Champion to Davidson, June 6, 1887, Davidson Correspondence.
[4] *Common Sense*, June 15, 1887.
[5] *Ibid.*, Sept. 15, 1887; *Labour Elector*, June 22, 1889.

argument of force, both because it is against our democratic principles that the few should coerce the many, and because any such attempt must be frustrated and is therefore inexpedient.

Champion still hoped that the Federation might serve as the new party. He presented a political program with proposals for complete adult suffrage, annual parliaments, the payment of M. P.'s, the abolition of hereditary authorities, free secondary and industrial education, an eight-hour day, and a graduated income tax. These measures, though drawn mainly from radicalism, would "facilitate further steps toward the ultimate goal of collective control over the means of production." [6]

Late in 1887, however, Champion fixed on the Labour Electoral Association as the main vehicle for independent labor politics. The Association had been formed the previous year by the Trades Union Congress to promote working-class parliamentary candidacies. Champion gained control of the London section and began to test a new political tactic. It consisted of questioning Tory and Liberal candidates at elections about their stands on issues vital to labor. The Association's support would go to the candidate who seemed more favorable to working-class interests. If neither candidate made adequate concessions, Champion would consider running an independent labor candidate. During the winter of 1887 Champion and his associates employed this tactic at several by-elections. Inspired by the Irish party in Parliament, Champion envisioned himself, in Henry Pelling's words, as "the Parnell of the labour movement, controlling a disciplined bloc of voters and eventually capable of holding the balance in the House of Commons between the two major parties, thus ensuring consideration for the special claims of labour." [7]

Meanwhile, Champion was attempting through his paper, *Common Sense*, and later the *Labour Elector*, to provide a theoretical justification for his course of action. Although he denounced the propaganda of the Federation as "windy rhetoric" and "senseless

[6] *Common Sense,* Sept. 15, 1887.
[7] Pelling, "Champion," p. 226.

rubbish," he praised Marx as the "greatest mind that ever espoused the cause of the workers . . . and as true a heart as ever beat in the breast of man." The masthead of the *Labour Elector* carried a quotation from Marx:

The economic subjection of the man of labor and the monopolization of the means of labor, that is the source of life, lies at the bottom of servitude in all its forms, of all social misery, mental degradation and political dependence. The economic emancipation of the working classes is therefore the great end to which every political movement ought to be subservient as a means.[8]

For Champion as for Hyndman, the core of Marxism lay in the doctrines of surplus value and the class struggle.

During 1888 and 1889 the circle around the *Labour Elector*, which now included several young trade union leaders, began to concentrate on the goal of the eight-hour day as the immediate and most practical expression of their Socialism. Here was the "first great step," for the restriction of working hours would check the drain of labor value to the capitalist. Tom Mann, one of Champion's associates, argued that "the whole of surplus value" could be "absorbed" through the "gradual reduction of working hours" until the "cooperative organization of industry becomes an accomplished fact." Champion also insisted, like Hyndman and Webb, that his proposals represented the "further extension of principles already enforced" in society.[9]

In the summer and autumn of 1889 the Champion group and other Social Democrats extended their agitation and organization to the unskilled workers. They helped the London gasworkers secure a reduction in their working hours from twelve to eight, and this success was soon emulated in the provinces. Then the London dockers, in the most dramatic industrial dispute of the period, won a substantial wage increase and better working conditions. "It is the Champion school of Socialists," a Liberal newspaper conceded, which has "scored most heavily." [10]

[8] *Labour Elector*, Nov., 1888.
[9] *Ibid.*, July 20, May 11, 1889.
[10] Quoted in *Labour Elector*, Oct. 5, 1889.

The place of Socialism in these labor disputes, however, was not at all clear. Hyndman observed, with reason, that the leaders of the dock strike, John Burns, Ben Tillett, Tom Mann, and Champion, had refused to "fly the Red flag." Yet Champion denied Frederic Harrison's assertion that they had jettisoned Socialism in favor of the "practical work of raising wages." "No jot of their principles or of their ultimate aims," he declared, had been abandoned by "Socialists of the saner kind." He cited the policy of the "old 'International' while it was guided by Karl Marx" to support his claim that the "class war" was implied in trade unionism.[11]

The next step in Champion's "Plan of Campaign" was to enroll all workers in trade unions and then to create a federation of unions.[12] Economic organization would serve as a firm basis for political power, but Champion warned that time was short. The gains of the new unions, won at a time of good trade, would be imperiled by the next downswing of the economic cycle unless the workers could protect themselves through vigorous political action. His fears were justified, for few of the new unions proved able to withstand the economic recession which began in the early nineties. Within a few months after the dock strike, however, Champion had lost the support of his most important working-class allies. Although he continued his efforts to shape the new political force, he was increasingly cut off from the Socialist and labor movement. After a series of rebuffs he left England early in 1894 to settle in Australia.

In the view of his friend, the novelist Frederick Rolfe, Champion "had been sponged upon for fifteen years by Socialistic cadgers, sucked dry, ruined, and cast out, a victim of Socialist jealousy and treachery." Socialism then became, according to Rolfe, a "headless monster . . . hunting for a brain to direct its forces." [13] Champion's estrangement from the movement can be traced more plausibly to

---

[11] *Ibid.*, Sept. 28, Nov. 16, 1889. Hyndman and his supporters thought the "new unions" were "as dangerous to us as the old" and represented at best "unconscious strugglings toward Socialism" (*Justice*, May 3, 1890).

[12] *Labour Elector*, Nov. 30, 1889.

[13] Frederick Rolfe (Baron Corvo), *Hadrian the Seventh*, Penguin Edition (Harmondsworth, 1963), p. 162.

his defects as a leader and to the difficulty of relating Socialist ideas to the interests and aspirations of the working classes.

With boldness and imagination, Champion had used his Marxism to search out a new political strategy for Socialists. He grasped, more clearly than either Hyndman or Morris, the nature of political power; he was relatively free from the moralistic and sentimental considerations that dominated many middle-class reformers. His political realism and cool, even cynical detachment, as well as his conception of leadership, were reflected in an article he wrote for the *Nineteenth Century* in 1890:

Given a great mass of uncultivated, ignorant, emotional, human beings, stirred by unrest, discontent, and a sense of injustice, but without trained minds to reason back to causes or even to put other complaints into coherent form, [and] you must have much confusion and discord. . . . Then the immensity and grandeur of the subject attracts fluent persons of a poetical temperament who scorn detailed argument and pipe a Paradise in which Kings, priests and policemen shall be no more seen. Loudest and most enthusiastic of all are the constitutional mongers, each with a new Atlantis, who darken counsel by setting off on the wrong scent that large proportion of mankind whose standard of intelligence is shown by the way they accept statements of a company prospectus, or a patent medicine advertisement. They either follow the few who know their own minds or act from unreasoning instinct.[14]

Champion no doubt included himself among those "few men" in society who were "neither ignorant or selfish" and could point out the "dangers years before they are seen by the common herd." But his elitist outlook helped to explain Champion's inability to win the confidence of the working-class leaders. Some distrusted him because he was "too fond of wire pulling," while others thought he exhibited the "dragooning spirit" of the "artillery officer." [15]

Champion was also the victim of his own realism. His concentration on the tangible benefits making up the "labor interest" and his

[14] H. H. Champion, "Protection as Labour Wants It," *Nineteenth Century*, XXXI (June 1892), p. 97.

[15] *Yorkshire Factory Times*, May 20, 1892; Joseph Burgess, *John Burns* (Glasgow, 1911), p. 135.

preoccupation with the immediate considerations of power led him to ignore vital elements in the making of a party or movement. Not only did he ignore the need for theory, despite his continuing commitment to Marxism, but he underestimated the force of more deep-seated attitudes and sentiments. His working-class associates of the late eighties still held views on such major national questions as trade, education, disestablishment, Ireland, and the Empire that were scarcely distinguishable from those of the radical wing of the Liberal party. They readily attached these views to Socialism. Failing to appreciate the strength of their customary loyalties and feelings, Champion wounded the sensibilities of his working-class allies. The actual break was occasioned by Champion's attacks on a Liberal journalist who had been sued for libel by some Tories. Yet even before this event Champion had antagonized the working-class leaders by advocating a protectionist trade policy which he considered the necessary consequence of the state's protection of the workers through a compulsory eight-hour day.[16] Champion's Tory background, like that of Hyndman, probably inclined him to think more in terms of an organic national policy than was customary for those within the Liberal or radical political tradition. But only after a series of miscalculations did Champion come to see the deep bonds of the workers to the Liberal party tradition as the greatest danger to the cause of working-class political independence.

Nevertheless, Champion had connected the cause of Socialism to the interests of the working classes. Such an adaptation was already implicit in Hyndman's utilitarianism; Champion had simply taken the step Hyndman had refused to take and accepted the legitimacy of the customary forms of working-class organization. A number of Social Democrats, particularly in London, were already beginning to make the Federation a significant force in the political and economic life of the metropolitan workers. Moreover, Champion's strategy, with its clear subordination of Socialist consciousness to the immediate struggles of the workers, corresponded closely to

[16] See his article, "An Eight Hours Law," *Nineteenth Century,* XXVI (Sept. 1889), 509–522.

the strategy being urged on the Socialists at this time by the leading authority on Marxism—Friedrich Engels.

Engels had not attempted to be active in the early development of British Socialism. After the death of Marx in 1883 he was occupied mainly with the still unpublished volumes of *Capital* and with Socialist affairs on the continent. Meanwhile, his initial hostility to Hyndman was confirmed by the growth of the Federation, which seemed to be led by "nothing but careerists, adventurers, and literary people." He was at first more hopeful about the Socialist League, but in the spring of 1886 Engels concluded that Morris was an "emotional Socialist" surrounded by "muddleheads" and "faddists." When the Federation gained prominence through its leadership of the unemployed, Engels was bitter. He attributed Hyndman's ability to "reap the harvest" to the "stupidity of the Socialist League," which would not "concern itself with the living movement." [17]

According to Engels, the British, like the American Marxists, conceived their theory as a "credo and not a guide to action." They failed to appreciate the necessity for dialectical interaction of theory and practice:

Both here and in America the people who more or less have the correct theory as to the dogmatic side of it, become a mere sect because they cannot conceive that living theory of action, or working with the working classes at every possible stage of its development, otherwise than as a collection of dogma to be learned by heart and recited like a conjurer's formula or a Catholic prayer. Thus the real movement is going on outside the sect and leaving it more and more.

Engels urged Socialists to participate directly in practical political and economic struggles. A Socialist outlook, he was confident, would gradually develop out of these efforts. It was crucial that the workers "have a movement of their own—no matter in what form . . . in which they are driven further by their own mistakes and learn

[17] Dona Torr, ed., *Marx and Engels: Selected Correspondence, 1846–1895* (New York, 1942), p. 442; Leonard Mins, ed., *Marx and Engels: Letters to Americans, 1846–1895* (New York, 1942), pp. 162, 165.

through their mistakes." [18] Engels shared the faith in the masses which he ascribed to Marx:

Marx entirely trusted to the intellectual development of the working class, which was sure to result from combined action and mutual discussion. The very events and vicissitudes of the struggle against capitalism, the defeats even more than the victories, could not help bringing home to men's minds the insufficiency of their various favorite nostrums and prepare the way for a more complete insight into the true conditions of working class emancipation.[19]

After 1885 Engels began to counsel a number of the British Socialists and working-class leaders on tactical and theoretical questions. He encouraged his friends in the Socialist League, the Avelings, Bax, and others, to strike off in a more practical direction. He welcomed enthusiastically the campaign for the eight-hour day and called it the "gateway into a genuine Socialist movement." [20] The new surge of unionism seemed to Engels the most significant development since the days of Chartism:

The old unions preserve the traditions of the time when they were founded, and look upon the wages system as a once for all established final fact, which they can at best modify in the interest of their members. The new Unions were founded at a time when the faith in the eternity of the wages system was severely shaken; their founders and promoters were Socialists either consciously or by feeling; the masses, whose adhesion gave them strength, were rough, neglected, looked down upon by the working class aristocracy; but they had this immense advantage, that *their minds were virgin soil,* entirely free from the inherited "respectable" bourgeois prejudices which hampered the brains of the better situated "old" unionists.[21]

Engels' confidence in the unskilled was misplaced. Indeed the absence of those organizational virtues which he labeled "bourgeois

[18] Torr, ed., *Marx and Engels: Selected Correspondence,* p. 450.

[19] Preface to the 1888 edition of the *Communist Manifesto;* quoted by Edward Thompson, *William Morris: Romantic to Revolutionary* (London, 1955), pp. 667–668.

[20] Quoted by Friedrich Buenger, *Engels und die Britische Sozialische Bewegung* (Berlin, 1962), p. 172.

[21] Torr, ed., *Marx and Engels: Selected Correspondence,* p. 465.

respectability" was partly responsible for the failure of most of the new unions to survive during the economic recession of the early nineties.[22] A Socialist consciousness grew more readily, as the Independent Labour party soon demonstrated, among the sections of the working classes that shared most fully middle-class moral and religious values. Engels welcomed the new working-class party in the North as the "most genuine expression of the movement thus far." Again he misunderstood the development. He saw Keir Hardie, the leader of the new party, as cunning and ambitious and the "great obstacle" to a true grasp of Socialism, and he was convinced that the workers "would either teach" their leaders or "throw them overboard." Before long, however, his enthusiasm for the Independent Labour Party faded. While the masses were "wrestling for consciousness," he wrote, the leaders continued to resist the theory of scientific Socialism. Indeed, in the final two years of his life, 1894 and 1895, Engels repeatedly distinguished between the "socialist instinct," which was becoming "ever stronger among the masses," and the "clear demands and ideas" he believed necessary. "The various old traditional memories," he observed, and "the lack of people able to turn this instinct into conscious action and to organize it all over the country, encourages . . . haziness of thought and local isolation of action." [23]

While Engels came to recognize something of the tenacity of traditional working-class attitudes and the difficulty of bringing the "Socialist instinct" to full consciousness, his Marxism provided no answers to these problems. It did not encourage serious inquiry into the psychology of the workers or consideration of the relationship between economic changes and inherited attitudes. He did attempt in the early nineties to qualify the rigid determinism, increasingly characteristic of the new generation of European Marxists, by granting some causal efficacy to ideas. But his scattered comments about

[22] The problems of the "new unions" in the early nineties are discussed in Desmond Crowley, "Origins of the Revolt of the British Labour Party from Liberalism, 1875–1906," Ph.D. dissertation, London School of Economics, 1952.

[23] Mins, ed., *Marx and Engels: Letters to Americans,* pp. 249, 262, 263; Torr, ed., *Marx and Engels: Selected Correspondence,* p. 507.

working-class mentality, and particularly the high hopes he placed on the unskilled workers, suggested a rationalistic, hedonistic, and mechanistic psychology as crude as that of any nineteenth-century utilitarian. Until his death in 1895 Engels remained wedded to notions which prevented him from understanding the actual development of the British workers.

Both Champion and Engels greatly underestimated the resistance customary working-class attitudes offered to a new Socialist strategy. Their miscalculations were repeated by J. L. Mahon, who attempted to apply Marxist-inspired political realism to the new and promising working-class activity in the North during the early nineties.[24] A few years earlier, amid the deepening uncertainty of the British Marxists, Mahon had turned to Engels for advice.

When Mahon sought out Engels in November 1884 he was nineteen and the youngest member of the Federation's executive. Earlier in the year he had given up his job as a working engineer to undertake Socialist agitation in Scotland. At the end of 1884 he followed Morris into the Socialist League, became its first secretary, and over the next three years proved to be its most successful provincial organizer. He was in close and continuing contact with various sections of British labor, particularly in the North and in Scotland. His experiences gradually convinced him that the League's policies were sterile. During the autumn of 1887 he stated his views forcefully in *Commonweal:*

Socialists generally must soon choose between broadening the lines of the movement so as to include the practical aspirations of the working class, or become a mere group of factions, preaching, it may be, pure enough principles, but preaching them to the winds and exercising no real influence with the masses. My view of the matter is . . . that the method of Socialist propaganda must not be merely or mainly preaching rigidly pure principles which the masses of the people cannot grasp, but

[24] Mahon's career is discussed in Thompson, *Morris,* pp. 551–564. The letters exchanged between Mahon and Engels are included in an appendix. For the correspondence between Mahon and Morris, see R. Page Arnot, *William Morris: The Man and the Myth* (London, 1964).

taking hold of the working class movement as it exists at present and gently and gradually molding it into a Socialist shape.[25]

Mahon was, in Edward Thompson's words, "one of the first of the pioneers to write and think in a creative way about the 'labour movement' as a whole." He viewed Socialism not as a creed superimposed upon the masses, but rather as "the most conscious and complete expression of the class struggle which existed in spontaneous and instinctive forms." [26] What was needed, Mahon concluded, was a plan to consolidate all sections of the labor movement and all Socialist groups. To this task he devoted himself.

Over the next two years Mahon participated in a variety of economic and political activities. He and Champion undertook an intensive Socialist campaign in Scotland toward the end of 1887. They and others were prominent in the campaign to elect Keir Hardie as an independent labor candidate in the Mid Lanark by-election in 1888. Afterward Mahon helped to organize the Scottish Labour party. He also worked closely with the Social Democratic organizer Tom Mann in developing Socialist groups among the North-eastern miners during 1888. At this point he severed his ties with the League and rejoined the Federation. Late in 1888 he published a "Labour Programme," giving clear priority to the immediate and practical interests of the workers. By the following year he was ready to undertake, in the plan for a "Labour Union," the building of a new working-class party. However, the surge of New Unionist activity during 1889 drew the more practically minded Socialists toward industrial organization. Mahon himself became involved in the organization of the London postal workers and led an abortive strike which greatly damaged his reputation in London labor circles.

Mahon's participation in the political and economic struggles of the working classes had led to a growing indifference to Socialist theory. He developed, in Thompson's words, "a half-spoken contempt of theory" and began to slide "down the opposite slope" from the purism of Morris into a belief in the spontaneous growth of

[25] *Commonweal,* Oct. 8, 1887, quoted in Thompson, *Morris,* p. 557.

[26] Thompson, *Morris,* p. 556. Mahon's strong espousal of Socialist ideas is seen in his pamphlet, *A Plan for Socialism* (Newcastle, 1887).

working-class interests.[27] Moreover, Mahon had decided by 1890 that only "an overwhelming force from the provinces" could save the movement from the mistakes of the London leaders. In the autumn of that year, at the invitation of his friend Maguire, Mahon joined the Socialists in Leeds.

Leeds, like the surrounding West Riding area, was dominated economically by woolen and worsted industries, but the workers, unlike the cotton workers in neighboring Lancashire, had never developed strong unions.[28] During the eighties increased mechanization, changes in the scale of manufacturing, and declining wages had stimulated new efforts to build a general union of woolen workers. The success of the New Unions in London in 1889 had also inspired the formation in Leeds of a Gasworker's and General Labourer's Union in which local Socialists assumed leading roles. With the appearance of a new weekly in 1889, the *Yorkshire Factory Times,* these efforts gained a larger measure of cohesion.

On his arrival in Leeds, Mahon set out to further the process of working-class consolidation. Some time earlier he had told Engels: "Our real immediate foes are the Trade Union leaders. We must fight these fellows in their own stronghold. . . . We must lay down a policy for Socialists to pursue inside the unions . . . foster a socialist ring there and get the leaders driven out." [29] This was pretty much the tactic Mahon followed. With Maguire's help he was elected assistant secretary of the Gasworker's Union and began to press the cause of Socialism and independent political action within the local Trades Council. In Leeds, as elsewhere in these years, the Trades Council drew together representatives of the various unions to consider common problems. Mahon soon collided with the

27 Thompson, *Morris,* p. 614.

28 The best account of developments in the West Riding is Edward Thompson, "Homage to Tom Maguire," in *Essays in Labour History, in Memory of G. D. H. Cole,* ed. Asa Briggs and John Saville (London 1960). Social and industrial characteristics of the region are described in Talbot Baines, *The Industrial North* (Leeds, 1928), and Percy Redfern, *Journey to Understanding* (London, 1946), pp. 36ff. Ben Turner, *About Myself* (London, 1930), provides a more personal account.

29 See Thompson, *Morris,* p. 861.

leaders of the older trade unions. Their chief spokesman, John Judge of the shoemakers' union, regarded him as an interloper, a "born general and not a common soldier," who wished to use the unions for purposes other than "protecting wages." [30] A series of disputes followed as Mahon attempted to realign working-class political support both in local governmental and parliamentary elections. The climax came in the summer of 1892, when Mahon, having secured financial backing from Champion, decided to stand as an independent labor candidate at a parliamentary by-election in South Leeds.

The by-election was important for Mahon and Champion. The campaign to create a new party had gained widespread support in the West Riding, and Champion was determined to take control of it and run it "for all it is worth." Their "only chance," he wrote Mahon, was "to go for the Liberals all along the line without gloves." Mahon's electoral campaign was aggressively anti-Gladstonian and aroused violent and almost solid opposition from the trade-unions in the area. At the last moment he was disqualified on a technicality, but the rift between him and most of the Leeds labor leaders was complete. Even the *Yorkshire Factory Times,* which had generally favored his position over that of Judge, turned against him:

Mahon's attempt to force an Independent Labour fight in South Leeds . . . has shown that the Labour party will have to educate and organize without the ranks of political parties. Personally, I can't say that Champion's method of forcing a Labour party over the heads of the people is desirable or likely to succeed. . . . Democracy will work out its own emancipation in its own dull clumsy fashion and gentlemen like Mr. Champion may be able to do much to help it on with the exercise of a bit of patience.[31]

Late in 1892 Mahon and Maguire gave up on the Trades Council and the unions (even the gasworkers were now torn by internal strife) and attempted, with some success, to form independent labor

30 *Yorkshire Factory Times,* Feb. 26, 1892.
31 Quoted by Thompson, "Homage to Maguire," pp. 315–316; *Yorkshire Factory Times,* Sept. 23, 1892.

clubs as the bases for a new working-class party. In January 1893, when the Independent Labour party was organized at nearby Bradford, Maguire and Mahon led the delegation from Leeds. Despite his close association with the now unpopular Champion, Mahon stood high in the voting for the party's administrative council. Yet his role at the conference indicated that Mahon had gone much further in sacrificing Socialist goals to the immediate interests of labor than the great majority of the delegates would permit. His chief contribution to the proceedings was an attempt to eliminate the Socialist goal of collective ownership and commit the new party simply to the aim of securing "the separate representation and protection of labor interests on public bodies." The delegates supported collective ownership over Mahon's amendment by a vote of 91 to 16.[32]

After the conference Mahon became president of the Leeds branch of the new party. He held the office only for a short time. When John Lister, the party's candidate at a by-election in Halifax, appealed for working-class votes by defining Socialism as "advanced liberalism," Mahon reacted strongly, for he believed that this appeal would compromise the independence of the party. Without consulting the branch membership he urged the Halifax workers to reject Lister.[33] Despite Maguire's defense of Mahon, he was suspended by the members of the Leeds branch and later left the movement.

Champion and Mahon broke through the impasse which British Marxists had entered during the eighties. The two leaders played down a distinct Socialist consciousness in favor of a direct political appeal to customary working-class interests. They put aside the central Marxist doctrines on which Hyndman insisted and gave up the utopian vision of Morris. But they also underestimated the force of those attitudes which most of the working-class leaders carried over from their earlier political allegiances. A Socialism thus

[32] Despite this opportunism Mahon continued to give Marxist lectures. See *Workmen's Times,* Jan. 21, 1893.
[33] *Ibid.,* Feb. 17, 1893.

stripped of many of its distinguishing ideas and cut off as well from existing habits of mind was incapable of inspiring a new movement.[34]

The "realists" had, nonetheless, scouted a new strategy. Meanwhile, the Ethical Socialists were developing a version of Socialism which appealed strongly to important sections of the working classes in the North. It remained for Socialist propagandists or labor leaders to connect the new strategy and the new ideology. The divergent careers of two working-class Marxist converts of the eighties, John Burns and Tom Mann, throw light on the process through which this linkup occurred.

Marxists Adrift: John Burns and Tom Mann

The Federation and the League had attracted a number of younger working-class leaders who found in Marxism a new explanation of economic injustice and a much broader conception of their class goals. They tended to be less interested in theoretical issues than in practical matters. Indeed, the practical possibilities opened up by the Marxist analysis of social development gradually drove the most prominent working-class converts away from the pioneer Socialist organizations. So it was with Burns and Mann.

Burns was a working engineer, steeped in London Secularism and political radicalism when he joined the Democratic Federation in 1883.[35] A fellow member of the Federation's branch at Battersea later described his early work as a propagandist:

His powerful and vibrant voice, which could be heard for a tremendous distance in the open air; his talent for epigrammatic and telling phrases; his physical strength and energy; his striking and magnetic personality; and his two trials and terms of imprisonment for defending the right of

---

[34] The absence of a vital Socialist ideology was especially evident in the Aberdeen ILP, which remained close to Champion in its outlook. See Kenneth Buckley, *Trade Unionism in Aberdeen* (Edinburgh, 1955), pp.160ff.

[35] The fullest biography is William Kent, *John Burns: Labour's Lost Leader* (London, 1950). There is a wealth of information not available elsewhere in Burgess, *Burns*. G. D. H. Cole's Fabian Society biography, *John Burns* (London, 1943), provides the fairest appraisal of his career.

free speech, all tended to mark him out as a man likely to become the great working class leader of his generation.[36]

Burns became during the mid-eighties the Federation's most effective stump speaker, serving as a kind of megaphone for the ideas of Hyndman and Champion. Yet he was increasingly unhappy with the policies of the Federation. As early as 1886 he began to consider the possibility of taking over the leadership of the new labor movement.[37] For a time, however, he followed Champion, helping him to develop a strategy of political independence based on an expanded and consolidated trade union movement. During 1887 and 1888 he stood, with Champion's support, at parliamentary by-elections and engaged in unionizing activity. At the first election for the London County Council, in March 1889, Burns was returned from the borough of Battersea. Later in the year, through his brilliant leadership in the dock strike, he became a national figure and a hero to many workingmen.

Burns had cut his ties with the Federation, but he remained an avowed Socialist and resisted Liberal efforts to draw him into their party. He had also transformed the Battersea branch of the Federation into an independent organization, the Battersea Labour League, loyal to him personally and capable of providing the financial support necessary for his political career. Free from the direct influence of a disciplined Socialist organization, Burns confronted alone the situation which many newly elected Socialists would face in the years ahead:

I had to choose between being an industrial Hal O' the Wynd, a mere advocate of abstract ideas, a propagandist of visionary aims and theories, and in so being reduce myself to the level of a faddist standing alone, free but impotent, or the practical pioneer of the advancing labor host, discovering and slowly winning a higher social, municipal and intellectual life.[38]

[36] W. Stephen Sanders, *Early Socialist Days* (London, 1927), p. 24.
[37] See Hyndman's introduction to Burgess, *Burns,* and p. 88.
[38] *Nineteenth Century*, XXXI (March 1892), 502. See Paul Thompson, "Liberals, Radicals and Labour in London 1889–1900," *Past and Present*, No. 27 (April 1964), 90.

As his statement suggested, Burns did not hesitate. He was, in his own words, a "socialist with conservative tendencies," deeply devoted to his native London. He decided to cooperate with middle-class reformers in utilizing the London County Council to improve the lot of the working classes.

His decision to work with non-Socialists inside the existing political machinery drew Burns close to the Fabians, and he joined the Society. The Webbs soon formed high hopes for his future as a Fabian. Beatrice regarded Burns as "essentially an intellectual man" who constantly tested "questions by intellectual methods rather than by sentimental considerations." She even saw Burns as a potential member of the Fabian "junta," alongside Webb, Wallas, and Shaw, and thought that he was the one man who might enable them to "dominate the reform movement." Burns failed them, perhaps as Beatrice concluded because of his intense jealousy of other labor leaders, his "incurable suspicion of middle class sympathizers," and his "instinctive fear of comradeship." [39] Burns, however, viewed the Fabian attitudes as patronizing and turned away.

Nor was Burns inclined to cooperate closely with the new working-class movement developing in the North, which promised a more substantial basis for a labor party. He was put off in part by the Ethical Socialism of many leaders outside of London. He had grown up in London and shared the Secularist outlook common to many of its working-class leaders. His strongly rationalistic and skeptical outlook separated him from moralistic Socialists. Moreover, his experiences with the Social Democrats had led Burns to view high-blown abstractions as injurious to the cause. The ethically inspired Socialists of the North seemed to him to be "arrant frauds." He felt they were also bypassing the trade-union structure, which still seemed the necessary basis for a new party. Burns charged that they were doing "everything in their power to disintegrate labor and trade unionism." And as the Independent Labour party developed during 1893 and 1894 he continued to denounce it as led by "faddists" and "adventurers" and "fanatical fools." [40]

[39] Beatrice Webb, *Our Partnership* (London, 1948), pp. 39–40.
[40] Quoted in Burgess, *Burns,* p. 172. For Burns' relations with the Fabians

Burns thus steered a course during the early nineties which increasingly separated him from the Socialist movement. It also drew him steadily back into the existing structure of party politics. In 1892 he had been elected to Parliament from Battersea as a Socialist and quickly came to see his role in the House of Commons as an extension of his work on the London County Council. "For some time to come," he wrote R. B. Cunninghame Graham, "the balance of advantages will be to work . . . with those whose political program goes most our way." [41] Burns cooperated closely with the radical wing of the Liberal party and set out to acquire the style and tone of parliamentary life. He concentrated on those measures which seemed to him to favor labor interests. Burns had not given up Champion's idea of a new political party based on the trade unions, and he worked for that goal within the Trades Union Congress as a member of its Parliamentary Committee. Indeed at the 1895 Congress he was able to drive a deeper wedge between the new Independent Labour party and the trade union movement by engineering the exclusion of several of its leaders, including Hardie, from subsequent congresses on the ground that they were not genuine trade unionists.

Burns, like Champion and Mahon, had sacrificed the clear espousal of Socialist principles to the possibilities for the immediate advance of working-class economic and political interests. He realistically viewed that advance in terms of the customary political radicalism of the London workers. Burns foresaw fairly well the subseqent course of the British labor movement. His own political career, which led in time to a cabinet post in a Liberal government, anticipated that blurring of lines between Socialism and liberalism which would characterize the later stages of the movement. Burns also assessed clearly the immediate prospects of the new Independent Labour party. It failed to persuade the trade unions to accept its

---

and other Socialist leaders see A. E. P. Duffy, "Differing Policies and Personal Rivalries in the Origins of the Independent Labour Party," *Victorian Studies,* VI (Sept. 1962), 43–65.

[41] Burns to R. B. Cunninghame Graham, July 29, 1892, John Burns Correspondence, British Museum, London.

program, suffered a complete defeat at the polls in 1895, and for several years traveled a course which bore little practical relevance to national political life. But his realism also cut Burns off from the struggle of the Socialists to develop a new consciousness and a new political party for the working classes. To share fully in this struggle demanded at times a capacity for adaptation which did not come easily to realists like Burns. No figure better illustrates this capacity than Tom Mann.

Mann joined the Battersea branch of the Federation in 1885 and soon became the most energetic of the Social Democratic organizers in the provinces.[42] He early took issue with Hyndman on the importance of trade unions, and Mann's pamphlet on the eight-hour day, written in 1886 at the request of Champion, helped to give new practical focus for discontented members of the Federation and the League. During the late eighties he cooperated with Mahon in forming Socialist groups among the Northeastern miners, investigated industrial abuses in London for Champion, and, after playing a leading role in the dock strike, became president of the dockers' union.

Impatient over the "time spent in theoretical speculation," Mann concluded by 1890 that trade unions were the best means of disciplining and educating the worker and making him "master of his fate." In talks up and down the country he urged workers to join unions and to secure control of local governing bodies and use them to rectify social wrongs. Mann did not share the enthusiasm of many working-class Socialists for an independent parliamentary party. But early in 1893 he agreed to become an independent labor candidate for Parliament in the Colne Valley constitutency of the West Riding. At the same time he demanded that his working-class

---

[42] Dona Torr's *Tom Mann* (London, 1956) ends with the dock strike. Two chapters and materials from a planned second volume have been printed in the "Our History" series of the Communist party of Great Britain. See "Tom Mann and His Times, 1890–92," *Our History* (London), Nos. 26–27 (Summer–Autumn 1962). Also see Tom Mann, *Memoirs* (London 1923).

supporters develop trade union organizations "as proof of sincerity" and "moral stamina." [43]

Mann thus permitted his own doubts about working-class parliamentary candidates to be overcome by the enthusiasm for an independent party developing in the North. He also allowed himself to be drawn into the new tide of popular Socialist propaganda, the ethical strain in which appealed strongly to Mann. In earlier years he had aspired to be a religious missionary, and his Socialism continued to draw much from Ruskin. During the early nineties, as he began to address audiences in Yorkshire and Lancashire, he altered his propaganda style, softened the militancy he had carried over from the Marxism of the Federation, and dropped those forms of language which might offend the religious sensibilities of the northern workers. In 1891 and 1892 Mann and Ben Tillett, another prominent dockers' leader, appeared frequently in the pulpits of Congregational chapels or on the platforms of the Brotherhood and Pleasant Sunday Afternoon groups.[44] Here they appealed directly to the sentiments of working-class men and women still tied, however tenuously, to the Nonconformist chapels.

The tendency for Mann and other Socialist speakers to recast the creed into quasi-Christian terms became increasingly pronounced in the years just ahead. It offended veteran Socialists like Glasier. The new men, he complained, had adopted the canon that they not only could "teach less than they believe but also many things which they do not believe."

I have heard Socialists whom I know to be "howling infidels" appeal so solemnly and unctuously to the identity of Socialism and Christianity and that without any reservation or explanation that one might have imagined their hearts were bursting full of the "grace of God" instead of their mouths being choked full of lies. . . . Thus it happens that the body and spirit of Socialist teachings, especially that given from Trade Union and

[43] *Labour Elector,* Jan. 4, 11, 1890; *Yorkshire Factory Times,* Aug. 28, 1891, Jan 6, 1893. See also the discussion in Torr, "Tom Mann," pp. 19ff.

[44] The addresses are reported in the Congregational journal, *Independent,* Nov., Dec. 1891.

political platforms, bears little resemblance to the concept of Socialism which is possessed by the teachers themselves.[45]

Mann remained for some time doubtful about the desirability of a new working-class party. He did not participate in the founding conference of the Independent Labour party early in 1893, but a year later he agreed to become its secretary. Over the next two and a half years his remarkable skills as an organizer and propagandist contributed much to the party's growth. In 1897, however, as working-class support for the party began to ebb, Mann resigned his post. He then threw himself into a campaign to combine trade unionism and political work on new grounds, not concerned with principles or "what school of politics a man belongs to" but simply "for the measures." Mann's new venture did not prosper, and shortly after the turn of the century he left for Australia and New Zealand where he continued to work as a labor and Socialist organizer.[46] Later he returned to England to launch the British syndicalist movement and participate in a series of industrial disputes before joining the Communist party in 1920.

"To me," wrote one of his early colleagues, "Tom Mann remains the Peter Pan of the Socialist movement, to whom life is a series of adventures and who resolutely refuses to grow up." [47] Although the judgment was one-sided, it caught something of the capricious quality of Mann's career and pointed to the special kind of realism in his work for the Socialist movement. Like Burns he had discarded fixed notions of Socialist theory or strategy in order to pursue practical possibilities. Burns, however, had anchored himself firmly in existing political institutions, but Mann tended to rush to those points where the labor cause seemed most promising at the moment. He chose to skirmish on the edges of the social system seeking a point for major penetration on behalf of working-class interests. He became peculiarly dependent on economic and political fluctuations. He was eager to exploit the waves of economic discontent or the gusts of

[45] *Labour Prophet,* Aug. 1893.
[46] *Clarion,* May 7, 1898; "Tom Mann in Australia, 1902–1909," *Our History,* No. 38 (Summer 1965).
[47] Sanders, *Early Socialist Days,* p. 53.

political enthusiasm, but equally disposed to turn away from a line of action when the realities of the immediate situation ceased to be favorable.

Yet there was a unifying purpose in Mann's activity, for he was devoted to the goal of working-class organization. His admiration for organization even led him on one occasion to consider entering the Anglican church in order to utilize it for the cause of labor. An Anglican friend had proposed that he assume a lay position, and Mann gave it serious thought before declining. It was "well understood," Mann wrote later, "that I did not accept the Thirty Nine Articles. What attracted me to the Established Church was the fact that it was about the most perfectly organized body in the country. I love organization." What seemed to one outraged clergyman the "hypocrisy of Tom Mann" was the behavior of a man for whom ideas or doctrines held little more than instrumental value.[48] Hence the relative ease with which he passed through a series of ideological allegiances, including Swedenborgianism, the teachings of Ruskin, Marxism, Ethical Socialism, and, later, syndicalism, before resting in Communism.

Mann's skill as an organizer was probably related to his comparative freedom from deep ideological commitment. There was, in fact, a sharp contrast between the impassioned rhetoric of Mann's platform work and his generally casual and detached view of himself off the platform. Engels, who liked Mann, noted an absence of firmness in his personality.[49] If the realism of Burns prevented him from developing much sympathy for the popular Socialist movement, Mann's different kind of realism drew him to the promising new points of working-class self-assertion only to deprive him of staying power. The careers of Burns and Mann help one to appreciate the

[48] *Labour Prophet,* June 1897. Also see Mann's discussion of this episode in his *Memoirs,* ch. 11; *Christian Weekly,* Oct. 7, Dec. 2, 1893; Mann's *Clarion* pamphlet, *A Socialist's View of the Churches* (London, 1896).

[49] Mann contrasts his platform style with that of Webb in a letter to Webb, Nov. 9, 1893, Passfield Papers, Library of Political and Economic Science, London. For Engels' comment see *Friedrich Engels–Paul and Laura Lafargue Correspondence, 1891–1895,* ed. Emile Bottigelli (Paris, 1956–1959), III, 340.

special qualities of the outstanding leader of popular Socialism, Keir Hardie.

Keir Hardie: The Realist as Ethical Prophet

Hardie traveled an arduous road in early life.[50] Born in humble circumstances in Scotland, he went to work at the age of eight. Later his experiences as a miner and his expulsion from the pits for unionizing activities nurtured a strong spirit of rebellion against the existing social and economic system. He continued his efforts to organize the miners while earning his living as a shopkeeper and as a local contributor to several Scottish newspapers. In 1886 he became the paid secretary of the newly formed Ayrshire Miners' Union and the following year started a monthly paper, the *Miner,* to advance the cause of labor throughout Scotland. An early issue referred to a "more perfect order of things wherein the laborer shall be rewarded in proportion to his work." [51] Hardie also hammered away in the early issues of the paper on the necessity for labor "to realize its own strength." The working classes, he argued, should advance their own interests regardless of traditional party loyalties.

Hardie's commitment to trade-union organization and political independence attracted the attention of Champion and his associates, who were doubtful about the reliability of Burns for their purposes. In August 1887, after careful coaching by Champion's Scottish ally, Cunninghame Graham, Hardie carried the cause of labor independence onto the floor of the Trades Union Congress with a sharp attack on the Liberal party allegiances of the older union leaders. He gained little initial support, but as he repeated the attacks at subsequent congresses a vigorous minority began to form around him. With the support of Champion's group Hardie contested the Mid

---

[50] The standard biography is William Stewart, *Keir Hardie* (London, 1921). David Lowe, *From Pit to Parliament* (London, 1923), is a better account for the period ending in 1900. Additional information on the early years is in Emrys Hughes, *Keir Hardie* (London, 1956). Also see G. D. H. Cole's Fabian pamphlet, *James Keir Hardie* (London, 1941), and Fred Reid, "Keir Hardie's Conversion to Socialism," in *Essays in Labour History, 1886–1923,* ed. Asa Briggs and John Saville (London, 1971), pp. 17–46.

[51] *Miner,* Jan. 1887.

Lanark by-election in 1888 in the first clear challenge to the Liberal party's hold on the working classes.[52] A short time later, Hardie and others formed the Scottish Labour party and attempted to advance Champion's political strategy. Hardie also allowed his *Miner* to be absorbed by the *Labour Elector* and joined its board of directors. But like Burns, Mann, and other working-class leaders, Hardie soon rejected Champion as a political guide.

Champion's strategy, however, was highly congenial to Hardie's own deeply ingrained sense of the class struggle and his belief in working-class political independence. Like other such Socialists, he was inclined to subordinate ideas to practical considerations. Hence his remarks to Engels in the spring of 1889:

We are a solid people and very practical, and not given to chasing bubbles. Mr. Graham's eight hour agitation has made more progress here in six months than the SDF has made in six years or could make in sixty years. We are not opposed to ideals and recognize to the full the need for them and their power of inspiring men, but we are more concerned with the realization of the ideal than in dreaming of it.[53]

In 1890, Hardie decided to give up his salaried position with the Scottish miners in order to commit himself fully to the cause of working-class political independence. "The paid official of an organization," he observed later, "cannot very well be a pioneer," for "his members in the bulk are sure to be against him." Hardie joined the Fabian Society in 1890, but his conviction that the working class had to develop its own leadership prevented close identification with the Fabians. Indeed, his Socialism, though eclectic, was strongly Marxist. This was evident in his Foreword to the rules of the Ayrshire Miners Union:

All wealth is created by Labor. Capital is part of this wealth, which instead of being consumed when created, is stored up and used for

---

[52] Burgess, *Burns,* p. 105. See James B. Kellas, "The Mid Lanark By-Election of 1888 and the Scottish Labour Party," *Parliamentary Affairs,* XVIII (1964–1965), 318–329; Desmond Crowley, "The Crofters' Party, 1885–1892," *Scottish Historical Review,* XLV (Oct. 1966), 110–126.

[53] Hardie to Engels, March 31, 1889, Friedrich Engels Correspondence, International Institute of Social History, Amsterdam.

assisting Labor to produce new wealth. Interest is a charge made by those who own capital for the use of it by those who [hire] Labor. Rent is a charge made on those who are willing to use it for the production of wealth. If all land and capital were owned by those who produce wealth, the wages of Labor would be the whole of the wealth produced by Labor; but as land and capital are owned by men who are not laborers and labor cannot be performed without them it follows that those who own land and capital are the masters of those who toil. Thus, capital which is created by Labor, has become the master of its creator.[54]

The Marxist doctrines of exploitation and the class struggle gave conscious form to Hardie's own experiences. But he continued to view working-class interests as did Burns in terms of contemporary political radicalism. In 1892, when the radicals in the West Ham South constituency of London quarreled with the local Liberal caucus, Hardie stepped in as their candidate for Parliament. The death of his Liberal opponent in the ensuing campaign enabled Hardie to capture the seat through a broad appeal to the Liberal voters. At this time he looked to Burns as the natural leader for a new working-class party, but when Burns ignored his appeals Hardie assumed the initiative.

Meanwhile Hardie's view of Socialism was changing markedly. His concern with the class struggle and class interests did not disappear, but was increasingly associated in his propaganda work with moralistic and religious appeal. While the shift cannot be traced with precision, it was strongly influenced by his growing familiarity with the ethically inspired popular Socialism of the North. Hardie's success in drawing together the strategy of the Marxist realists and the rhetoric of the Ethical Socialists would make him the leader of the new Socialist political party.

Ethical Socialism engaged ideas and feelings within Hardie which had not previously been clearly related to his activity as a working-class leader. Although his parents had been Secularists, Hardie was converted to Christianity as a young man. His religious development after he joined his minister in Cummock in a schismatic move-

---

[54] Hardie is quoted by Lowe, *Pit to Parliament,* p. 23; and Francis Johnson, *Keir Hardie's Socialism* (Leicester, 1922), p. 6.

ment was ever more liberal. The schismatic chapel had joined the "Evangelical Union" of James Morrison, a Scottish religious reformer who had advocated freer views of divine grace and man's will than did traditional Calvinism. Indeed, the outlook of this chapel, where Hardie served as a lay preacher, was much like that of advanced Congregationalism in England. But the congregation in Cummock did not survive; as in several similar developments, a number of the members redirected their religious and moral feelings into the Socialist movement.[55] Hardie never abandoned his ethical version of Christianity, but he came to regard the theological and institutional forms of the faith as obstacles to spiritual sincerity. His "inherent, spiritual emotionalism," as a biographer described it, broadened into an "imaginative catholicity of spirit which rendered him responsive to every expression of religious feeling which seemed to him sincere," including the "votaries of spiritualism and theosophy." Meanwhile, influences like Carlyle, Ruskin, Ernest Renan, Morris, and perhaps most of all, as Hardie himself claimed, the simple humanitarianism of Robert Burns strengthened his moralistic outlook.[56]

It was not until Hardie plunged into the campaign to create an independent labor party in 1892 that his Socialist propaganda took on the ethical and utopian quality with which it was subsequently identified. Sam Hobson, who served as Hardie's secretary in these years, later recalled the special religious and moral climate into which the organizers of the new party had entered:

When I first began to move amongst Yorkshire and Lancashire folk I felt in a new world. I was puzzled as to why the I.L.P. propaganda gained such instant acceptance in these two counties while the other industrial centers lagged behind. It was certainly not the intellectual appeal for of that the I.L.P. speakers were innocent. They always spoke of the appeal to the heart; their speeches were a blend of religion and sentiment—sentiment which generally lapsed into sentimentalism. . . . I

[55] For an attempt to relate Hardie's political views to his religious beliefs see Donald Carswell, *Brother Scots* (New York, n.d.), pp. 166ff. For an example of redirected feelings see Alexander Webster, *Memories of Ministry* (London, 1913), pp. 30–41.

[56] Stewart, *Hardie*, p. 98; *Review of Reviews*, XXXIII (June 1906), 570–571.

soon realized that the I.L.P. had appeared at a moment in time when Yorkshire Nonconformity was in a process of disruption. . . . The I.L.P. accordingly set out to capture the soul of Nonconformity and Yorkshire was the battle ground.[57]

Hardie, like Mann, rapidly recast his Socialism into terms which appealed to the workers in the North. He possessed, in fact, a rare gift for sensing the tone of his audiences.

For myself, I usually began a speech, literally, in fear and trembling. . . . I never get in touch with my subject until I am thoroughly in touch with my audience. . . . When the hall is good and the audience indulgent a genial thaw sets in, and as it works its way through me I cease to be a separate person. I absorb and am absorbed by my audience. In spirit we seem to melt and fuse into one, and I am not speaking to them, but through them, and my thoughts are not my thoughts but their thoughts, and we are on the most comfortable and confidential terms one with another.[58]

During 1892, Hardie began to appropriate the symbols and meanings of Christianity for the Socialist cause and, in his words, to develop "an educated sentiment in the rank and file of the nation." The "Christianity of the schools," he declared at Bradford in October, was passing away. It was "bound up in the cerements of a dead and lifeless theology" and "awaited decent burial." The leaders of the Socialist and labor movements had come to "resuscitate the Christianity of Christ." A few weeks later he insisted that "Christ taught his disciples no prayer for a beautiful life in some problematical world beyond the grave but a prayer for the good things of this life." In the months ahead Hardie developed the idea that Socialism was simply a new form of the Christian gospel:

The spirit of progress which was to shake off the earthly shackles which bound men to sensuality and raise them a stage higher in the evolving of the perfect man is also in our midst today. But instead of calling it Christianity we call it Socialism. . . . The religious form may still exist

[57] S. G. Hobson, *Pilgrims to the Left* (London, 1938), p. 40.
[58] *Labour Leader,* Feb. 28, 1903.

but once again the spirit has passed away and found its embodiment else-where.[59]

Hardie retained his concern for working-class interests, which he viewed largely in terms of advanced radicalism, amended by such proposals as the eight-hour day, the right to work, and the broader goal of collective ownership. But he had raised the cause of labor to the level of moral and religious imperatives and imparted something of the utopian spirit of Morris to practical political agitation. Hardie's Socialism also found its justification more and more in the intuitive and emotional sides of man's consciousness. It meant, as in Glasier, a tendency to ignore objective principles. "Thoroughgoing sincerity cannot fail of its purpose," Hardie insisted, for "mankind always responds to earnestness. Were it otherwise there were no immutable principle of righteousness in the Universe." [60]

Back in London Hyndman complained of the "queer jumble of Asiatic mysticism and supernatural juggling which we call Christianity put forward by Keir Hardie and Tom Mann as the basis of a social and economic propaganda." Perhaps there was in Hardie, as in Mann, a strong element of conscious calculation in all this. Hardie was convinced that "mere abstraction" would "never move masses of people," and he attempted in rhetoric and even in his personal appearance to engage the feelings and imaginations of the workers. He was aware of what Engels called the need for the new working-class leader to "hawk" his person "constantly before the public." [61] Hardie's entrance into the House of Commons wearing

[59] Johnson, *Hardie's Socialism*, p. 8; *Bradford Labour Journal*, Oct. 14, Nov. 4, 1892; *Labour Leader*, May 2, 1896. Fred Reid has pointed out that Hardie first employed the style of a "pulpit orator" in his South West Ham Campaign of 1882 (*Bulletin for the Society of Labour History*, XVI [Spring 1968], 33).

[60] Quoted in Lowe, *Pit to Parliament*, p. 74.

[61] Quoted in Chushichi Tsuzuki, *H. M. Hyndman and British Socialism* (London, 1961), p. 100, and in Johnson, *Hardie's Socialism*, p. 9. A hostile observer contended that Hardie tried to look older and, with his "broad brimmed sombrero," corncob pipe, and flowing tie, assumed the "mantle of a proletarian prophet in the cast off rags of Victorian Bohemia" (Carswell, *Brother Scots*, p. 188).

tweeds and a cloth cap and his somewhat Bohemian, even Neo-Raphaelite style of dress helped to dramatize his independence and identification with the working classes.

Hardie's dual appeal to class interests and religious sentiment proved especially effective in those sections of the working class still tied to the Liberal party and, at least by sentiment, to the Nonconformist chapel. G. D. H. Cole maintained that no other appeal would have succeeded:

To wean them from Liberalism, which also had its stronghold in the chapels, required the presentation of Socialism as an ethical gospel. On no other terms would they have responded, and no leader who had not been like minded with themselves would have appealed to them with any hope of success. Keir Hardie was like minded with them.[62]

Hardie was more successful than any other Socialist propagandist in uniting the political strategy of the realists to the ethical and utopian aspirations nurtured by Morris and the Ethical Socialists. But the relationship between these two sides of the movement remained vague. The theoretical linkage provided by Marx had been lost, save in the rather narrow and dogmatic form preserved by the Social Democrats. And while the Fabians were providing new ideas and practical proposals, they discouraged both the realist and ethical emphases in Socialism. The new Socialism of the North, however, in which a realist strategy was loosely joined with a utopian appeal, inspired the Independent Labour party. The new party quickly became the most important vehicle for the advance of Socialism.

Formation and Early Growth of the Independent Labour Party

A major strike by woolen workers at the large Manningham Mills in Bradford, lasting from December 1890 to May 1891, helped to consolidate the movement for political independence in the West Riding.[63] Relations between the workers and the employers had been deteriorating because of the increased size of factories and firms and

---

[62] Cole, *Hardie*, p. 4.

[63] The crucial importance of cooperation between the trades councils and the leaders of the movement for working-class political independence is stressed in Thompson, "Homage to Maguire," pp. 302–309.

the consequent loss of sense of common interest. Deepening conflicts within the Liberal party and the declining appeal of the Nonconformist chapel, both of which had served to bind the classes together, contributed further to the estrangement. When the Manningham strike failed, the workers decided to defend their interests by political methods. They founded a "Labour Union" dedicated to independent political action and later in 1891 tested the new policy successfully in local elections. Soon other "Labor Unions" were formed in various parts of the West Riding.

The new spirit of working-class solidarity in Bradford and the surrounding region found its clearest expression in the rapid proliferation of labor clubs.[64] These clubs, which excluded Liberal and Tory party members, provided a variety of social and cultural activities for working-class families. But they served mainly as centers for political discussion. Many of them, in contrast to the old political clubs, refused to sell alcoholic drinks so as to maintain a high level of political seriousness. Here the spokesmen for Ethical Socialism, as well as Fabian and other speakers, found eager and attentive audiences. Here, too, was a firm basis of support when the working-class leaders in Bradford decided in 1892 to put up an independent candidate at the general election. They first invited Blatchford to contest the seat, but he withdrew and was replaced by Tillett. The election demonstrated that the workers were capable of challenging the older political parties. Supported by the local Trades Council, Tillett drew 2,749 votes compared to 3,306 and 3,053 respectively for his Liberal and Conservative opponents.

Meanwhile, Joseph Burgess in his weekly *Workman's Times* was carrying on a campaign to develop local rosters for a new party. By September there was sufficient support to plan for an organizational conference at Bradford in January 1893.

The Bradford conference drew on nearly all the forms of Socialist activity developed during the preceding ten years. From the Federation came its dynamic Lancashire organizer, Joseph Terrett, though only as an observer. Former members of the Socialist

[64] The growth of the clubs can best be followed in the *Bradford Labour Journal* during the closing months of 1892.

League were prominent—Jowett, Maguire, Mahon, and Leonard Hall, who appeared as delegates of local independent labor parties. Aveling was there on behalf of the London Eight Hours League. Blatchford and Katharine Conway stood out among those who had contributed to the growth of Ethical Socialism; the Fabian Society sent Shaw and De Mattos. Champion, still hoping to play a leading role in the new party, was kept away at the last moment by illness. The presence of Ben Tillett and James Sexton reflected the impact of the New Unionism, though most of its leaders were absent. Hardie, one of several delegates from the Scottish Labour party, served as chairman through most of the proceedings. But the conference was made up chiefly, in Pelling's words, of the "intelligent, respectable trade unionists of the new labor clubs." [65] A third of the one hundred and twenty delegates came from the West Riding and nearly as many from Lancashire.

The proceedings at Bradford indicated the extent to which Socialist ideas had influenced the delegates. Proposals to limit the party's program to the immediate interests of the working classes were defeated, and the delegates committed themselves to the goal of the collectivization of the means of production, distribution, and exchange. For the immediate future, however, the party's program stressed the legal eight-hour day, public provision of work for the unemployed, the taxation of unearned incomes, and various social welfare measures. The delegates did adopt the word "Labour" rather than "Socialist" as the key term in the party's title and thus blurred its Socialist image in order to broaden its appeal. "The new party," Katharine Conway explained, "had to appeal to an electorate which had as yet no full understanding of Socialism"; it was "not right to ask these men to call themselves Socialists" at the outset.[66]

The delegates adopted a federal structure for the party, hoping that this would facilitate one of their major goals, the affiliation of trade-unions. The strong opposition to centralized authority within the party also reflected the ultrademocratic outlook present in the

[65] Henry Pelling, *The Origins of the Labour Party* (London, 1954), p. 122.
[66] *Ibid.*, p. 173.

new wave of popular Socialism. The new party's administrative council was denied power to initiate policy. It "should confine itself to the instructions given it by the annual conferences." And in a move which somewhat diminished the influence of Hardie during the party's first year, the delegates decided not to elect a permanent chairman. The belief in the direct and spontaneous workings of democracy which underlay these arrangements distinguished the new party from the traditional political parties.

The Bradford conference was relatively free from the ethical and religious rhetoric so prominent in popular Socialist propaganda. But the question of electoral tactics inevitably raised the problem of the party's primary objectives. The Manchester delegation, headed by Blatchford, led a fight to commit the party to the primary goal of making conscious Socialists. They urged the conference to adopt a clause from their own constitution which bound all members to abstain from voting in elections where no Socialist candidate was standing. In his spirited defense of the "fourth clause," as it was called, Blatchford restated his belief in a party of righteous individuals:

He regarded Liberals and Tories as the enemies of the people. When he said a man was his enemy he meant he hated him and would fight him to the death. He could not understand why one should take such a man's hand. He considered it a stain on the Labour Party to have any dealings with the Liberals. He would as soon have dealings with the devil.[67]

Actually there was much to commend the policy from a purely practical standpoint, for in order to attract the mass of the workers the ILP needed to demonstrate its independence. There was a strong temptation in areas where the working classes had traditionally voted Liberal for the local branches of the ILP to reach electoral agreements with the Liberals.[68] The Liberals would refrain from contesting a seat sought by the ILP in return for the workers' support in other constituencies. But such agreements would diminish the ILP's chance of detaching the workers from the Liberal party. Moreover,

[67] Independent Labour Party, *Report of the First General Conference* (Glasgow, 1893), p. 15.
[68] The minutes of the ILP's national administrative council disclose several episodes of this sort. Much of the trouble centered on Halifax.

such a policy would also endanger the party's appeal to those sections of the working classes, particularly in Lancashire, which had tended to vote Conservative.

And yet the attempt to guarantee independence by urging the ILP members to abstain from voting in contests where they did not have a candidate posed a dilemma. The paucity of party resources would limit the number of candidates the ILP could put up at the next parliamentary election. Hence adoption of the "fourth clause" entailed a disenfranchisement of all ILP members outside of constituencies where the party had candidates. Progressive Liberal or Tory candidates would lose support, and labor interests would suffer.

The Bradford conference failed to settle this tactical issue; it left the decision to the local ILP in municipal elections. For national elections the decision would be left to a special party conference. During the next few years, however, the ILP leaders urged a policy of abstention. They sought to maintain rigorous independence and expressed strong hostility toward the older parties. Nevertheless, at the local level there were a number of attempts to make electoral deals with the Liberals. Noting these efforts, Champion warned, shortly before his departure from England, that the Liberal party would "try to absorb the ILP" for it had a "strong stomach" and could "swallow anything." [69]

The controversy over the "fourth clause" brought to the surface the tension, central to the subsequent history of the ILP, between those who wished to stress the party's Socialist vision and those who emphasized the immediate interests of the workers. But for several years that tension remained dormant. The party's propagandists and organizers could combine the two appeals in their efforts to win support. Margaret McMillan described their hopes:

The ILP reached forth not only to the skilled and semi-skilled but to a new and vast army of mute and lonely sufferers who hung like a dead weight on the skirts of the working class bodies, and who had not only hampered but wrecked their work in the past, the unemployed, the rear

[69] Quoted in Pelling, "Champion," p. 235.

of the great organism called Labor. It had been like the emprisoned tail of a creature whose lively head is free of the trap. In vain was the head advanced again and again with lively hope. It was doomed by its own members; and these defeats would not end till the whole of the working class below them could be freed together. This belief was the impulse of the ILP.[70]

The initial response was encouraging. At the end of the first year the party claimed four hundred branches, though the paying membership was still less than five thousand.[71] But the ILP did not get the hoped-for support from the trade unions, practically none of which affiliated. At the Trades Union Congress in September 1893 Hardie also failed in a bid to give the ILP access to the new fund which the trade unionists had set up to support parliamentary candidates. At succeeding congresses there were further setbacks. Even the New Unions, counted on to mobilize the masses of the unskilled, provided little help. Most of these unions declined sharply in the early nineties, unable to protect their members against economic recession. The decay in their fortunes did bring some of their leaders—Mann, Pete Curran, J. R. Clynes, Fred Hammil, Tillett, and James Sexton—into more active roles in the ILP. However, the party drew the bulk of its support from the skilled workers and mainly those between twenty-two and thirty-three years of age.[72] The composition of the party branches varied with the region, but the following description of a branch in Glasgow was fairly typical:

Except for an odd teacher and a few shop assistants, the members were all working men and their wives. For the most part the men belonged to the skilled trades as in England and were nearly always known as exceptionally good and steady working men. They were active trade unionists to a man. The ILP was not attracting as yet what are called the "unskilled workers". . . . The great majority were total abstainers. There

[70] Margaret McMillan, *The Life of Rachel McMillan* (London, 1927), pp. 85–86.

[71] See Pelling, *Labour Party*, p. 243.

[72] *Labour Annual* (Manchester, 1894). See Mann's report on the ILP.

was a strong element of Puritanism in their makeup. It was to these that the ILP owed its extraordinary influence.[73]

While the ILP drew mainly from the skilled and better-off workers, its growth often reflected, as in the West Riding, the weakness of trade union organization and the determination of local leaders to rely on politics instead. Indeed, in some regions, such as the Scottish coal areas, the growth of the ILP may have retarded the development of trade unions, as some union leaders charged. There was also some correlation between ILP support and the changing form of industrial activity. In Sheffield, for example, the party's following came not from the "old crafts" or "lighter trades," but from workers in the newer "heavy trades . . . who had no tradition of collaboration with the Liberal-Radical caucus." The unskilled, the irregularly employed, and the slum dwellers remained almost completely impervious to the ILP appeal. Party organizers discovered that the "indigent have neither time nor opportunity to think out social problems for themselves." [74]

The growth of the ILP settled early into fairly well defined geographical regions. Lancashire and the West Riding, the initial centers of strength, remained predominant. Support also developed in Scotland and the industrial sections of the Midlands, but London proved less responsive than its population might have promised. Of the 300 branches claimed at the 1895 conference Lancashire and Yorkshire had 175, including the largest and most prosperous. Indeed, at the second annual conference in 1894 at Manchester, several northern leaders, having made preparations behind the scenes, reconstructed the administrative council to correspond more closely to the ILP's geographical support.[75] Lancashire and Yorkshire, Burgess complained, "practically determined the whole of the

[73] John Paton, *Proletarian Pilgrimage* (London, 1936), p. 199.

[74] Sidney Pollard, *History of Labour in Sheffield* (Liverpool, 1959), p. 198; *Labour Leader*, Sept. 1895).

[75] Russell Smart, *Labour Leader*, May 15, 1908, refers to a meeting called for this purpose. Also see the comment by Alfred Settles, *ibid.*, May 29, 1908. The key step in the reconstruction at the 1894 conference occurred when the delegates passed, by a vote of 35 to 33 a recommendation by the newly appointed standing orders committee, composed almost entirely of Northern dele-

allotment of seats" on the new council.[76] To some this power play seemed unworthy of a party of principle which aspired to be national in scope. Others were embittered at the Manchester conference by the repudiation of Champion, who was there as an observer. The bitterness was directed mainly toward Hardie, who filled the newly created post of chairman. Feelings remained sufficiently strong in Aberdeen to prevent Hardie's candidacy there at a by-election in 1896. Indeed, during these years Hardie was the target of charges of undemocratic practices and power seeking.[77]

The practical problems involved in building a party organization and the personal rivalries which soon developed disillusioned those who viewed Socialism primarily as a moral crusade. "I feel very sick," Blatchford confessed in 1894, "of the British workingman and his leaders and also of the dirty lies, tricks, and intrigues of the lousy political crew." Could they do anything with such a "rabble rout?" Could they do what Christ, who "died for these creatures nearly 2000 years ago . . . failed to do?" [78] Blatchford was not as disillusioned as this outburst suggested, but his confidence in the ILP had begun to fade. Hardie's decision to start a weekly paper of his own in 1894 also added the obstacle of journalistic rivalry to friendly relations between the two leaders. Increasingly, in fact, Blatchford saw himself as above party, and he and his associates began to work toward Socialist unity.

With the emergence of the ILP the Socialist movement had divided into three sections, each with its own conception of a new Socialist consciousness. The Social Democrats held fast to their form of Marxism and continued to preach a highly rationalistic version of the doctrines of exploitation and the class struggle; they scorned the Socialism of the new party as sentimental. The Fabian leaders

---

gates, to elect members of the council henceforth simply by the vote of the delegates. This enabled the preponderant voting strength of the Yorkshire and Lancashire delegates to prevail.

[76] Quoted in Pelling, *Labour Party*, p. 161.

[77] Percy Widdrington's letters to Enid Stacy in 1895 reflect the latter's strong criticism of some of Hardie's practices (P. E. T. Widdrington–Enid Stacy Correspondence, Maurice Reckitt, London).

[78] Blatchford to A. M. Thompson, Robert Blatchford–A. M. Thompson Correspondence, Manchester Central Reference Library, Manchester.

on the other hand, now fixed in their gradualist and administrative conception of Socialism, had little sympathy for the ethical and utopian aspirations of the ILP propagandists.

Yet these differences, so marked at the level of national leadership, often faded out at the local political level. The electoral program the Federation presented to the workers in London or elsewhere was usually indistinguishable from that of the ILP. Particularly in the North, where the Social Democrats had shared in the surge of popular Socialism, their members often cooperated with the ILP branches in demonstrations and local elections. Even the Fabians dropped for a time their skepticism about working-class political independence and attempted, in their pamphlets. "To Your Tents, O Israel" and "Plan of Campaign for Labour," to provide guidance for the new political force.

Most of the Social Democrats, the Fabians, and the members of the ILP shared a strong sense of participating in a common movement. This sense often gave a special bitterness to their disagreements and rivalries, but it also encouraged many forms of cooperation. The advance of the movement might even take precedence over the loyalty of individuals to their own organization. Thus Joe Terrett, by far the Federation's most effective organizer in the North during the early nineties, turned several branches of the Federation into branches of the ILP. For this he was dismissed.[79] But Terrett was simply responding to local sensibilities and opportunities.

Moreover, the ILP was weak in theory and largely dependent on the other sections of the movement for ideas. Often its propagandists turned to the literature of the Social Democrats, for they found the Marxist account of economic exploitation simpler or more convincing than the Fabian explanations. The Marxist doctrine of surplus value, or ideas clearly derived from it, appeared in several

[79] Terrett used a pseudonym, A. G. Wolfe, to conceal his identity as a Socialist organizer in order to avoid persecution. During 1892 and 1893 he delivered hundreds of talks for the Social Democratic Federation in Lancashire and started twenty new branches. For his dismissal, see *Justice,* May 19, 1894. Terrett remained a Social Democrat. See the biographical sketch in the *Social Democrat,* Aug. 1899. James Leatham also helped to form several ILP branches where the prospects seemed more promising. See *Gateway, XXXII* (April, May 1944).

of the early ILP tracts. Some members of the ILP referred to themselves as Marxists, but the propaganda drew more from the Fabians.
Most ILP leaders were members of the Society, and the party's
branches relied heavily on the lectures, tracts, and book boxes provided by the London Fabians. Indeed, Hardie urged the London
Fabians to stick to their role as a "purely educational agency," and
he argued that the Fabian policy of permeating other political organizations was "a positive danger to the Socialist movement." [80]

Within a short time, however, the ILP had become the most important Socialist organization. As the general election of 1895
approached, Beatrice Webb thought that the ILP had "utterly check-
mated" the policy of permeation and left the Fabians "sitting
with their hands in their laps." Despite their membership gains the
Social Democrats had now been clearly outmaneuvered in the struggle
to create a broadly based Socialist party. They were able to put
up only four candidates at the general election while the ILP
put up twenty-eight. Yet all of these candidates, including Hardie,
were defeated. Beatrice Webb was confident that the ILP had "completed its suicide," leaving the Fabians free to "begin afresh on the
old lines." [81]

During its first two and a half years, however, the ILP had
sunk roots sufficiently deep to sustain it through the difficult years
ahead. The tenacity of the new party derived in part from its involvement in local politics and was also sustained by a small band
of organizers and speakers, including both nationally known figures
such as Hardie, the Glasiers, Enid Stacy, and Carolyn Martyn and
countless obscure men and women working at the local level. They
succeeded in giving the rank and file of the party not only a new
sense of their own interests but a belief in a higher Socialist mission
on behalf of a more humane and cooperative social order.

The interaction between Marxist ideas and the British reform move-

[80] See H. Russell Smart, *The Independent Labour Party: Its Program and
Policy* (Manchester, 1893); and James Sexton, *Sir James Sexton, Agitator*
(London, 1936). A Liverpool branch of the ILP was busy studying *Capital* in
1895. See the *Labour Chronicle* (Liverpool), Jan. 1, 1895. Hardie's talk before
the Fabians is in *Keir Hardie's Speeches and Writings,* ed. Emrys Hughes
(Glasgow, 1928), pp. 39ff.
[81] Beatrice Webb, *Our Partnership* (London, 1948), pp. 124–127.

ments of the eighties had produced three distinct forms of Socialist consciousness. Hyndman had translated the ideas of Marx into familiar utilitarian terms and developed, through the Social Democratic Federation, a militant but abstract conception of working-class interests. The Fabians, following Webb's lead, had also come to rely mainly on utilitarian modes of thought, but had discarded the idea of the class struggle, limited the scope of Socialist concern, and identified Socialist advance with the evolution of existing institutions and the public consciousness of administrators and political leaders. The disciples of Morris had translated his utopian form of Marxism into popular terms and connected the Socialist vision with the moral and religious sentiments of those sections of the lower classes which had been closely tied to the Nonconformist chapels. In the Independent Labour party, inspired largely by the strategy of the Marxist realists, Ethical Socialism found a political vehicle.

The development of Socialist ideas had stubbornly resisted the direction of any single leader or organization. Indeed, to Edward Carpenter, the movement seemed "like a great river, fed by many currents, with none guiding its destinies." [82] More specifically, the growth of the movement had contradicted the Marxist expectation that a working-class consciousness would emerge, informed by Marxist understanding of social development. Rather, Socialism gained popular support only by reverting to modes of thought that were essentially romantic; interest in theory gave way to the assertion of moral feelings. But in this way Socialism found significant points of growth in British life.

Not all of those who had accepted the Socialist vision were willing to entrust their hopes to the political process. During the early nineties some Socialists were seeking alternative paths toward the new order. They expressed in part a deepening disillusionment with the ILP as it attempted to translate its Socialist ideas into an effective political ideology and strategy. They were also seeking to realize the deeper impulses of the Socialist consciousness.

[82] Edward Carpenter, *My Days and Dreams* (London, 1916), p. 246.

PART III

THE CHALLENGE
OF POLITICS

8
Divergent Strategies

Socialists who shared the conviction of Morris and others that the integrity of their principles was more important than political advance followed several alternative strategies in the early nineties. One small group contemplated a course of violence in the belief that the new Socialist man only awaited liberation from a corrupt social system. They were convinced that the solidity of prevailing social arrangements must necessarily dissolve in the light of Socialist truths. Others attempted to destroy the claims of the existing social order through withdrawal; they experimented with forms of communal life. A much larger section of the movement sought to accentuate the Socialist consciousness by giving it a religious form; this strategy drew not only on feelings pervasive within the movement, but on the peculiar religious situation of many members of the working class in the North.

These divergent strategies had little impact on the course of the movement, but they are of considerable importance in understanding popular Socialism. Here several of its strongest impulses became more explicit; at the same time they underwent a more extreme, though simplistic development. Their continuing vitality intensified the dilemmas of the Socialist leaders who attempted in the late nineties to accommodate the movement to the exigencies of the political process.

Rejection of Politics, Anarchism, and Tolstoyism

A turn toward violence, more verbal than physical, appeared among the group which had wrested control of the Socialist League from Morris. By 1890 they had taken over *Commonweal* and, supported by branches in Norwich, Sheffield, Leeds, and Glasgow, began teaching "propaganda by deed." In August, with the support of *émigré* anarchists in London, they held an "Anti-Parliamentary Conference" to discuss tactics. The "first act of the Revolution," according to a delegate, Frank Kitz, an editor of *Commonweal,* "ought to be to open the prison door." Kitz also urged the delegates to "preach to the thieves, paupers, and prostitutes" for they were less attached to the old social order. To Fred Charles, a delegate from Sheffield, it seemed clear that the spirit of revolt was spreading in the lower classes. He noted the riots which had accompanied the recent strike of gasworkers in Leeds: "The very children looted the provision shops for their fathers who were fighting in the streets. The women collected stones for the men to throw. If only we spread ourselves a bit in the provinces we should light a fire that would end the whole damned thing." [1]

The views of Kitz and Charles were crude but recognizable outgrowths of Morris' ideas. There was the same simple confidence in the basic incorruptibility of man, particularly those least infected by the mores of bourgeois society. Here too was the hope, expressed earlier by Morris, that the whole institutional apparatus might be swept away in a spontaneous upsurge of destructive energy. The outcome of this kind of Socialist reductionism may be followed briefly in the development of Charles.

Charles was a type of person, rare in the British Socialist movement, who was almost totally alienated from society. He had pioneered for Socialism in Norwich during the eighties, using a small legacy to start a cafe and support a discussion group. The group soon became a branch of the Socialist League, but its short history was stormy. Charles was frequently the center of controversy. Though deeply committed to the cause and ready to sacrifice whatever he possessed for a comrade, he had a way of putting everyone at

---

[1] The meeting is reported in *Commonweal,* Aug. 16, 1890. His full name was Fred Charles Slaughter, but after joining the movement he dropped his surname.

loggerheads.[2] In 1890 he left Norwich. Lacking regular social ties, he drifted to other centers of League activity—to Sheffield and then to Walsall. There in 1892 he was implicated, along with several other anarchists, in a scheme to manufacture a bomb for export to Russia. Charles was tried and sentenced to ten years in prison.[3]

The "Walsall Conspiracy" brought the League's anarchists under the close scrutiny of the authorities. In April 1892, *Commonweal* was suppressed by the police for inflammatory articles and its editors, David Nicoll and Charles Mowbray, arrested. The remaining members of the League dispersed. Already a number of them including Fred Henderson, Tom Barclay, and H. B. Samuels, had made their peace with the new political wing of the movement. Others formed ties with the London anarchist group associated with the paper *Freedom,* inspired largely by the ideas of Kropotkin. Dominated by the outlook of continental *emigrés,* the London anarchists maintained tenuous contact with the wider Socialist movement in the years ahead.[4]

There were gentler forms of anarchism in England. From the beginning some Socialists had dreamed of breaking away from conventional society in order to form new communities. Like Owen earlier, they hoped to convert society by example. This bent was particularly strong among the Bristol Socialists where Carpenter, the prophet of the simple life, had exercised a major influence. One of the Bristol Socialists, Helena Born, left England in 1890 and pursued

[2] George Hukin to Edward Carpenter, Jan. 15, 1891, Edward Carpenter Correspondence and Papers, Sheffield Public Library, Sheffield.

[3] The Walsall episode and the end of the League are discussed in Edward Thompson, *William Morris: Romantic to Revolutionary* (London, 1955), pp. 675–687. Charles was released after seven and a half years. He was met at the prison gate by a wealthy woman with whom he had been corresponding. They married, took a tour on the continent, and subsequently settled near Oxford. Charles retained some contact with the movement, was active in the affairs of Ruskin Hall, and later joined the Whiteway colony. See Nellie Shaw, *Whiteway* (London, 1935), pp. 163ff.

[4] See the chapters on Kropotkin and Stepniak in James W. Hulse, *Revolutionists in London* (Oxford, 1970).

the utopian vision all the way to California. Others from Bristol, Katharine Conway, Enid Stacy, and Dan Irving, joined a cooperative community set up in the North of England by a Unitarian clergyman, H. V. Mills, in 1892. The community was not anarchist in inspiration, but the Socialists saw it as a unique opportunity to illustrate the deepest truths of their faith. They were soon disillusioned. After rebelling against the "autocratic" methods of Mills, the Socialists were forcibly expelled.[5]

The Fellowship of the New Life also carried forward the aspiration after a new form of communal life. During the late eighties its leaders had increasingly turned to the ethical writings of Kant and T. H. Green and emphasized "our fundamental moral law" as the standard for judging the economic system.[6] For a time they conducted an experiment in cooperative living in the Bloomsbury section of London and took part in the Ethical movement. But in the early nineties the Fellowship began to dwindle away, partly because some of its more active members were participating in a new effort to develop a higher moral life, inspired by the teachings of Tolstoy.

The Tolstoyan movement gave fresh expression to many of the attitudes and values underlying popular Socialism. Tolstoy's simple New Testament ethic, his emphasis on daily contact with nature, and his insistence on the need for physical labor appealed particularly to men of the lower middle classes who were caught up in the routines of commercial life. Indeed, in the writings of this foreign prophet, significant features of Ruskin's message reappeared. The *Clarion* soon recognized the relevance of Tolstoy for Ethical Socialists and began to spread the new ideas through its serialized versions of Tolstoy's *Life and Teachings of Jesus* and his *Resurrection*. Meanwhile, Tolstoy had found a British apostle for his gospel in a former Congregational minister, J. C. Kenworthy.

---

[5] See the biographical sketch in the preface of Helena Born, *Whitman's Ideal Democracy and Other Writings,* ed. Helen Tuffs (Boston, 1907). Mill's project was based on ideas developed in his book *Poverty and the State* (London, 1886). For descriptions see *Clarion,* June 4, 1892, and *Justice,* Sept. 24, 1892. Also see Laurence Thompson, *The Enthusiasts: A Biography of John and Katharine Bruce Glasier* (London, 1971), pp. 75–77.

[6] See Maurice Adams, *The Ethic of Social Reform* (London, 1887).

Kenworthy had been active in the Ruskin Society in Liverpool before concluding that it was morally impotent.[7] Moving to London he joined the Fellowship of the New Life and then discovered Tolstoy. He also worked for a time with Bruce Wallace and his "Brotherhood movement," which hoped to subvert the capitalist system through the creation of a "voluntary Cooperative Commonwealth" made up of altruists. Unlike Wallace, however, Kenworthy agreed with Tolstoy that political methods must be repudiated:

In the atmosphere of politics, the upright reformer cannot live and work; he loses honesty, purpose and sight of his ends. It is impossible to fight the system with its own weapons, one cannot touch pitch without being defiled. Those who are most intimate with the Labor movement best know the helplessness of labor against a corrupt propertied class in Parliament; they know that the only successful political action is that which will result from the creation of a sound public opinion, which will sweep away the whole machinery of government.[8]

In the fall of 1896, Kenworthy and some members of his Brotherhood Church in Croydon began to build a new model community on twenty-three acres of land at Purleigh in Essex. Members of the Croydon church belonged for the most part to the ILP or the Fabian Society. Kenworthy viewed the new colony as an integral and pure expression of the larger Socialist movement:

Small local and intense movements may always be discovered in association with every wider and more superficial movement of the people toward social reform. We ought not to be surprised to find at the heart of the present Socialist movement, a body of people who elect, as the Purleigh colonists do,—to *live* Socialism.[9]

[7] There is a biographical sketch of Kenworthy in the *Labour Annual* (London, 1896). W. H. G. Armytage, *Heavens Below* (Toronto, 1961), pp. 342–358, contains the fullest account of the Tolstoyan movement in England. Also see Percy Redfern, *Journey to Understanding* (London, 1946), pp. 49–78, 91–105; and Aylmer Maude, *Life of Tolstoy* (London, 1910), pp. 546ff.

[8] J. C. Kenworthy, *The Anatomy of Misery* (2nd ed.; London, 1900), p. 91. The volume, first published in 1893, was dedicated to Keir Hardie, who described it as "both a text book on political economy and a gospel according to Morris, Ruskin and Tolstoy" (*Labour Leader,* Sept. 22, 1900).

[9] *Commonweal,* Nov. 1898 (an Anglican publication edited by Canon Scott Holland).

After a visit to Russia, Kenworthy secured Tolstoy's blessing. For four years the group struggled to become economically viable on an agricultural basis. The colonists constructed a number of buildings, including a large greenhouse, started an apple orchard, and developed several acres of market gardens. The fifteen residents during the first years were mostly unmarried, middle-class young men, in several cases refugees from commercial and clerical life in London. But the Purleigh colony also became a center for Russian *émigrés* and, through the work of Aylmer Maude, a source for the dissemination of Tolstoy's writings in England.

By means of continuing discussion the colonists hoped to develop a common outlook. Tolstoy was their prophet, and they agreed that all coercion should be eliminated from human relationships. But they could not agree on the procedures for reaching that goal, particularly the terms for admitting new members. Should they accept only those who would be "serviceable to the community" and share its philosophical outlook or should they eliminate all restrictions at the outset and concentrate on building a "right relation between man and man"? [10] The dispute led to a schism and the formation of a new colony at Whiteway near Gloucester. Weakened by the loss, the Purleigh group struggled on until 1900 when some newcomers from Lancashire, having "starved through a winter in a barn," came down with smallpox. Health authorities then closed the colony. According to Maude, another "important factor in smashing the colony was a gift of nine hundred pounds. When that came there was not a young man in the place who did not straight way want to get married." [11]

The experiment at Whiteway was financed mainly by S. V. Bracher, a Gloucester journalist and Tolstoy convert. Composed of nine men, five women, and two children, the group attempted to organize an agricultural settlement along much the same lines as

[10] *New Order*, Sept. 1898. This monthly paper, begun by Kenworthy in 1895, contains a number of articles and reports on the experiment. The Purleigh colony is also discussed in the *Clarion*, Aug. 20, 1898, and in the *Social Democrat*, Sept. 1901.

[11] Redfern, *Journey*, p. 93; *Ethical World*, May 19, 1900.

Purleigh. They also admitted members without considering their suitability for the new life. But at Whiteway the sex question, prominent in the Purleigh discussions from the beginning, proved to be especially disruptive. When several "free unions" were formed Bracher and his wife were offended and attempted, unsuccessfully, to regain their title to the property. One of the first acts of the group had been to burn the title deed; the land, they declared, had been "sent by the Supreme Being for the use of man and therefore should be free to everyone." [12] The quarrel dismayed Kenworthy, who denounced the group for bringing discredit to his teachings. There were further difficulties as the colonists were taken advantage of by neighbors and visitors. But after the individual members were given their own plots of land the Whiteway colony achieved a degree of stability and economic efficiency which enabled it to survive into the 1930s.

Tolstoyan and "Brotherhood" ideals also inspired experiments in the North of England. Here the economic basis was industrial or commercial rather than agricultural. In Leeds the leader was D. B. Foster, who had been a lay preacher in the Wesleyan Methodist church and a small manufacturer before joining the ILP. He then came under the influence of Kenworthy and Wallace. His discovery of their form of Socialism led him, in 1897, to break with his church and also to renounce his position in the social and economic order. Convinced of the overwhelming evil of capitalism, Foster determined to be one of the workers and "live on their level." The following year he joined another disciple of Kenworthy, Albert Gibson, who owned a bicycle and electrical business, to set up a workshop on "brotherhood lines." They permitted the workers to come and go as they pleased and combined work in the shop with "religious and philosophical discussions." The venture soon proved uneconomic. When Foster sought to restore the discipline of "regular hours," the workers resisted and the experiment collapsed.[13]

At Blackburn several lectures delivered by Kenworthy, under

---

[12] *New Order,* Sept. 1899. The colony's history is related in Shaw, *Whiteway.*
[13]*New Order,* June, July 1898. Foster described his development in *Socialism and the Christ and the Truth* (Leeds, 1921).

the auspices of the local ILP, inspired a group of Socialists to follow Tolstoy's creed. Tom Ferris, a participant in the Leeds enterprise, opened a "brotherhood" electric shop and tried to run it without the use of money. All money, he explained, "is an expression of fear that our needs will not be supplied"; it is "fear of our fellow man" that lies beneath "nearly all evil and misery." [14] Love could emerge as the true bond of human relations only when all remnants of fear and its corollary, force, were removed. Ferris attempted to replace currency transactions with the bartering of services and goods though for a time his associates were allowed to be less fastidious in the handling of money. But this effort to live without "external rules" soon broke down. Another member of the Blackburn Socialists started a free school in a cottage a few miles out of town in order to "have done with the commercial system and work for love alone." Gifts from sympathizers kept the school going for a time.

The Socialist experimenters in new communal forms recognized in Tolstoy's teachings the natural outcome of ideas central to their own movement. Through their experiments they were asserting the sovereignty of the ethical ideal and seeking to bring human behavior into correspondence with it. They were also asserting the power of man's consciousness over institutions and attempting to eliminate external forms of coercion from social life. Such an outlook was incompatible with conventional political activity; indeed, this deviation from the main stream of the Socialist movement was in part a reflection of political disillusionment. In the difficult years after 1895, some Socialists concluded that Tolstoy was right in warning that the struggle for political power inevitably produced a "bankruptcy of the Socialist ideal." At least one of the Tolstoyan Socialists had become aware, too, of the threat which the political and administrative tendencies within the movement posed to the efforts to cultivate a new personal morality:

For now, in 1900, after six socialist years, I was becoming conscious of a still more determining force, a fixed state of mind. I was beginning

14 *New Order,* Aug. 1899.

to find it impossible to think of any social good to be done except through state or municipal or other authoritarian large scale organizations and their funds. The capacity to see a more social world began to appear only in terms of establishment and regulation by law; for all real faith in individual power was vanishing.[15]

Yet those Socialists who attempted, through experiments in cooperative living, to test the moral power of the individual often experienced profound disenchantment. Edith Lees, a participant in the cooperative household of the Fellowship of the New Life, concluded that the "robes of ethical splendor," the constant moral self-scrutiny, did not reach very deeply into individual motivation: "The whole wonder and glory of that house was that all the people there were miles beyond their preaching. All the most beautiful things that happened were quite unconscious. The stupid and dull things were chiefly the things done on principle." The Tolstoyans also learned that "to live Socialism," at least in the context of Victorian England, might entail grave personal risks. Having discarded the constraints of conventional society in favor of personal moral directives, the anarchists frequently had difficulty maintaining their mental balance. Maude observed: "Partly owing to the strain it put upon men's minds and partly because every strenuous movement attracts some ill-balanced people, there was much insanity at Purleigh. At least five who lived and stayed at the Colony while I was there were subsequently put under medical supervision on account of their mental condition." [16] Kenworthy himself, after another visit to Tolstoy and further propaganda work, entered a lunatic asylum.

Others, however, looked back on the experience as a "valuable beginning" in the "search for rightness of life." It provided fresh inspiration for cultivating a richer social existence. Indeed, the moral and social aspirations of the Tolstoyans contributed directly to the new thinking about community planning under way in England by the turn of the century.[17]

[15] Redfern, *Journey*, pp. 96, 102.

[16] Edith Lees, *Attainment* (London, 1909), p. 309; Maude, *Tolstoy*, p. 546.

[17] Redfern, *Journey*, p. 104. The connection with community planning is traced in Armytage, *Heavens Below*, pp. 370ff.

Most Socialist leaders were hostile to the communal enclaves within the movement. To both the Fabians and the Social Democrats the Tolstoyan ideas and strategy were naive; to the *Clarion* and the ILP leaders the experiments were premature. But the faith which underlay the experiments pervaded the Socialist movement. A number of Socialists attempted to give this faith religious form; some believed that a "religion of Socialism" would be necessary to preserve the new consciousness from the narrowing and materializing influence of politics.

The "Religion of Socialism": John Trevor and the Labour Churches

Popular Socialism in Britain drew much vitality from what De Man called the "eschatological sentiment"—the promise of a radically different way of life. This hope, expressed most vividly in *News from Nowhere* and *Merrie England,* found many forms in the movement. Thus in Leicester during the mid-eighties, Tom Barclay envisioned the "last great battle of the world" bringing a "paradise of purity, of concord, of love." He argued that the reforms of Lycurgus in Sparta had demonstrated mankind's capacity to "overcome rotten capitalism and institute equality." For Glasier the dream of man's perfectibility was supported by the "immemorial myth of the Golden Age." [18] More often the Socialist propagandists drew on Biblical imagery in portraying the future.

The awakening of this social hope was frequently accompanied by a quasi-religious sense of conversion. H. W. Hobart, a Social Democrat leader, described his dramatic acceptance of Socialism after hearing a lecture by Herbert Burrows on the "Morality of Revolution":

I had at that time not sufficiently shaken off my religious prejudices to consent willingly to give up my attendance at the Mission Hall where I used to sing in the choir, but after a sharp conscientious struggle I went. I listened in rapt attention to the new gospel . . . and was trans-

[18] Henry De Man, *Psychology of Socialism* (New York, 1928), pp. 133ff; Socialist League Correspondence and Papers, #176, International Institute of Social History, Amsterdam. See Glasier's "The Legend of the Golden Age," *Labour Leader,* April 29, May 6, 1920.

formed with astonishment. . . . The argument and the reasoning of the lecturer convinced me of the truth of his gospel but the prejudice I had incepted from various sources seemed to hold me back from declaring my convictions. A second appeal from the Chairman had an electrifying effect. When he asked again whether anyone would like to join the branch I said, "Yes I would." [19]

Joining the movement might bring social ostracism and economic discrimination, but the convert often experienced a new and exhilarating sense of righteousness. "Our zeal and enthusiasm throve" upon the feeling of being cast out, a Scottish Socialist recalled. "We acquired the air of men set apart; we walked along with a tense air and set expression. We conceived we were the stuff of martyrs." [20]

Almost from the beginning Socialists had attempted to provide ceremonial and symbolic expressions of their faith. They might, like Eleanor Marx in 1885, try to appropriate a traditional festival such as Christmas to celebrate "the death of darkness and the birth of light" represented by Socialism. Or they might oppose the old Christian symbolism with their own. The "Red Flag," a *Justice* editorial observed, was replacing the cross as the emblem beneath which men were striving for a "regenerated world." In the annual May Day demonstrations Socialists found the most effective way of giving an objective, almost ritualistic form to their sense of solidarity. James Leatham attempted to explain the meaning of the occasion:

As the churches celebrate Christmas and Easter so should the workers celebrate May Day . . . with enthusiastic demonstration and exhortations. . . . I would have every Socialist, even the poorest, save his pennies for months before hand. . . so that he might travel one hundred miles if need be to attend some magnificent festival of the New Earth and the New Man. . . . No party can afford to neglect its festivals. Festivals furnish a ceremonial and mechanical aid in retrospection and introspection. . . . They give outward and visible sign to the inward and spiritual significance of the great principles which at ordinary times are mere words.[21]

[19] *Justice*, Nov. 19, 1894.
[20] John Paton, *Proletarian Pilgrimage* (London, 1935), p. 116.
[21] *Commonweal*, Dec. 11, 1885; *Justice*, Dec. 24, April 20, 1895.

Socialist leaders claimed that their faith produced a quickening of conscience. No doubt many shared the experience of moral uplift reported by the Fabian benefactor, Henry Hutchinson. "Under the pulpit I had been deaf and unreceptive," he wrote, but as he turned toward Socialism his sympathy for the "essential Christian doctrine" of humanitarianism revived. A number of ILP branches followed the example of the *Clarion* groups and carried on charitable activity. There was even an attempt to establish an annual "Self Denial week" within the movement, during which Socialists were to fast in order to help the needy. The promptings of Socialist principles might generate severe conflicts as the individual's loyalty to the cause clashed with conventional social expectations. The *Clarion* presented a series of "cases of conscience" in which young Socialists related their moral dilemmas as they prepared for careers in the competitive world of commerce. The demands of the movement also alienated some converts from their families. "My father forbade me in the house," Joseph Toole of Manchester recalled, and "challenged me to fight with bare fists." Socialist leaders discussed the question of whether "love, wife, children, home" should be renounced for the sake of the brotherhood. Katharine Conway urged total commitment:

As the early Christians founded Brotherhoods and Sisterhoods so in a sense must we if we are to convert the people. . . . In the birth of the movement there is a great need of lives absolutely consecrated to the work with no home ties to bind them to one spot more than another, and for no need for earning more than a bare subsistence wage. . . . It is a new band of pilgrims who are needed today to go through the length and breadth of Great Britain.[22]

The self-sacrificing enthusiasm exhibited by the Socialists often evoked the admiration and envy of orthodox religious leaders. The Socialists, Canon Scott Holland declared, were "the only people with

[22] Henry Hutchinson, *Socialism in Its Relation to Christianity* (Derby, 1891); *Clarion*, June 23, July 7, 28, 1894. The "cases of conscience" appeared during July and August 1894. See as well Joseph Toole, *Fighting through Life* (London, 1935), pp. 84–85; *Workman's Times*, March 25, 1893.

any touch of the prophetic spirit." [23] For many ministers of organized religion in these years, faced with the increasing alienation of the lower classes and often discouraged by the irrelevance of conventional religious life to pressing social problems, the Socialist movement seemed to possess a spiritual vigor far superior to that of their own congregations. This was the conclusion of John Trevor, a Unitarian minister in Manchester who decided in 1891 that the Socialist movement held greater promise for man's religious future than did his own church. He attempted to give the "religion of Socialism" an institutional form.

Trevor's early years were marked by a painful struggle to escape from the anxieties associated with Calvinist theology. "A continual fear of hell," he wrote later, kept his youthful nerves in a "state of severe tension." Yet his later revulsion to orthodox religion was tempered by appreciation for the "tremendous soul drama" behind its forms. He remained unwilling to accept "any cheap interpretation of human existence." [24]

The path toward a new faith was difficult. He developed a "morbid sense of exile, loneliness, and self suspicion" and in 1877, after he had begun to train to be an architect, he suffered a breakdown. Urged by his doctor to take a sea voyage, Trevor traveled to Australia. At the same time he determined to face the "whole problem of religion . . . afresh, and with no Bible as my guide." From Australia he went to America, where he studied for a time at a Unitarian seminary. He discovered the writings of Emerson and gained a "confidence in the soundness of life," as well as a feeling of "his oneness with the Universe." Emerson's essay on "Nature" presented Trevor with a fresh challenge: "The foregoing generations beheld God and nature face to face; we through their eyes. Why should not we have a poetry and philosophy of insight, and not of tradition, and a religion of revelation to us, and not a

[23] Quoted by Frederick Rogers, *Labour, Life, and Literature* (London, 1913), p. 141.

[24] John Trevor's autobiography, *My Quest for God* (London, 1898), is one of the most revealing accounts of the spiritual travails of a late Victorian. The citations here are taken from the second edition (Horsted Keynes, 1908), pp. 23, 10.

history of theirs? Why should not we also enjoy an original relation to the universe?" Trevor now began to see his task. "Men need new anchors forged," he wrote to a friend in England, particularly "those simple heads who want a faith they can believe and amidst the wrangle of sects cannot find." [25]

Trevor returned to England in 1879 but not until ten years later did he develop the spiritual confidence necessary to undertake his mission. After a year's study at a Unitarian college in London he became assistant to Philip Wicksteed, the Unitarian minister of Little Portland Street Chapel. Trevor gained much from his eighteen months' association with Wicksteed. A specialist on economic questions, Wicksteed sharpened Trevor's growing awareness of the social problem. But Trevor did not become fully conscious of the "helplessness of the Churches in facing the world's problems" until he became minister of Upper Brook Street Chapel in Manchester in 1890. After a year he concluded that Unitarianism was bankrupt. His church seemed a "prison" to his soul, its "four walls like the four walls of a grave." As the "deadness" of this last refuge of the traditional faith weighed upon him, Trevor turned to the new social and ethical idealism developing among the working classes.

Trevor had earlier been repelled by the Socialists in London; their creed seemed to teach that men might be made better by being made more comfortable. But he also believed that society was in "a state of chaos—just held together by its old clothes, liable to burst into shreds at any moment." Only a "new life could save it." Once in Manchester he discovered the new life in a branch of the Socialist League. One of its meetings, held "in the rain on a busy street corner," profoundly impressed him. He decided that he would have to "leave the Church and go out into the world . . . in my quest for the living God." [26]

Two events in the spring of 1891 brought Trevor's discontent with Unitarianism and his admiration of the Socialists into new focus. At a Unitarian conference in London he heard Ben Tillett appeal to clergymen to "provide churches where the people could get

[25] *Ibid.*, pp. 63, 135, 141–142.
[26] *Ibid.*, pp. 220, 226, 219, 234.

what they needed." If they did not, Tillett warned, the "workers would provide churches for themselves." A short time later Trevor talked to a working man who had ceased to attend the Brook Street chapel because he "could not breathe freely" in it. During the sleepless night which followed, Trevor developed the idea of a radically different kind of church designed for the working classes.

Having failed to win over his Unitarian congregation to the venture, Trevor secured financial backing from Wicksteed and others in London. Early in October the new "Labour church" held its first service at the Chorlton Town Hall, Manchester. A well-filled hall heard opening music from a string band, and, after a prayer by Trevor, listened to a reading of James Russell Lowell's poem "On the Capture of Fugitive Slaves." A Unitarian minister from Hyde, Harold Rylett, then read the fifth chapter of Isaiah. Following a choir rendition of "England Arise," the popular Socialist hymn of the day, Trevor delivered the sermon. He noted the lethargy of the traditional churches and spoke of the need to bring "religion into the struggle" for the emancipation of labor. It was necessary, he concluded, for the working classes to "start a religious movement of their own outside the churches, which would allow them to live a righteous and godly life and yet secure the freedom for which they lived." [27]

The new Labour church appealed strongly to Manchester Socialists. On the second Sunday, when Robert Blatchford gave the address, several thousand were turned away. The *Workman's Times* described his audience as typical of the thousands who had become "fascinated . . . with the broader hope and future prospects of humanity" presented in his *Chronicle* articles. They had come to "regard him in the light of a prophet and savior of men."

In the following months Trevor gradually clarified his ideas of the new church's mission. It was to bring to full consciousness the new religious spirit he saw developing in the lower classes. Although Socialist agitators and strike leaders might appear to be atheists, they

[27] There is a description in the *Workman's Times,* Oct. 9, 1891.

had "the real life of the moral order of the universe dwelling in them." The labor and Socialist movement, Trevor insisted, was "the greatest religious movement of our time." It was the task of the Labour church to "set free the tremendous power of religious enthusiasm and joy" pent up within it.[28]

Trevor believed, like Morris and Carpenter, that his age was "spiritually exhausted." The "civilized world was worn out," and a "new religion and a new social energy must come to the rescue." Although the "thought of Jesus" was an anachronism, there were signs of a "new religious sentiment arising in the hearts of the people." In human evolution, Trevor wrote, "the highest is the latest"; mankind was at "the dawning of a new spiritual age." The Socialist movement represented its clearest manifestation:

In the midst of English Socialism alone do I see any sign of religion being able to stand securely alone, without Priest, without parson, without creed, without Tradition, without Bible; firmly based, as Socialism itself is, in the heart of the living facts of today, capable of revising its conditions without losing its life, committed irrevocably therefore to continued growth and progress.

While the historic churches "were weeping over the lapsed masses," Trevor claimed, the new Labour churches would "discover among them the moving power of God's spirit and the day-dawn of a new religious life and love." [29]

Trevor accepted the Socialist formula of the nationalization of the means of production, distribution, and exchange as the "great constructive principle of future industrial and social development." But for him the essence of Socialism lay in a "growing yearning of man toward man." It would bring a widening spirit of human sympathy and brotherhood, gathering up elements in the Christian tradition and yet developing a "new and deeper . . . pagan joy of life." Trevor repudiated the Christian doctrine of "original sin and human depravity," confident of an underlying divine evolution

---

[28] *Ibid.*, Oct. 16, 23, 1891.
[29] *Clarion*, Aug. 11, 1893; John Trevor, "The Labour Church in England," *Labour Church Tracts*, No. 4 (London, 1896), p. 52.

and "unconscious religion" which needed only to break into full consciousness. But while he believed that the next stage of man's spiritual evolution would bring a fuller realization of the ethic of love and brotherhood, Trevor did not equate ethics with religion. "The Ethical flag," he wrote, "flies at half mast and signifies death in the upper reaches." True religion required a "God relationship" and a capacity for "seeing far more deeply into the facts of life . . . and the significance of our moral struggles and defeats." [30] Moreover, ethical enthusiasm would not carry the Socialists far, Trevor warned, unless it was supplemented with the "intellectual acumen of the Fabian society." A Fabian member himself, Trevor hoped that the Labour church might reconcile and unite the moral and the rational sides of the movement.

Trevor started a monthly magazine, the *Labour Prophet,* in 1892 to advance the Labour church. Already a number of other churches had been organized, and in 1893 a Labour church union was formed.[31] But Trevor did not attempt to give strong leadership to the movement. He believed that the churches should develop spontaneously as "growing points [in] the evolution of Humanity Godward." He possessed, as a friend put it, an "ingrained distrust of established things." His distrust included, as with so many Ethical Socialists, nearly all forms of external control and authority. Trevor preferred to see himself as a prophet without "power and place":

The possession of power with its attendant limitations and disabilities seemed to me entirely inconsistent with that living free relation which I desired to hold toward the movement. I wished to be a strong influence but I came to see in the work I was attempting that the less power a

[30] John Trevor, "Our First Principle," *Labour Church Tracts,* No. 3 (London, 1894), pp. 46. Also see *Labour Prophet,* Oct. 1893.

[31] The best published account of the Labour churches is the chapter in K. S. Inglis, *Churches and the Working Classes in Victorian England* (London, 1963). Also see Henry Pelling, *The Origins of the Labour Party* (London, 1954), Ch. 7; and Eric Hobsbawm, *Primitive Rebels* (Manchester, 1959), pp. 126ff. I am also indebted to the Ph.D dissertation of David Summers, "The Labour Church and Allied Movements of the Late Nineteenth and Early Twentieth Century," University of Edinburgh, 1956.

man has the more wholesome will be his influence and the more durable the results while . . . his own growth will be less endangered.[32]

Trevor's own spiritual growth proceeded in the face of great personal difficulties in these years. Two of his children died, the second suddenly in the summer of 1894. Later that year his distraught wife followed the child to the grave. Trevor himself suffered periodic physical breakdowns and spent much of his time in retreat in the Cheshire countryside. Yet he felt a continuing "growth of illumination" and during 1894 gained his "highest experience of the presence of God":

Suddenly without warning I felt I was in heaven—an intense state of peace and joy and assurance indescribably intense, accompanied by a sense of being bathed in a warm glow of light as though this external condition had been brought about by internal effect—a feeling of having passed clearly beyond the body though the scene around me stood out more clearly and as if nearer to me than before by reason of the illumination in the midst of which I seemed to be placed.[33]

But the extent to which Trevor was able to communicate his experiences to others proved limited. His unwillingness to exercise strong leadership and his belief in spontaneity encouraged the diversity which characterized the Labour churches.

The churches originated in a great variety of circumstances. In one case a church was started by gasworkers; in another a group of Swedenborgians took the initiative. Several were inspired by the immanentist theology and the social activism characteristic of advanced Nonconformity. In Oldham a Congressional minister, already known for his progressive social outlook, won the confidence of local Socialists and virtually abandoned Christian forms in favor of those of the Labour church. In Bolton, B. J. Harker, minister of the old Dukes Alley Congregational Church, now stranded in a working-class area, decided to transform it into a Labour church "as far as the constitution" of Congregationalism permitted.[34] In time the

---

[32] Trevor, *Quest,* p. 258.

[33] *Ibid.,* p. 268. William James used Trevor's account in *The Varieties of Religious Experience,* Modern Library Edition (New York, n.d.), pp. 387–389.

[34] *Labour Prophet,* July, Sept. 1894; May, June 1892.

Bolton church entered fully into the new movement. The Bradford Labour church, one of the strongest, was started by Fred Jowett and several other active Congregationalists after they concluded that the close identification of local Nonconformists with the Liberal party and the employer class made a new religious start desirable.

Most often the Labour churches were organized by ILP branches as a part of their political and social activities. Labour church growth corresponded very closely to the spread of the new party. Yorkshire and Lancashire contained most of the congregations, though the geographical range was wide. It extended from Arbroath in North Scotland to Cardiff in South Wales. The social composition of the churches was usually much like that of a typical ILP branch. A description of a church "in the North" was probably characteristic: "I attended several meetings. . . . [They were] packed with a respectable, responsible audience, not to be confounded with one of the Salvation Army type. . . . The bulk were men, decently dressed artisans and mechanics, some of the higher grades, all, unless the look belied them, full of earnest expectancy." [35]

The leadership of the Labour church movement, both nationally and locally, usually came from middle-class men and women who had earlier been active in orthodox denominations. Fred Brocklehurst, next to Trevor the most important figure in the movement, had studied at Cambridge preparatory to taking orders in the Church of England. J. A. Fallows, who provided the funds and much of the inspiration for the church in Birmingham, was the son of a local alderman and had also planned to become an Anglican clergyman. Miss K. M. M. Scott, who helped in the work of expansion as "pioneer secretary," was a member of an Anglican sisterhood before joining the movement.[36] Men and women of Noncomformist religious background were even more prominent among the leadership and particularly within the rank and file. A. J. Waldegrave, for example, became a Labour church leader in London after

[35] *Spectator*, April 21, 1894.

[36] *Workman's Times*, March 10, 1894. On Brocklehurst's break with the church see *Labour Leader*, April 17, 1894, July 28, 1895.

deciding that his work in a Wesleyan mission was "completely futile."

I had been losing my belief in the central Christian doctrines and I had been enlarging my knowledge of the economic aspects of society. . . . By now when I attended a Methodist church service . . . it all seemed desperately unreal. Yet I knew that at the heart of the religion which had led my old fellow men and myself to say "The love of Christ constraineth us" was a deep reality and I wanted to have it continue such, both in my mind and in that of others. . . . I got in touch with a half dozen who were forming the Tottenham Labour Church. . . . Like myself and like most of those I believe who took the initiative in forming other Labour Churches they were discontented Nonconformists. . . . I continued to indulge in the hope of there arising a great new Church which would be completely free from bondage to the past, with its outworn creeds and fossilized traditions; would be a home for man's highest aspirations and finest spiritual instincts; would be a powerhouse supplying energy for strenuous moral endeavor and would devote itself to a peaceful revolution in social conditions on a basis of Socialist principles.[37]

The Labour churches were usually led by men and women who had ceased to be Christian, but the rank and file of the membership held a wide variety of religious views. In some places the members retained their affiliations with orthodox chapels, and the Labour church meetings were scheduled so as not to conflict with the regular chapel services.[38] When a Southampton Labour church was attacked for "harbouring agnostics, atheists, and infidels," its leaders replied that the majority of members were "believing Christians." Margaret McMillan's description of the Bradford congregation indicated the range of outlooks within a given church:

It departed from all the customs of the other churches, though we tried more and more to conform and please our various fellow worshippers.

[37] Letter from Mr. Waldegrave to David Summers, Sept. 25, 1953; used by courtesy of Mr. Summers.

[38] Conversation with Mrs. Annie Hilton of Middleton, Lancashire. Mrs. Hilton was active in the formation of several Labour churches in the Manchester area.

The Swedenborgians repeated the Lord's Prayer with the Christians. The Social Democrats did nothing of the kind. The old chapel goers, or some of them, enjoyed the hymns but the Secularists did not enjoy them. The lecture was the thing . . . all waited for that. . . . In spite of their differences they did form one real party, united by a single hope.[39]

As this description suggests, Labour church services resembled those of the chapels although the element of worship was greatly diminished. The question of prayer provoked considerable controversy. Trevor urged the use of prayer; it was, he argued, compatible with all forms of belief and unbelief. In some churches it was abandoned completely. The person conducting the service might read passages from the Bible; more often the Labour church leaders relied on a new scripture based on the writings of such secular prophets as Mazzini, Emerson, Carlyle, and Ruskin or the Socialists, Morris and Carpenter. Hymn singing was popular and later the churches developed their own song book, in which themes of moral exhortation largely displaced the older religious emphases on praise and adoration.

The lecture, as Margaret McMillan observed, was the "thing they all waited for." Since the Labour churches repudiated the idea of a clergy, their pulpits often had a different speaker each Sunday. Leading propagandists, Hardie, the Glasiers, Mann, Margaret McMillan, Enid Stacy, and Carolyn Martyn were in particular demand; in some cases they were booked up for a year in advance. To Labour church audiences they delivered talks much like those they gave from the propaganda rostrums of the Socialist movement. More distinctly religious or ethical themes appeared in the sermons of less prominent speakers, though here too there was a wide range of styles and views. The sermons almost invariably attacked the traditional dualism between the sacred and the secular and particularly the sharp distinction evangelicals had tended to draw between religious and political concerns. Thus Fred Henderson, in one of the most popular Labour church addresses, cited the prophet Amos as

[39] *Labour Prophet,* May 1895; Margaret McMillan, *The Life of Rachel McMillan* (London, 1927), pp. 75–7.

one who had attempted to "re-establish religion as a principle of conduct" and "claim the whole range of human activity as being subject to its teachings." The individual sin, with which the older churches were preoccupied, Henderson argued, was "for the most part only a knot in the vast network and entanglement of social and industrial conditions." John Tamlyn of Burnley, a Secularist speaker during the eighties, agreed. Using the fifty-fifth chapter of Isaiah as a text, Tamlyn criticized the theologians for having "fought shy of giving any bodily sense" to the words of Isaiah. The architect Raymond Unwin, a close friend of Morris, argued that religion should supply motives for the "upswinging within our society of a new society based on other ideals and . . . fresh social relationships." Waldegrave emphasized the power of the "religion of Socialism" to bring a new "consciousness of the oneness of life," of the "worth and unity of all things." [40]

Labour church speakers judged religious activity almost entirely in terms of its contribution to social justice; they were little concerned with the personal, redemptive meaning of religious faith. This strong preoccupation with social reform opened the Labour church platforms to almost anyone with a cause to plead. Appeals on behalf of "vegetarianism," "anti-vivisection," "theosophy," "Ethical Culture," "Tolstoyism," "cooperative dress-making," "Esperanto," and against the "tactics of Scotland Yard" were only a few of the topics which confronted Labour church audiences. Most often the Labour church addresses drew heavily on the program and the ideals of the ILP. The inner story of Trevor's movement lay in his unsuccessful struggle to prevent the churches from becoming captive to the ends of the party.

Trevor shared the view, expressed so frequently on the Labour church platform, that political life needed a new infusion of moral and religious idealism. He denounced the "base, equally damnable hypocrisy of separating politics from the rest of man's life," but he also believed in the special mission of the Labour church. He had

[40] Fred Henderson, *Politics in the Pulpit* (Norwich, n.d.) pp. 8, 14; *Labour Prophet,* March 1895, March, 1898; A. J. Waldegrave, "The Religion of Socialism," copy of manuscript in possession of David Summers.

joined with Blatchford in forming the Manchester branch of the ILP partly because he hoped this would free the Labour church for its proper work. In his conviction that the new church and the new party had separate roles Trevor received support from Hardie. The Labour church, Hardie observed, was a "great feeder for Socialism," but he argued, in a curious reversion to orthodox religious attitudes, that "it would be fatal . . . to identify it with any political party." [41]

From the beginning Trevor had worried lest their close ties with the ILP tempt its leaders to use the Labour churches to draw people who were not attracted to the party "by the usual methods." His fears were borne out. A founder of the Dundee Labour church, David Lowe, recalled that their church not only "kept the religious element in the cause robust" but "it allowed lecturers to obtain a hearing on Sunday." [42] Sam Hobson helped to form a Labour church in Cardiff because the Sunday meetings of the Socialists had invited charges that they desecrating the Sabbath.

In vain our assurances that Socialism was our religion—the religion of humanity. It was not very convincing. But when we founded our own church, dragging in an enticing clause from the Lord's Prayer as our basis, that particular criticism was silenced. They found they must meet us on theological grounds.[43]

Almost from the beginning some Labour church leaders saw their churches mainly as a means of advancing the labor and Socialist cause. This was Brocklehurst's view. Their "peculiar mission," he declared in 1893, was simply the "Labour program at its best," the "socialization of wealth through the election of independent labor candidates to all representative bodies." A year later he sharpened his attack on Trevor's view:

The portals of the Labour Church should be as wide as the labour movement. Neither religious faith nor want of religious faith should debar any man from joining our ranks. It is the heighth of folly . . . to

[41] *Workman's Times,* Nov. 7, 1891; *Labour Prophet,* June 1897.

[42] *Labour Prophet,* Feb. 1895; David Lowe, *Souvenirs of Scottish Labour* (Glasgow, 1919), p. 97.

[43] S. G. Hobson, *Pilgrim to the Left* (London, 1938), p. 41.

attempt to create another theological church. . . . Our work and our mission . . . lies in the practical work around us. . . . In the fulfillment of such duties we shall preach both Socialism and the eternal truths of religion and thus vindicate our claims to be a Socialist Labour Church.[44]

By 1895, Trevor had concluded that the development of the ILP was hostile to spiritual growth:

To a man who has any sense of the vast range of life, and of the intricate interaction of the laws of human progress, the ILP must of necessity appear to be attempting the salvation of the world in appalling cheap fashion. Making converts at the low price of a penny a head, winning elections by listening to tickling speeches, attempting to bottle up all the elements of man's personal and social life in one resounding formula, paying no attention to the vast issues outside and having no life or thought outside of it, failing to recognize the forces making for progress in other spheres of life, jealous and suspicious of any extension of their own principles where they touch men's deeper needs and higher aspirations—all this I have been watching with perplexity and sorrow the past twelve months.[45]

Trevor continued to deplore the tendency toward "political supremacy" and sought new ways to enhance the ethical and religious aspects of Socialism. But the view that the Labour church "should be a fighting machine for labor above all else" steadily gained the upper hand. Those Labour church leaders who sought to deepen the spiritual life of the churches tended to antagonize the labor politicians. In Bolton a large section of the membership broke away because the Labour church was "getting too religious." Elsewhere, Labour church groups were turned out of their halls on Sunday evenings because the local ILP wanted to hold a meeting. Several leaders of the Labour churches began to see their function as simply to provide a common platform where "all sections of the Socialist party may meet upon neutral ground to discuss and consider the truths of Socialism." [46]

44 *Labour Prophet,* Oct. 1893; Feb. 1894.
45 *Ibid.,* Feb. 1895.
46 *Ibid.,* Sept. 1898; Feb. 1898; *Clarion,* Sept. 22, 1897.

By 1896 the Labour churches were losing ground; the *Labour Prophet* launched an inquiry into the reasons for the "slow progress we are making." Trevor called for a clearer statement of their religious significance and their relationship to the Socialist movement. But while the leaders of the strongest churches, D. B. Foster in Leeds, H. V. Herford in Manchester, James Sims in Bolton, Edwin Halford in Bradford, and A. J. Waldegrave in London, shared his views, they also recognized that a more precise statement of belief would alienate many members. Trevor concluded once more that they must fall back on a trust "in our own natural development towards God." But he set out over the next few years to remedy the lack of qualified speakers, which he believed was the greatest problem. "We have a new religious message for the world," he lamented, "but we have practically no messengers to deliver it and so it remains dumb in our midst." [47] He also noted the limitations of "itinerant speakers":

[They] tend to puff rather than build up. . . . They are not as a rule of much help in those more intimate and sacred relationships which especially require religion for their highest development. . . . The young, who are confronted with all the temptations and difficulties of life, the middle aged who are beset with trial, bereavement and loss and the aged who in weakness and pain, are slowly passing to their long home, find no helpful and inspiring ministry in the Labour Church.[48]

Trevor did not believe in "discipleship," insisting that "life is the great teacher." But after retiring to a farm in southern England in 1898 he invited young Labour church leaders to visit him for brief periods of time in order to receive informal religious instruction. Through conversation and deeper study of the writings of such figures as Arnold, Ruskin, Carlyle, Carpenter, Emerson, Whitman, and Mazzini, they prepared themselves to deal more effectively with the religious needs of their congregations. The plan did not succeed, however, and before long Trevor severed his ties with the churches.

---

[47] *Labour Prophet,* Dec. 1896; Jan. 1897; *Labour Church Record,* Jan. 1899. This publication, a quarterly, replaced the *Labour Prophet* at the end of 1898.
[48] *Labour Church Record,* Jan. 1899.

He was in fact looking beyond the Socialist movement and developing millennial views which, like Carpenter's, entailed a more radical break with traditional moral and religious ideas.[49]

During the late nineties support for the Labour churches fell off sharply. Their decline was to some extent a reflection of the ebbing force of the Socialist movement generally. But it also indicated the weakness of those ethical and religious impulses which Trevor and others had attempted to nurture within the churches. The Labour churches had failed to make the "religion of Socialism" a self-sustaining force rising above the more mundane preoccupations of the movement.

The "religion of Socialism" did find one additional vehicle in these years. The slowing down of the movement after 1895 led some Socialists to place their hopes for a new society on the next generation. In the growth of the Socialist Sunday Schools the ethical idealism within popular Socialism assumed its simplest and most naive form.

The idea of inculcating their principles into the young and sparing them "all that we have had to unlearn" was as natural to the Socialists as it had been to the Owenites and Secularists before them. Early in the life of the Socialist League its "Propaganda Committee" had recommended the formation of a "Children's Sunday School," and Eleanor Marx engaged in a brief experiment of this kind.[50] In 1891 one of Hyndman's associates, Hunter Watts, raised the problem of bringing up their children as Social Democrats. "Can I find it in my conscience," he wrote in *Justice,* "to let them attend the usual Sunday School where they will be taught all the old balderdash, knowing all the time that to be a true Social Democrat they must unlearn it all again." Watts' suggestion that they organize Sunday Schools evoked little initial response. A year later Mary Grey of the Battersea branch of the Federation announced that she had

[49] *Labour Annual* (Manchester, 1900), the article on the Labour churches. Trevor's later thought was expressed in an essay, *The One Life* (Horsted Keynes, 1908).

[50] *Justice,* May 16, 1891; *Commonweal,* Sept. 1885. The only account of this side of the movement is F. Reid, "Socialist Sunday Schools in Britain, 1892–1939," *International Review of Social History,* XI (1966), 18–47.

formed such a school in order "to capture the children." "We intend," she declared, to teach them "about the moral part of Socialism." [51] Other Social Democratic branches followed the Battersea example and joined to form a "Socialist Sunday School Union." Later Mary Grey described an outing of the children from the various London schools:

We started from the hall at nine in brakes with red flags flying, with children singing the songs of the Revolution (and) . . . distributing *Justices* . . . the children picked wild flowers and there was a prize for the best bunch. . . . Coming home they sang all the way and repeatedly called for three cheers for the Socialist Revolution. We gave them biscuits and grapes coming home and a bag of sweets when they got out of the brakes. They were all happy, not a dissatisfied one among them.[52]

Socialist Sunday Schools grew even more readily out of the various forms of Ethical Socialism. The Cinderella clubs, started by Blatchford, developed into Socialist Sunday Schools in a number of towns in Lancashire and the West Riding. Other schools in the North could trace their source to a "kind of young folks fellowship" called the "Crusaders," which Keir Hardie inspired through a weekly column in the *Labour Leader*. Activities for children came naturally to ILP branches, appealing as they did to the social and cultural interests of working-class families. Leaders of the Labour churches also promoted the growth of the schools as an integral part of their mission and in several cases the schools survived the disappearance of the sponsoring church.

The Socialist Sunday School usually carried the distinctive imprint of the variant of Socialism, Marxist or Ethical, which had inspired it. If the teachers were "strong Social Democrats," an observer wrote, "the teaching is naturally more materialistic" than in schools connected with the ILP. The latter "leaned more to ethical teaching." A. P. Hazell's *Red Catechism for Socialist Children* conveyed the simple Marxist message: "Who creates all the wealth? The working

[51] *Justice*, May 16, 1891, Dec. 17, 1892. There are further details in the *Young Socialist*, Nov. 1896. Also see Reid, "Socialist Sunday Schools."
[52] *Justice*, Sept. 8, 1894.

class. Who creates all poverty? Our Capitalist society. . . . What is a wage slave? A person who works for a wage and gives all he earns to a capitalist." The ethically oriented schools also appealed to justice, but they stressed the importance of love. Their teachers were usually men and women who had "worshipped at the shrine of orthodoxy," and they adapted the techniques of orthodox Sunday Schools to inculcate a Socialist moral. They might also adapt fairy tales for this purpose. Thus the "big bad wolf of capitalism" would find himself defeated by the "fairy Godmother of Socialism." Instruction also included simple Socialist ideas about social and economic questions, but it stressed the conventional moral sentiments together with strong opposition to the "competitive spirit" of capitalism. The Socialist "Ten Commandments" exalted the virtues of love, mercy, courtesy, learning, respect for parents, and justice, while reminding the child that "the good things of the earth are produced by labour." Those who enjoyed this wealth without working for it were "stealing the bread of the workers." [53]

By the turn of the century the juvenile phase of the movement was becoming more cohesive. It found a more or less official journal in the *Young Socialist,* started in 1900 by a group in Glasgow. Clusters of schools in Yorkshire, Lancashire, and Cheshire also formed regional unions and cooperated in developing common teaching materials and techniques. During the years just ahead the schools expanded to over a hundred and reached between four and five thousand children each week.

In the teachings of the Socialist Sunday Schools the ideas of the Ethical Socialists were reduced to their simplest terms. Here once more was the "sacred belief in a future state of bliss here in this world," a world where war and poverty would be abolished, and crime, "the result of unjust social conditions," unknown.[54] Again the key to the future lay in the growth of "the moral sentiment—divested of

[53] *Ibid.,* April 28, 1906; A. P. Hazell, *The Red Catechism for Socialist Children* (London, 1908), p. 8; *Young Socialist,* July 1902; Reid, "Socialist Sunday Schools," p. 46.

[54] *Young Socialist,* March 1911. Also see Lizzie Glasier and Alfred Russell, *Socialist Sunday Schools, What and Why?* (Glasgow, 1907).

supernaturalism," for Socialism was the "law of the Religion of Love" which had "absorbed all the highest teachings of the ages."

While the simple idealism of Ethical Socialism persisted within the Sunday Schools it did so in a form safely removed from the complexities and difficulties of the adult world. But the confidence in man's moral sentiments and the distrust of institutional authority, common to both the Tolstoyans and those who sought to develop a "religion of Socialism," continued to be vital elements in the wider movement. These attitudes were especially strong in the ILP where they were expressed in suspicion of leadership and centralized authority. This strain in popular Socialism complicated the tactical problems that faced the ILP leaders as they attempted in the late nineties to bring the party closer to the political process.

9
The Testing Years, 1895–1900

After the general election of 1895 the political climate in Britain was not congenial for the spread of Socialism. The triumph of the Conservatives and the heightened interest in imperial affairs directed attention away from domestic problems and confronted the Socialists with a powerful emotional counterappeal. Moreover, the rising level of employment dissipated much of the social and economic discontent which had aided the movement a few years earlier. For a year or more after the election the Socialist movement continued to grow as both the Federation and the ILP recorded substantial increases in the numbers of branches and members. But during the second half of 1896 the movement lost its impetus. Soon there were complaints of "backsliding" and expressions of regret that "so many should have burnt out in those first five years of conflict." [1] Over the next three years, despite growth in several geographical areas, nearly half of the ILP branches ceased to exist and many of the remaining branches shrank in size. The Federation proved somewhat more tenacious, but by the end of the century it had experienced a comparable decline.

The new situation provided a severe ordeal for the Socialists, testing the quality and the practical relevance of their faith. For some it was a time of discouragement and even disillusionment; for others it was a time to re-examine their political prospects. This was especially true of the ILP, which had become the main political

---

[1] See James Connel, "How to Prevent Backsliding," *Labour Leader,* April 17, 1897; and *Manchester,* a monthly of the Manchester and Salford ILP, July 1900.

vehicle for the movement. Its leaders, particularly James Ramsay MacDonald, now set out to develop policies more closely related to British political life.

Decline of Socialist Enthusiasm

By 1897 the Socialist movement was suffering from what Hardie called a "backlash of apathy." [2] It became more difficult to arouse the interest of working-class audiences, and the zeal of many active Socialists dropped off sharply. During 1896 death removed a number of leaders and propagandists, including Morris, Carolyn Martyn, Tom Maguire, Edward Fay of the *Clarion,* and the pamphleteer Samuel Washington. Other deaths followed soon—Tom McCarthy, a Social Democrat and a leader of the London dockers, and Edward Pankhurst, a key figure in the Manchester ILP. Eleanor Marx took her life early in 1898 after her betrayal by Aveling, and the latter died a few months later. Two hardworking propagandists, Fred Brocklehurst and Harry Snell, suffered physical breakdowns while Blatchford, Katharine Glasier, and Enid Stacy withdrew from active propaganda work for varying periods. Tom Mann, Ben Tillett, and Pete Curran, three of the ILP's most effective organizers and speakers, turned away from Socialist politics in these years to concentrate once more on building up trade unions. By 1901 only half of those who had been "on the road" for Socialism six years earlier were speaking regularly. Even Hardie approached despair. Death and resignation, he wrote, were removing the "props on which the movement rested. Small wonder if betimes amid the gloom a chilling sense of fear creeps into the stoutest hearts. But there can be no going back." [3]

[2] Hardie used this phrase in the *Labour Leader,* Nov. 28, 1896.

[3] *Young Oxford,* Feb. 1901. Blatchford occupied himself mainly with literary topics and stories during these years, leaving political and editorial policy largely to Thompson. Katharine Glasier retired from platform work for two years, during which time she had her first child. Enid Stacy married P. E. T. Widdrington in 1897 and spoke little for the movement during the next two years. Brocklehurst was forced to take an extended vacation, "utterly exhausted in body and spirit" (*Clarion,* Feb. 6, 1896). Mann resigned as general secretary of the party in January 1897. Curran resigned from the ILP council in

There were other signs of disillusionment and mental exhaustion. Brocklehurst warned young recruits against "wasting their time in peripatetic lecturing" and letting the movement "starve" them. Enid Stacy cautioned against a "too close acquaintance with practical politics and constant propaganda work." Critics within the ILP began to complain of the party's intellectual poverty and its excessive reliance on "raw recruits" as speakers. Their young men, a local leader declared, would be "doing more useful work if they stayed home and studied their subject." Others deplored the absence of fresh ideas and the failure to provide for "nourishing the brains" of their speakers. Self-doubt troubled even the most dedicated of the Ethical Socialists. Before her death Carolyn Martyn had begun to fear that she taught only "cunningly devised fables," and she eagerly accepted a Fabian offer of financial support for several months of formal study of economics. But after her period of study she still confessed to a deepening sense of "futility," of becoming "just a speaking machine, which receives impressions and reduces them to words without volition and almost without motive on my part." She died after ignoring repeated warnings that the pace of her activity was destroying her. For a woman, a friend observed, such a career often brought bodily death while "in men it might be delayed only to induce final mental and moral ruin." [4]

Tom Maguire's last years also show that personal toll. He had retired into the background as the movement in Leeds floundered in factionalism. Lacking steady employment or family ties, he lived more and more at the labor club, drinking and reminiscing. Carpenter, who knew him well, observed that "his life was really rather lonely and wanting in the elements which are more or less necessary to everyone." Hence "the void of personal affection trying delusively to fill itself by the conviviality of the cup." Maguire's "weakness of habit"

July 1898, and Tillett was forced to take a long rest early in 1897 to "recover strength" (*Labour Leader,* Jan. 9, 1897). Hardie is quoted by David Lowe, *From Pit to Parliament* (London, 1923), p. 147.

[4] *Young Oxford,* May 1901; *Labour Prophet,* Jan. 1899; *Ethical World,* Oct. 8, 1898; Lena Wallis, *Life and Letters of Carolyn Martyn* (London, 1898), p. 58; Fyvie Mayo, *Recollections* (London, 1910), p. 226.

grew upon him and contributed to his death from pneumonia in 1896. In a posthumously published article, Maguire wrote of the "idealists" who came to "the people and were spurned." Though he still saw a Socialist revolution at hand, he conceded that society would work out "its own destiny . . . using very little head in the process." The sense of defeat was, in at least one case, too difficult to bear. Tom Smedley, the fiery young editor of the *Nottingham Socialist Echo,* committed suicide in 1898 after expressing his discouragement over the poor attendance at recent meetings. "If Socialism was not going to sweep all before it, life had nothing to make it attractive." [5]

In a brilliant essay, "The Illusions of Socialism," Shaw caught something of the inward drama of popular Socialism at this time and the peculiar hazards it held for the young convert:

We are told of the personal change, the transfigured, lighted up face, the sudden accession of self-respect, the joyful self-sacrifice, the new eloquence and earnestness of the young working man who has been rescued from a purposeless, automatic loafing through life, by the call of the gospel of Socialism. . . . These transfigurations are very remarkable and touching to the observer who has not had any opportunities of following them up. They are as common in Socialist propaganda campaigns as in the Salvation Army. But to the old hand, they are dangerous symptoms of a too rapid and facile exaltation. If they are followed by a long campaign of insatiable and urgent public speaking, indoors and out, several times a week, they end in a peculiar exhaustion and emptiness of mind and character, leaving their victim a dull and hopeless windbag, opinionated without opinions, and conceited without qualities.[6]

Hardie also acknowledged the "terrible cost at which the work was done. Men cannot live at high pressure, seething continuously in a cauldron of excitement, cut adrift from home influences . . . without suffering a deterioration." [7]

[5] Edward Carpenter, ed., *Tom Maguire: A Remembrance* (Manchester, 1895), p. xiii; *Labour Leader,* Dec. 19, 1896, Aug. 27, 1898.
[6] George Bernard Shaw, "The Illusions of Socialism," *Forecasts of the Coming Century,* ed. Edward Carpenter (Manchester, 1897), p. 157.
[7] *Labour Leader,* Sept. 30, 1899.

The morale of the rank and file also fell during the late nineties, as working-class adherents tended to revert to more conventional patterns of behavior and self-interest. The change was seen in the growing drinking problem in ILP clubs, for the extent of drinking was usually inversely proportionate to the interest in serious political or propaganda effort. When an ILP club allowed drink to come in its quality often declined, so the party's administrative council observed, "to the level of the unlicensed public house patronized by our political opponents." Some ILP branches also suffered from the growing "football madness" and the mania for spectator sports and gambling among the working classes. "Cycling, football, and other forms of personal recreation," Glasier noted, "have cost us the zealous services of many admirable propagandists." The loss of discipline and enthusiasm among the ILP membership was reflected too in the party's financial difficulties. Wages generally were rising in these years, but the ILP leaders complained that they were forced to beg for dues. Nearly half of the branches were delinquent each year and Hardie turned increasingly to a few wealthy sympathizers for funds.[8]

The consolidation of ILP branches in the larger industrial centers also indicated an ebbing of local vitality. The administrative council's report of 1899 observed that "many of the branches have found that just in proportion as the principles of our party have taken root in their neighborhood, more and more difficulty is experienced in rendering small club meetings attractive or useful." But this was something of a rationalization. As the new secretary, John Penny, noted, most branches were made up of "a serious little group of Socialist politicians" surrounded by "lighter men and women" who were "kept in the party branch partly by sentiment and partly by amusement."[9] As the less serious members fell away the remnants drew together in consolidated branches.

[8] *ILP News*, Sept. 1898, March, 1902, July, 1899. During the spring and summer of 1900 only a third of the approximately 190 branches were paying dues regularly. Among those who made sizable donations to the party were Joseph Cadbury, the chocolate manufacturer; Joseph Fels, the American soapmaker; and James Allen, a Glasgow shipbuilder.

[9] Independent Labour Party, *Report of the Annual Conference* (Manchester, 1899); *Clarion*, Jan. 24, 1902.

To Harry Snell, who was almost constantly on the road for Socialism during the mid-nineties, it seemed clear that the movement had suffered a "moral disaster." He was convinced that the Socialists had relied too much on transient gusts of "sentiment or passion" and had failed to develop the intellectual and moral strength necessary to sustain the movement. The "overworked and ill-paid agitators" had exhausted their stock of thought and resorted to "aimless enthusiasm." In 1898 Snell accepted an offer to become a full-time lecturer for the Ethical Culture movement, which had much in common with Ethical Socialism. Although its composition was mainly middle class, its leader, Stanton Coit, possessed confidence in the power of moral ideas and was seeking to bring the various Ethical societies into a close relationship with the Socialist movement. For Snell the Ethical movement promised a higher standard of teaching and personal discipline as well as a new body of "trained lecturers . . . focusing on people's needs all their knowledge, enthusiasm, and love." But Snell did not abandon the Socialist movement, and in the years ahead he stood as an ILP candidate and entered Parliament.[10]

Similar disillusionment drove Stephan Sanders toward the Ethical movement. He had been involved in local Socialist and labor politics in London since the mid-eighties, serving for a time as secretary to Burns. But the results had been disheartening. A "few years of good trade," Sanders observed, had proved sufficient to "soothe the working classes into a slumbering apathy." He noted that many of those who had embraced Socialism as a new religious fellowship now saw it as no more than a means of securing working-class representation; it was simply a "political or economic tendency" to be "slowly and cautiously worked out by experts in administration." Sanders attributed the decline in Socialist idealism to an excessive appeal to class and material interests, which "bred a rancorous spirit of dissension and suspicion." He insisted that the true basis for "a great democratic movement" was moral rather than political or economic, and he hoped the Ethical societies would provide the moral inspiration lacking in Socialism.[11]

[10] *Ethical World,* Oct. 8, 1898.
[11] *Ibid.,* Nov. 18, 1899.

The death, exhaustion, or desertion of many of the movement's most active workers, together with the ebbing enthusiasm in the rank and file, forced the ILP leaders to reconsider their policies. The sense of riding the crest of an irresistible wave of reform gave way to a more realistic appraisal of the party's position in society. As early as the fall of 1896 Hardie admitted that the party had reached a critical stage in its development. Indeed, it was a "matter of life and death to know not only what next to do but how to do it." Yet Hardie defended the existing policy. The ILP's "most precious possession" was the "fighting power" which came from its "integrity and independence." He warned against the Liberal offers of "working arrangements," which were "sure to come," and he expressed concern lest deals be "made privately by individuals without the cognizance of the movement generally." [12]

Hardie's view of social and political developments altered little in these years. "Commercialism," he wrote, was bringing men "face to face with world wide revolution" for it was clear that life was becoming "more difficult for the masses of the people." In Marxist fashion, he asserted that "all forms of government in the world" had for "their primary object the protection of property and the subjugation by force of the common people." Yet the workers possessed the power to "capture the State machinery" and "change the ownership of land and capital." The task of the ILP was still to "place the issue clearly before the people." Hardie predicted that "jelly fish Liberalism" would be "crushed out" in the coming "struggle between Commercialism and Socialism," and within ten years a general election "would have Socialism for its chief issue." [13] In 1898, when several leading Socialists suggested the possibility of co-operating with the "democratic men" in Parliament, Hardie reacted vigorously:

I can afford to wait for the advent of the Independent Socialists in parliament, if need be I can go down to the grave without seeing one there, but I would not be a party to betraying the Socialist movement

[12] *Labour Leader,* Nov. 28, 1896.
[13] Emrys Hughes, ed., *Keir Hardie's Speeches and Writings* (Glasgow, 1928), p. 60.

into the hands of its enemies. . . . What is the chief aim of a Socialist organization—surely to make Socialists. Everything else must in the nature of things be subordinated to this. . . . When Socialism gets mixed up with all other kinds of "isms" it is robbed of its power.[14]

Yet Hardie's insistence on rigorous independence was increasingly at odds with the ILP's actual development. In its efforts to penetrate new sections of the working classes the party was becoming ever more solicitous of the feelings of the non-Socialists. The ILP leaders were more than ever convinced that a strong working-class party would require the financial and other resources of the trade unions, hence the importance of the ILP's campaign to convert the strongly organized miners.

Socialist propaganda had made comparatively little headway among the miners. Only in the Scottish fields, where the Socialists did not encounter a strongly entrenched trade union organization, had the ILP attracted a significant following. In Durham and Northumberland a few ILP branches were started in 1894 and 1895 in the wake of industrial disputes, but they did not grow. Wales was no better. The mining areas there held, according to the administrative council's report of 1895, only a few Socialists living "an isolated life in the dreary desert of narrow non-conformity and bigoted Liberalism." [15]

In 1896 the council decided to devote a substantial part of the party's resources to a campaign to win over the miners. New organizers were appointed, first Tom Taylor, and a year later, Willie Wright. Both were ex-miners, and Wright had turned down an opportunity to become an Anglican clergyman in order to work as a Socialist propagandist. During 1897 and 1898 he and his wife traveled extensively through the mining areas of Wales and, aided by a long and bitter industrial dispute, helped to increase the number of ILP

---

[14] *Labour Leader,* Aug. 24, 1898.
[15] On Socialist growth in the Scottish mining areas see R. Page Arnot, *A History of the Scottish Miners* (London, 1955), pp. 91–97. For the Northeast see R. A. Welbourne, *The Miners Union of Durham and Northumberland* (Cambridge, 1923). The council report is in *Labour Leader,* Nov. 23, 1895.

branches in the area from two to thirty.[16] Few of these branches survived, but the campaign paved the way for more solid ILP growth after the turn of the century.

ILP speakers and the *Clarion* van also toured the mining areas of the North in these years. But the difficulty of winning over the miners and the consequences of a direct assault on existing political loyalties were demonstrated in October 1897 when the ILP contested a by-election in a mining constituency in northern Yorkshire. Barnsley, where the ILP candidate, Pete Curran, challenged both the Liberal and the Conservatives, was the "capital city of the Miners' Federation of Great Britain." [17] It was also a stronghold of those trade-unionists, led by the Federation's president Ben Pickard, who continued to view the Liberal party as the proper political vehicle for advancing labor interests. The by-election campaign witnessed a bitter confrontation between the old and the new conceptions of working-class political action. The ILP sent its best speakers into the contest, while the miners' leaders fought back vigorously against what seemed to them an effort to divide the labor vote.

The ILP poll of little over a thousand votes out of the eleven thousand cast was disappointing; it was less than half the average number secured by ILP candidates in the three preceding by-election contests. Hardie admitted, moreover, that most of Curran's votes had probably come from the Conservatives. "Barnsley," he wrote to a friend, is "altogether the worst thing we have done." It was clear that the episode had damaged the party's relations with the trade unions. The ILP's failure to contest other by-elections over the next three years reflected in large part a fear that electoral efforts would antagonize trade-unionists. It had become evident, Russell Smart, the editor of the *ILP News,* observed, that "progress

[16] *Manchester,* Jan. 1901; Henry Pelling, *The Origins of the Labour Party* (London, 1954), p. 192.

[17] For the changing attitude of the Northeastern miners toward Hardie and the ILP see Tom Richardson's reminiscences in *Labour Leader,* May 31, 1912. There is an account of the campaign in R. Page Arnot, *The Miners,* I: *1898–1910* (London, 1948), pp. 300–302. Also see Philip Poirier, *The Advent of the British Labour Party* (London, 1958), pp. 69–70.

on Parliamentary lines is impossible" until trade unionism is "prepared to move." "Until it does," he added, "we shall have to wait." [18]

The ILP's deepening involvement in local government also encouraged a more moderate and opportunistic political policy. By 1900 the party could count nearly four hundred of its members on town and county councils, boards of guardians, and school boards. Indeed the extent to which the party succeeded in realigning the working-class vote in several areas, particularly in the West Riding, is an important qualification to the general story of Socialist decline in the late nineties. But experience in local government also gave many Socialist leaders a clearer understanding of the limits and possibilities of political action. It was "seldom given to anyone," Jowett observed after eight years' work on the Bradford city council, "to be at once an idealist and an administrator." [19]

When Socialists serving on local governing bodies refused to compromise their principles so as to work with non-Socialists, they might injure the immediate interests of the workers. Such was the case in West Ham after cooperation between the Social Democrats and the ILP groups there produced a Socialist-Labour majority on the borough council in 1899. Joe Terrett, now a leader among the local Social Democrats, expressed the spirit in which they approached the work of the council:

We never pretended to be a "Progressive" council. We were a Socialist council—our municipal struggle was a phase in the class struggle against the exploiters and not in any sense a petty affair of local government reform. If we had had our way, in five years we should have made landlordism a practical impossibility in the borough, or at least thoroughly clipped its wings.[20]

[18] Hardie quoted by Lowe, *Pit to Parliament,* p. 117; *ILP News,* Nov. 6, 1897.
[19] *Clarion,* April 13, 1901.
[20] *Ibid.,* May 4, 1901. The episode was the subject of extensive discussion, mostly critical, in the *Clarion* from March to December 1901. There is also a critical evaluation of the affair by Percy Alden in the *Fabian News,* June 1901. For a detailed and sympathetic account, see Paul Thompson, *Socialists, Liberals, and Labour* (London, 1967), pp. 132–135.

The outcome was a year of acrimonious debate within the council, punctuated by noisy scenes, and the defeat of the Socialist and labor forces at the next election.

The growing Socialist and labor representation on local government bodies also revealed that the "supply of suitable men" for this kind of work was "becoming exhausted." [21] Only in rare cases could the ILP or other groups give their representatives financial support. Moreover, few working men possessed the leisure or the training necessary to deal with the often complex problems of local government. The Fabians helped some. Their tracts and lectures contained specialized information and proposals. In 1899 the Fabians joined the ILP in sponsoring annual conferences of "elected persons" to consider problems in local government and practical administration.

Concern with the problem of preparing working men for larger responsibilities as citizens underlay the founding of Ruskin Hall, the new "labour college" at Oxford, in 1899. The American founders, Walter Vrooman and Charles Beard, gained the support of trade unions, cooperatives, and other working-class associations in selecting and usually supporting promising young men for a year's study of history, political science, and political economy. Socialists numbered about a quarter of the first hundred students, while nearly half were "radicals." The general secretary of Ruskin Hall described the college's purpose: "Most of our students arrive as young enthusiasts with advanced beliefs and limitless ideals, led to their opinions by their hearts rather than their heads. We seek to leave the enthusiasm undimmed but controlled by scientific knowledge." [22] During the years ahead the college drew closer to the Socialist movement and came to mirror the tensions which arose within it.

After 1896, as Socialist enthusiasm subsided, the ILP began, in part unwittingly, in part through choice, to reconcile itself to the dominant economic and political attitudes among the working classes. The adjustment was not easy, for the party derived much of

[21] See Smart's discussion of the problem in *Young Oxford*, Dec., 1900.
[22] *Young Oxford*, Dec., 1900. For the story of the founding of Ruskin Hall, see *Ethical World*, March 4, 1899.

its coherence and morale from an idealism which condemned the existing order. Incorporated into the ILP constitution, this idealism— if lived up to—placed severe limits on the tactical maneuverability of its leaders. Nevertheless, in these years the ILP began to develop a stronger leadership and found in Ramsay MacDonald a person well equipped for the delicate task of strategic and ideological accommodation.

The Process of Political Accommodation and the Role of Ramsay MacDonald

The ILP constitution reflected its socialist ideology. It was suspicious of centralized authority and was designed to facilitate the immediate expression of the political wisdom which Ethical Socialists thought sprang almost spontaneously from the people. "Disband every Socialist organization," Blatchford wrote in 1896, "and get rid of every prominent writer and speaker in the Socialist movement, and I believe that the march of Socialism would continue without serious impediment." [23] Blatchford and many Ethical Socialists often expressed their suspicion of leaders by referring to Walt Whitman's strictures against the "never ending audacity of elected persons."

In the constitution of the ILP the direct voice of the rank and file was protected by denying the national administrative council a policy-making role; it was envisioned simply as an agency to carry out decisions made at the annual party conferences. In matters not covered by conference decisions, authority resided in the local branches. The distrust of strong leadership led in 1896 to a downgrading of the office of president, created in 1894, to that of chairman, an action which nearly caused Hardie to resign the post.

The ultrademocratic bent of the ILP did not produce weak leadership but a tendency toward oligarchical control. The process was gradual and informal and left the party's constitution intact. It was marked by a measure of subterfuge and evasion among the leaders and by periodic outbursts of resentment among the rank and file. An early stage in this development occurred during the controversy over "Socialist unity."

[23] *Clarion*, April 18, 1896.

Efforts to bring the ILP and the Federation together in a single organization culminated in July 1897 when representatives of the two bodies recommended fusion if the memberships approved.[24] A referendum of ILP members brought a favorable response from 85 per cent of the six thousand members voting. The Federation's members also approved. The vote within the ILP demonstrated the strength of Socialist feeling in its rank and file and their sense of participating in a common movement. Most ILP leaders, however, saw the vote as awkward and dangerous. If the ILP became closely identified with the more militant Social Democrats the party's distance from the trade union leadership would inevitably increase. Hardie and the other members of the adminstrative council decided not to implement the vote, but to propose their own alternative at the next party conference. In the meantime, Hardie used his column in the *Labour Leader* to criticize the fusion proposal. At the ILP conference in 1898 the council proposed a scheme of federation in which the two parties would retain their separate identities. Glasier, on behalf of the council, delivered an address against the fusion plan.

Glasier brought the full rhetorical force of his Ethical Socialism to bear on the issue. He spoke of Socialism as a "marvelously pervading and encompassing power," in the face of which men were as "reeds shaken in the wind of its coming." He warned against any step which might "confine or constrain" its message, for it was "a great delusion to imagine that identity of principle" would hold "men or organizations together." Association was possible only through love, sympathy, and "harmony of disposition":

There is no disguising that the ways of the SDF are not our ways. If I may say so, the ways of the SDF are more doctrinaire, more Calvinistic, more aggressively sectarian than the ILP. The SDF has failed to touch the heart of the people. Its strange disregard of the religious, moral and aesthetic sentiments of the people is an overwhelming defect.[25]

[24] See Pelling, *Labour Party,* pp. 187–189.
[25] Independent Labour Party, *Report of the Annual Conference* (Manchester, 1898).

Glasier's statement touched on real differences between the two organizations, but it obscured the basic issues. As he admitted, the question was not one of principle. Marxist and ethical approaches to Socialism mingled inconsistently within the rank and file of the two bodies, and the groups often cooperated in electoral contests and other local ventures. Moreover, the poll demonstrated the willingness of most Socialists to ignore the contrasts stressed by Glasier. What was at stake, as Hardie indicated in his chairman's address, was the effect which fusion with the Federation would have on the party's rising prospects of an electoral alliance with the trade-unions. Confronted with this presentation of the issue, the delegates voted overwhelmingly against the plan. If the choice lay between Socialist unity and a trade-union alliance, it was clear that a majority was willing to follow the leaders.

The decision against fusion was closely related to the council's recommendation, at the 1898 conference, that the ILP change its electoral policy. Until this time that policy had been clear and simple—to engage in parliamentary contests wherever financial resources and local morale permitted. The ILP sought to win the largest possible aggregate vote in competition with the other parties. The vote would be an accurate measure of the party's following. But with the experience of the Barnsley by-election still fresh, the council's report noted the danger of the existing policy to the party's political objectives. Although the delegates voted to delete this section of the report, they did call on the council to reformulate the electoral policy. The editor of the *ILP News,* Russell Smart, sought to interpret the action of the conference:

From the tone of the debate at the Conference it is evident that the branches are disposed to place a self denying ordinance upon themselves, if need be, so that the efforts of the organization as a whole may be directed to achieving actual victory at the polls, rather than a multitude of defeats. . . . Strong feeling is growing up against spending immense sums of money to ascertain the nominal growth of our movement. . . . There was further an unmistakeable recognition of the enormous disadvantages our party and the cause of Socialism and labour suffers by the absence of a single voice in Parliament. A dozen or so energetic men in the House of Commons would, in the opinion of many, at once lift our party into a position of influence and power, and re-energize all the activities of the nation.[26]

The 1898 conference was critical in the development of the ILP for it witnessed the emergence of much stronger direction from the top and opened the way to a more flexible electoral policy. These developments did not go unchallenged. Several branches, angered by the council's treatment of the fusion issue, went over to the Federation. There were also complaints of "bossism." Later in the year the Newcastle ILP sent out a circular to the other branches of the party attacking the administrative council for "reprehensible and undemocratic tactics" in frustrating "the desires of a majority of the members." [27]

During the months following the 1898 conference Ramsay Mac-Donald began to exercise a decisive influence on the party's growth by taking the initiative in developing a policy which would connect the ILP more closely to the economic interests and political attitudes of the working classes. MacDonald's growing influence also served to strengthen the Fabian elements in the ILP outlook and play down the visionary and utopian consciousness of many of the party's most dedicated members.

No biographer has yet unraveled the diverse strands of experience and thought which shaped MacDonald's early development.[28] Few Socialists equaled his exposure to the varied facets of the movement during its first ten years. In 1885, at the age of nineteen, he had left his home in Scotland to take a clerical position in Bristol. He was already immersed in the writings of Carlyle, Ruskin, Emerson, Thoreau, and George and soon joined the local Socialist society. He later recalled the experience:

[26] *ILP News,* May, 1898.

[27] *ILP News,* Aug. 1898; Minutes of the National Administrative Council of the Independent Labour Party, Jan. 30, 1899, Archives of the Independent Labour Party, Bristol. The minutes of the ILP council during the months following the conference indicate the defection of groups at Walthamstow, Bolton, and Treharis.

[28] The best study is Lord Elton, *The Life of James Ramsay MacDonald* (London, 1939).

We had all the enthusiasm of the early Christians in those days. We were few and the gospel was new. The second coming was at hand. . . . In the happy virgin days of the SDF. . . . That coffee shop was our cathedral; its odors were the smells of sacrifices which were being offered up to Demos; we were the new order of High Priests.[29]

MacDonald moved to London in 1886, where he spoke for the Social Democrats, participated in a short-lived schismatic group, and joined the Fellowship of the New Life. He became secretary of the Fellowship and took part in its experiment in cooperative living in Bloomsbury Square. Meantime, MacDonald was also exploring conventional avenues of social advance. He studied biological science, hoping to win a scholarship, until overwork resulted in a physical breakdown and forced a change of direction. In 1888 he secured a position as secretary to a Liberal Member of Parliament and over the next four years gained intimate knowledge of practical politics. By the early nineties MacDonald moved in the London circles of progressive journalists, young Liberal politicians, and reformers of various ideological shadings. He was active in the Fabian Society, served as secretary for the Rainbow Circle, and became associate editor of the *Progressive Review*. After studying the writings of Emanuel Swedenborg for some time he found in the Ethical movement a congenial atmosphere for the religious and ethical search in which he was engaged, like so many of his contemporaries.

Between 1885 and 1895 MacDonald moved from the utopian and ethically charged enthusiasm common to many early Socialists to the political borderlands where Fabians and other Socialists mingled on easy terms with advanced Liberals and radicals. To his friend J. A. Hobson, MacDonald seemed in the nineties "a radical with Socialist sympathies." [30] But his independent outlook toward the major issues of the day emerged most clearly in his writings for the *Ethical Review* at the end of the decade and distinguished him clearly from both the Fabian leaders and the prominent men of the ILP with whom he was closely associated.

MacDonald rejected the emphasis of Webb and other Fabians on

[29] *Labour Leader,* Dec. 23, 1904.
[30] J. A. Hobson, *Confessions of an Economic Heretic* (London, 1938), p. 51.

reform from the top. He quarreled bitterly with Webb over the uses of the Hutchinson money, arguing that the funds should support expanded propaganda and contribute to the growth of a new popular party. Social progress, he wrote later, would not "spring from the generosity of the enlightened, but from the common intelligence." The "cooperative commonwealth" could rise only on the basis of "improved quality of citizenship" produced by educating men in "social duties and civic virtues." MacDonald looked to the Ethical movement, in which he had become increasingly active during the late nineties, to aid this growth by fostering an "ethical intelligence of ever sharpening keenness." [31]

MacDonald, however, did not share the extreme optimism of the Ethical movement. He felt more keenly the loss of older spiritual guidelines. His compatriot, John Davidson, the poetic voice of late Victorian nihilism, seemed to MacDonald the true "mirror of the age." "Being unprotected from the bewildering movements" of thought and "responsive to every one of a liberating nature," Davidson "left nothing sacred from his touch." Perhaps MacDonald's Scottish Calvinist background accounted for the pessimistic strain in his social outlook; certainly he remained wary of what he referred to as "the flaws of human nature and the evils of the human condition." [32]

Though committed to the Ethical movement as the true claimant to the "Protestant succession" MacDonald did not believe that its ethical ideals could be realized by political means. The extent to which acts of parliament could express "moral convictions" was very limited. Social problems were extremely complex; men worked with materials where the "results . . . were rarely foreseen with accuracy." Men should "abandon all hope of perfecting democratic machinery to such a degree that it will produce ethical results." The ideal was "always a possible factor in the situation," but it was "generally latent, a modifying influence rather than an active guide." Although MacDonald criticized his Fabian colleagues for their re-

[31] See A. M. McBriar, *Fabian Socialism and English Politics, 1884–1918* (Cambridge, 1962), pp. 292–293; J. R. MacDonald, "The People in Power," *Ethical Democracy*, ed. Stanton Coit (London, 1900), pp. 61, 72.

[32] *Ethical World*, Jan. 15, 1898; MacDonald, "People in Power," p. 68.

luctance to commit themselves fully to popular propaganda, he shared some of their distrust of "popular inspiration." Thirty years' experience with the democratic franchise, he wrote in 1899, had destroyed the "delusion that the instincts of the average men can be trusted to keep within him political enthusiasm and indicate to him the most desirable line of political action." [33]

MacDonald had joined the ILP in 1894 after a local Liberal caucus rejected his bid to become a parliamentary candidate in Southampton. From the outset his relationship to the new party was strange, reflecting his somewhat circuitous intellectual and political development. His experience with the utopian and doctrinaire sides of the movement had left him with few of the visionary hopes which characterized many of the most active Socialists. Close contact with Liberal politicians and London reformers had also given him a political and intellectual sophistication rare in the ILP. MacDonald had studied the new party carefully, and he recognized the strong practical drives which underlay its Socialist enthusiasm. Indeed, he believed that the ILP was not so much a "child of Socialism" as an outcome of "a desire for Labour representation among Liberals." It had "attached itself to Socialism" in order to establish its independent existence. Given this view of the party, MacDonald could not share its utopianism. To Enid Stacy, one of his closest friends, he joked of his relationship to the party. He referred to himself as one "planted on the borders of Socialism," "a muddled attempt" at a Machiavellian politician, and "the traitor of the Labour movement." [34]

From the beginning MacDonald was viewed with distrust inside the ILP. When the new party adopted him as a candiate at Southampton, a number of the local Socialists left the ILP and joined the Federation. "Suspicion of him was so great in the early days," Tom Johnston recalled, that "when he did something of which we all approved . . . some crossed themselves as fearing an imminent catastrophe and reminded us of the wooden horse of Troy." Mac-

[33] "People in Power," pp. 70, 67–68.
[34] Quoted by Anne Fremantle, *This Little Band of Prophets* (New York, 1960), pp. 129, 133.

Donald, on the other hand, was critical of ILP policies. The defeat in 1895 seemed to him to demonstrate the incapacity of Hardie and other leaders.[35] Addressing a Socialist group in Rochdale a year later, he urged a basic change in the party's outlook and tactics. His remarks were summarized by a local reporter:

The Speaker appealed for Socialists more frequently to put themselves in the position of the man in the street, who is on the whole sympathetic but who does not want to follow out economic complexities. We can talk Socialism seriously to him and we will likely disgust him; we may gas sentimentalities to him and we may capture a member who will only be one more impossibilist in our movement; we may show him what we can do now, show him that we are as interested as he is in doing the smaller things that lie at our feet, and he will become a valuable supporter. . . . He therefore urgently recommended the alliance of the Independent Labour Party with the two or three leading questions in progressive politics at the moment. We have to preach Socialism and familiarise the public with our opinions and general standpoint, on the one hand, and on the other, we are to convince the general progressivist who is not an out and out Socialist that in our hands the minor, as we think, reforms are quite safe. The high superiority of so many Socialists to the political interests of their day was all very well when a nucleus of chosen souls was being formed for the Party. Now we want a little more generosity, a little closer application to facts, a little more recognition of our duty as a political party.[36]

MacDonald's ability was soon recognized and in 1895 he was nearly elected to the administrative council. Following the death of Carolyn Martyn the next year, he took her place on the council. MacDonald attempted to explain the council's changing role after the critical conference of 1898.

In an open letter to the party he observed that the council "with some reluctance, had agreed to overstep its real function and issue a statement of its own position" on the fusion question. But MacDonald also contended that while the council had a "humble con-

---

[35] *Forward,* April 16, 1910; Herbert Samuel, *Memoirs* (London, 1945), p. 26.
[36] *Rochdale Labour News,* Oct. 1896; quoted by Elton, *MacDonald,* pp. 214–215.

ception of its duties," there was a "widespread feeling" that it should provide more leadership. He noted the tendency, "growing stronger every year," for the branches to refer more and more matters to the council. MacDonald deplored this practice and observed that it was impossible for a council meeting only four times a year to engage in a "close detailed businesslike following out of work." [37] MacDonald was probably right about the limitations of the administrative council, but neither the annual conferences nor the local branches could really control the party's development. In the absence of well-defined executive power, the day-to-day policies were formulated mainly by the most active members on the subcommittees of the council. Three men were most influential—Hardie and Glasier, who earned their living by speaking and writing for the movement, and MacDonald, who, following his marriage to Margaret Gladstone in 1896, possessed the financial means to devote full time to politics and journalism.

During the fall of 1898, MacDonald began to bridge the gap between the party's Socialist goals and its efforts to win the trade unionists over to the idea of independent political action. He drew up a statement in which he skillfully obscured the conflict between the party's Socialist principles and its political strategy by identifying the ILP more closely with the radical Liberalism of most of the trade union leaders. The statement, which indicated MacDonald's continuing debt to Fabianism, was revised by Hardie, endorsed by the council, and published in the *Nineteenth Century* in January 1899. It revealed how ILP policy was being adjusted to existing political conditions.

MacDonald restated the characteristic ILP view that the Liberal party had lost a unifying purpose and vitality and would soon be absorbed by the Tories. It was absolutely necessary, therefore, to preserve the ILP's independence. But the ILP also stood in "the true line of the progressive apostolic succession" and it needed to reach the "sympathetic elements" in both the old parties. This could be done, MacDonald argued, only through the "slow process

[37] *ILP News,* July 1898.

of spreading ideas." He denounced the "utopian" attempts to found "ideal communities cut off from the general life of society" and advocated the "transformation of the whole social fabric" through "adaptations and rearrangements." "Our originality," he wrote, "consists rather in the width of our application of old principles than in the discovery of new ones."

The first six years of the ILP's existence, according to Mac-Donald, were primarily educative. The "great necessity of the time" had been to restate the truth that "parties stood on principles, not on programs." Having accomplished this task the ILP could "give better expression nationally, as the separate branches had done locally, to the evolutionary and experimental character of British Socialism." It "could now afford to identify [itself] with those questions of immediate reform upon which Radicals and Socialists alike agreed, with less fear of allowing our aims to be obscured and the party to be swallowed up in the ranks of the shiftless opportunist." The ILP intended to complete the work of political democracy and build a "golden bridge of palliation" to social democracy. MacDonald gave priority to two measures. To make the "popular will . . . supreme in the nation," the House of Lords would have to be abolished. To begin laying the foundations of social democracy, the party would press for the eight-hour day. The way would then be clear for the state to take over property and initiate large-scale public enterprises.

Finally, MacDonald discussed the possible threat to the ILP's independence contained in an appeal to "progressive electors." He distinguished independence from isolation and pointed to the local alliances the party had made with groups "whose aims it could trust," such as trade-unions and cooperative societies. "We can apply the rule of the practical politician that it is wise to work with those who are willing to go along with us, however skeptical they may be of the later stages of our proposals." If the ILP wished to appeal to "independent democratic support," however, it should announce well in advance the constituencies it planned to contest at the coming general election. MacDonald's phrasing of the party's electoral intentions held both an invitation and a warning to Liberals to leave the ILP candidate free for straight fights with Conservatives in a number of contests.[38]

The published statement, signed by MacDonald and Hardie, did not arouse much direct comment within the party. However, Smart chose this time to utter a new warning against alliances.[39] Even if successful they might be "fatal to the ultimate achievement of Socialist hopes." Socialist MP's who "gained seats by Liberal support" would have to "retain that support" and "therefore would be fighting in fetters." Rather than gain admittance to Parliament on such terms the ILP should, Smart argued, prefer exclusion for a generation if necessary.

At the annual conference two months later the council reaffirmed its opposition to arrangements with the Liberals. This would generate distrust in its ranks and suspicion among the Conservative working men whom the ILP also hoped to attract. But the council implemented the more realistic turn in ILP thinking by recommending that the party concentrate its resources in twenty-five constituencies at the next general election and pay special attention to those centers which had "proved themselves in local elections."[40] Where such proof existed, however, there was often evidence as well of deals between the ILP branch and local Liberals.[41] The ILP leaders were traveling a difficult road in attempting to harmonize the demands of independence and Socialist idealism with the customary political attitudes of the bulk of the working classes.

Meanwhile, developments in British society at large were converting many trade-union leaders to the ILP belief in working-class political independence. With the slackening of the labor and Socialist advance after 1895 the employer class had mounted a counteroffensive. It was dramatized in the stunning defeat of one of the most powerful unions, the Amalgamated Society of Engineers,

[38] J. Keir Hardie and J. R. MacDonald, "The Independent Labour Party's Programme," *Nineteenth Century*, XLV (Jan. 1899), pp. 20–38.

[39] *ILP News*, Jan. 1899.

[40] Glasier to the parliamentary committee of the administrative council, late 1899, John Bruce Glasier Correspondence, Archives of the Independent Labour Party, Bristol.

[41] See the editorial in the *ILP News*, Nov. 1900.

after a prolonged lockout in 1897. The shock of this defeat and new signs that the legal system might be utilized to defend the interests of property against the claims of the unions heightened interest in a resolution prepared by the ILP leaders for the Trades Union Congress in 1899. It called for a conference of delegates from Socialist, trade union, and other working-class organizations to consider ways of securing an increased number of labor representatives in the next parliament.[42]

Many trade-union leaders had been gradually discarding the individualistic outlook characteristic of the older radicalism in favor of pragmatic collectivism. During the nineties the Trades Union Congresses had adopted a series of measures favoring some form of nationalization. This emerging collectivist sentiment among the trade unionists provided some support for the resolution calling for a conference of Socialists and union representatives. But it was also clear that the attitude of the unions toward political action had undergone a marked change.

The conference in February 1900, which created the Labour Representation Committee, has been examined in several studies.[43] But two features of the conference were of special significance in the development of the Socialist movement. First, Hardie and MacDonald, who headed the ILP delegation, readily subordinated Socialist principles to the practical goals of the trade union representatives. First principles could be foregone, Hardie assured ILP members, confident that "we and they are almost one . . . on all questions of practical interest." [44] Hardie was again the pragmatic realist of the eighties as he and MacDonald skillfully negotiated a middle course between the efforts of the Social Democrats to identify the new organization clearly with Socialist doctrines and the reluctance of the more moderate trade-union leaders to sever their ties with the Liberal party. Secondly, having secured the principle of political

---

[42] The conference proposal closely followed a plan developed by Hardie several years earlier. See Pelling, *Labour Party,* pp. 213ff.

[43] See Frank Bealey and Henry Pelling, *Labour and Politics* (London, 1958), pp. 30ff; and Poirier, *Advent of Labour,* pp. 77–99.

[44] Quoted in William Stewart, *Keir Hardie* (London, 1921), pp. 156–157.

independence, the ILP leaders were able to place themselves in a strong and influential position in the new body. MacDonald was elected secretary of the Labour Representation Committee and several other ILP men, including Hardie, were appointed to the twelve-man executive. Through hard work and careful attention to the desires of their non-Socialist allies, MacDonald and Hardie guided the trade unionists toward political independence.

At the ILP conference which followed the organization of the joint committee Hardie denied that the alliance meant any "lowering of our ideals," and he asked for "confidence and forebearance." [45] The unions, he argued, worked for the "same end as the ILP, the economic enfranchisement of the masses," even though they had "not yet reached the stage at which we have arrived." Nothing was needed "save the lapse of time and a program of education to level up all to the realization of the fact that in Socialism alone can the freedom of the worker be secured." The ILP rank and file was little disposed to question Hardie's reasoning. Anxieties about the fate of Socialist ideals or consciousness in the new alliance were, with few exceptions, overwhelmed by the excitement over achieving the party's primary tactical objective. Moreover, the party now desperately needed new impetus. The outbreak of the Boer War and the surge of jingoistic feeling had diminished further the appeal of Socialist propaganda.

The ILP leaders claimed a membership of nearly thirteen thousand at the February meeting with the trade-unionists. But this figure, though probably double the actual number of dues-paying members, was far below the total of a few years earlier. During the spring and summer of 1900 the number continued to decline. Some ILP leaders began to despair of the party's future. In "case after case" party officials found branches apathetic toward the work of developing candidates for the approaching general election.[46]

[45] *Labour Leader,* April 28, 1900.

[46] There are no reliable membership figures for either the ILP or the Federation. The leaders of both organizations habitually exaggerated their numbers. When it affiliated with the Labour Representation Committee, the ILP claimed 13,000 members, but at its annual conference the delegates represented only

The new electoral alliance with the unions did little to check the declining strength of the party and by September, when the Conservative government announced a new election, the ILP had only seven candidacies ready. Three others were arranged before the election, but the total of ten was still far short of the number anticipated two years earlier. Five additional candidates were put up under the auspices of the Labour Representation Committee.

The election results were disappointing. ILP leaders boasted that the average poll of thirty-seven hundred votes gained by their candidates was more than double the average in 1895. These figures were deceptive, for the ILP put up only one-third the number of candidates run in 1895, nearly all of them in especially promising constituencies.[47] Indeed, ILP candidates were, with one exception, serious contenders only where they did not face Liberal opposition and where they received substantial Liberal support.[48] The single exception was Hardie's unexpected victory in Merthyr, Wales, which had a unique local explanation.[49] In Preston and Halifax, the only constituencies where the Liberals left the ILP with a straight fight

---

4,000 paying members. It is unlikely that the total was more than 7,500. Pelling estimates the Federation's strength at about one-fourth of the 9,000 it claimed when it affiliated with the Labour Representation Committee (Bealey and Pelling, *Labour and Politics*, p. 165). The ILP secretary, Penny, gives a very depressing report of the party's position in the *Labour Annual* (1901). See *ILP News*, Sept. 1900, for a comment on Brocklehurst's proposal for a new party. Subsequently Brocklehurst joined others, for the most part Fabians and radicals, in forming the National Democratic League. See also Minutes of the National Administrative Council of the Independent Labour Party, May 28, 1900.

[47] For accounts of the election and the results see Poirier, *Advent of Labour*, pp. 118–137; Bealey and Pelling, *Labour and Politics*, pp. 41–50; G. D. H. Cole, *British Working Class Politics, 1832–1914* (London, 1941), pp. 160–166.

[48] At Preston, a two-seat constituency, Hardie, who ran here as well as at Merthyr, drew nearly 5,000 votes as against over 8,000 for each of his two Conservative opponents. At West Bradford, Jowett lost by only forty-one votes in a straight fight with a Conservative. At Blackburn, a two-seat constituency, Snowden drew over 7,000 votes as against the polls of over 9,000 and 11,000 for his Conservative opponents.

[49] Hardie was elected by Liberal votes in this double constituency when one of the two Liberal candidates antagonized the strongly antiwar working-class electorate. See Bealey and Pelling, *Labour and Politics*, pp. 46–49.

with Conservatives in both 1895 and 1900, the ILP's percentage of the vote remained virtually the same. Yet the election campaign raised the ILP from "its doldrums." By the early months of 1901 the party was growing once more.[50]

The trials of the late nineties indicated the limited extent to which Socialism, after the promising surge early in the decade, had penetrated the working classes. Most of its working-class supporters had reverted to conventional patterns of behavior and outlook. The hope of developing a mass party vanished or at least receded into the future. The ILP proved tough and resilient. It carried the Socialist message into new working-class areas and in several of the older centers of support it put down roots by asserting working-class interests in local government. Meanwhile, the party began to approximate the organization and the practices of the traditional political parties; it developed more centralized leadership as well as greater flexibility. And through its political alliance with the trade-unionists it began to draw new strength from non-Socialist sources.

The struggle for a Socialist consciousness continued, but the ILP's accommodation to the political process and its alliance with the trade unionists altered the nature of the struggle. Henceforth the Socialists within the ILP would be faced with growing opposition between their principles and the political development of their party. And in the ensuing conflict between Socialist consciousness and politics the claims of the latter would increasingly predominate.

[50] *Labour Leader,* March 23, 1901.

Conclusion

Marxist ideas entered late Victorian Britain and imparted new inspiration to indigenous currents of social thought. In the process, however, the theoretical coherence of Marxism was lost—divided between its rationalistic drive and its ethical or visionary bent. The former blended easily with the native utilitarianism; the latter merged with modes of thought which were essentially romantic. The fate of Marxism in the 1880s thus confirmed the earlier divergence within British thought and culture.

That divergence expressed contrasting responses to the massive economic and social changes in Britain during the nineteenth century. The utilitarians accepted the changes and attempted to extend the rationalistic ethos which accompained the process of industrialization; the social romantics rejected the emerging industrial order in favor of imaginary models of society drawn largely from the past. The Socialist movement not only perpetuated these ambivalent responses to social change, but provided a context in which to work out their implications. At the same time the earlier dilemmas of the utilitarian and romantic forms of consciousness, dilemmas which Marx had attempted to overcome by means of the dialectic, reappeared.

The limitations of a utilitarian or rationalistic approach to social reconstruction became evident in the development of both the Social Democrats and the Fabians. Such an approach tended to assume the dominant values or modes of human satisfaction implicit in the existing social order; it ruled out ethical, aesthetic, or philosophical claims which questioned that order. Marx had dismissed the utilitarianism underlying the Socialism of both Hyndman and Webb as a "sophistical rationalization of existing society." [1] His hostile judgment anticipated the narrowing of his aspiration by those British Socialists who accommodated their creed to the utilitarian tradition of social thought.

The Social Democratic and the Fabian forms of accommodation were quite different. The former were confident that Marxism provided a scientifically valid analysis of capitalism and a reliable picture of coming social and political developments. They thought their main task was to rescue the workers from the particularistic aspirations nurtured by prevailing associations and to impart a broader and more rational concept of working-class interests. The Social Democrats proved unduly optimistic about the capacity or willingness of the workers to respond, but they did prepare the way for fresh working-class political initiative. The Fabians, having discarded the crucial Marxist doctrines of class and exploitation, conceived of Socialist theory in more dynamic and adaptive terms. In Socialism they saw the extension of the rational and moral possibilities of existing institutions. While the Social Democrats were faithful to the Marxist insistence on the need to organize the working classes and concentrated on the growth of a class-conscious proletariat, the Fabians set out to infiltrate and enlighten traditional political agencies. Both bodies, however, wished to achieve the society envisioned in nineteenth-century utilitarianism—a society which would be more efficient and more just in its distribution of the goods and services made possible by the modern economic order.

Neither the Social Democratic nor Fabian memberships submitted easily to the narrowing of Socialist concern. The doctrinaire style, sectarian ethos, and continuing disputes about religious questions within the Federation suggested the play of nonutilitarian impulses and the tenuous hold of Hyndman's rationalistic theoretical commitment; the Federation's theoretical position was continually threatened by aspirations which were incompatible with its utilitar-

---

[1] See the appendix in Sidney Hook, *From Hegel to Marx* (Ann Arbor, 1962), p. 316.

ianism. Hence the periodic defection of those who questioned, in ethical, aesthetic, or religious terms, the bases of the modern social order which the Social Democrats were seeking to modify. So too with the Fabians. Resistance to the gradual disengagement of the Society's Socialism from basic philosophical claims was less visible. It was apparent in the highly erratic paths of members like Besant, Shaw, and Clarke, and the sense of the constriction of possibilities, effected by Webb, produced continuing tension within the Society.

The deeper drama in the developing Socialist consciousness unfolded among those who had rejected utilitarian forms of thought. They drew mainly on romantic and for the most part nostalgic reactions against the advancing industrial society. But these Socialists also carried over Carlyle and Ruskin's recognition of the losses entailed in the growth of modern capitalism; traditional conceptions of personal worth, social morality, amd political obligation were all called into question by the development of a social order in which economic productivity and impersonal market relationships became dominant. Moreover, the later romanticism of Ruskin and Morris presented the outlines of a creative social vision. These sons of the affluent middle classes had become sensitive to modes of human satisfaction and possibilities for human fulfillment which lay beyond the horizons of their parents. Morris turned to Marxism because it promised the means of reinstating and implementing that vision.

The fusion Morris effected between the romantic vision and Marxism opened up new avenues for British Socialist development. But it also sharpened the divorce between consciousness and objective social reality which had characterized the thought of Carlyle and Ruskin. Indeed, from the Marxist standpoint the Socialism of Morris was regressive—a relapse into the subjectivism and idealism from which Marx had attempted to rescue earlier Socialist reformers. Moreover, the aesthetic and ethical impulses underlying Morris' Socialism soon revealed other limitations, for Morris carried much further the tendency (evident in Carlyle and Ruskin) toward eliminating clear acknowledgment of those impulses in men which did not harmonize with their desire for fellowship and beauty. Indeed,

Morris virtually dissolved moral claims in aesthetic feeling and made this feeling sovereign in human consciousness. He also tended to render the moral and aesthetic sentiments self-sufficient and independent of both objective social realities and other psychological factors. It was a self-stultifying outcome and challenged the creative spirits of the post-Victorian generation to renew the search into man's inner life and the nature of his social existence. Thus Yeats and D. H. Lawrence, both of whom entered for a time into Socialist discussion groups, turned away from the movement in their singular quests for a more authentic understanding of modern man.

Insofar as the more prominent Socialist followers of Morris avoided the impasses into which his aesthtic reductionism led and retained the vision of a qualitatively different social order, they fell back on the moral sentiments released by a disintegrating religious tradition. The aesthetic gospel of Morris and Ruskin tended to fade out or degenerate into a form of hedonism (found, for example, in some of the Clarion clubs) which drew energy away from the movement. But a Socialist consciousness which had come to center on the moral and religious feelings, divorced from the old matrix of doctrine and ritual, was as vulnerable as Morris' utopianism. In Ethical Socialism, too, exaggeration of the power of the moral sentiments and depreciation of the force of objective social circumstances led to the disillusionment which overcame a number of Socialist propagandists after 1895.

British Socialists pursued various strategies in their efforts to overcome the gap between their vision of a radically new order of life and the recalcitrance of historical reality. A few had retreated further into the recesses of consciousness, seeking to give Socialism a deeper psychological or metaphysical anchorage. Bax sought to provide this in his notion of the "alogical," Carpenter in his belief in a cosmic or higher consciousness, and Davidson in his insistence on a common metaphysical ground beneath the moral sentiments. Trevor, too, for all his hostility to theological and metaphysical formulations, was seeking to tap religious sources of energy for the cause.

Other Socialists turned outward and attempted to shape social reality to the forms demanded by their moral feelings. Such a turn might, as for those who contemplated a violent assault on the existing order, require a preliminary act of destruction. It might, as in the Tolstoyan and other Socialist colonies, bring withdrawal from conventional society and attempts to construct radically new forms of human association. But both strategies—toward deeper psychological or ontological levels of experience on the one hand and toward a total reconstruction of objective social forms on the other— failed to discover motives or energies capable of sustaining the Socialist consciousness.

The Ethical Socialists escaped from the impasse into which their moralistically centered outlook had led only by following the route urged by Marx and Engels into direct involvement with the economic and political struggles of the working classes. The way was prepared by those Marxists of the late eighties who had broken with the pioneering Socialist organizations to develop a more realistic strategy. But the passage of Socialist ideas to the working classes meant further attenuation of Socialist consciousness. Just as the Marxists sacrificed much of their theoretical content in the process, so too the Ethical Socialists subordinated their distinctive claims to the customary interests of politically awakened sections of the working class. In this way the visionary element in British Socialism tended to fade out or to serve, as in Mann or Hardie, mainly as a means of mobilizing the workers for common action. What remained was a highly eclectic conception of Socialism compounded of Marxist, Fabian, and Ethical elements. It retained the general goals of collectivization or common ownership. But it lacked the cutting edge of serious theoretical analysis of existing society and it had lost the reach, exemplified most fully in Morris, for creative alternatives to prevailing modes of social and personal satisfaction. Through this process, however, the Socialist movement brought a new working-class political party into existence.

The filtering of their ideas to the British working classes did not, as Marx and Engels anticipated, bring a single, coherent Socialist consciousness. Indeed, Marxist ideas entered creatively into the working-class movement only through the breakup of the distinctive synthesis which Marx had constructed. By means of that breakup, however, disparate native thought traditions received from Marxism fresh impetus and meaning.

Those sections of the working classes which gained a new political orientation from the Socialist movement were not, as Engels suggested, simply giving conscious form to class "instincts." They were building in part on the attitudes and values developed earlier in the working-class efforts to achieve economic justice and self-respect in the new industrial order. But they were also escaping to some extent from the confines of class and attempting to use a legacy of thought and imagination provided by the nineteenth-century intellectuals who had reflected most deeply on the nature and possibilities of the social changes under way. Whether in its utilitarian or its romantic form, Socialism introduced its working-class adherents to a century-long dialogue about the meaning of industrial society which transcended class limits. Indeed, between those members of the working classes who had acquired strong Socialist convictions and those who emphasized more immediate and tangible class interests there was an opposition which grew in the years ahead. The blend of the two outlooks within the ILP enabled it to carry out the complex maneuver of political disengagement and return necessary to launch a new party. While the romantic Socialist vision created a sense of distance from the older political parties and generated new political energies, the practical side of the ILP's program paved the way for its electoral alliance with the trade-union leaders. But the alliance in turn further restrained the development of a Socialist consciousness in any deep or systematic sense of the term.

The dissolution of British Marxism has been explained in terms of the defects of its British spokesmen, of the engrained "bourgeois" habits of mind of the British workers, or of the special features of British institutional development. The fate of British Marxism may be traced more plausibly, however, to the dilemmas inherent in the attempt to achieve the kind of integral or dialectial relationship between consciousness and social development envisioned by Marx. Wherever Marxists have attempted to fulfill the promise of their dialectic in modern history, they have confronted a seemingly inescapable opposition between the inner dynamics of consciousness and the compulsions of economic, social, and political institutions.

The fate of Marxism in late Victorian Britain was not an isolated and idiosyncratic phenomenon. It anticipated the wider development of Marxism in the twentieth century. Later European Marxism has followed much the same pattern of breakdown and reassimilation which took place in Britain. Where continental Marxists drew substantial sections of the working classes into social democratic parties and entered fully into the parliamentary process, these parties have tended to recapitulate the early development of working-class Socialism in Britain and slough off distinctively Marxist doctrines. Where the leaders of Marxist-inspired parties refused, often under pressure from international Communism, to surrender their doctrines, or their "consciousness," they have suffered from the intellectual paralysis characteristic of Hyndman's organization. And insofar as later Marxist intellectuals attempted, like Morris, to reassert the ethical and visionary impulses implicit in the foundations of the creed, they have lost contact with the actual historical development of Marxist-inspired movements or parties. Twentieth-century Socialist thinkers, such as Georg Lukacs, Henry De Man, Ignazio Silone, Jean Paul Sartre, Ernst Bloch, and Leszek Kolakowski, have all found it necessary to choose between the inner claims of consciousness and the dictates of those guarding the orthodox forms of Marxism. Where they have accepted the claims of consciousness Marxist thinkers have also entered into renewed dialogue with other schools of European thought.

The Marxist drive for a new consciousness was Promethean; it meant a struggle to attain a philosophical understanding so close to action that the old "cleavage between ideal and reality" would disappear.[2] Here was the most fundamental of all the utopian elements in Marxism; in the British movement it found expression in the belief of Bax and Carpenter that "consciousness" as man had experienced it in the past would be superseded. The Marxist vision assumed, however, a linear and teleological view of consciousness,

[2] George Lichtheim, *Marxism* (London, 1961), p. 406.

or history, which modern thought with its extreme plurality has made less credible. The place of archaic and visionary forms of consciousness in the political upheavals of the twentieth century, moreover, has forced men to recognize the perils that lie in men's most generous wishes. These experiences have suggested that any radical resolution of the tension between man's consciousness and his social forms is likely to destroy those qualities which are most ennobling in man. Perhaps, as some Marxists have argued, the deeper wisdom in their conception of the dialectic lay simply in its creative, transcending impulse.[3] If so, the Marxist dialectic reinstated the older wisdom of the Hebraic-Christian tradition, as well as the more modest imperatives of the liberal political ethos—that men must constantly transform their historical existence without, however, claiming finality for their ideas or their social institutions.

[3] See for example, Roger Garaudy's interpretation of "dialectical supersession" in *Marxism in the Twentieth Century,* trans. René Hague (New York, 1971), pp. 103ff.

Unpublished Sources

Bibliographies for British Socialism during this period can be found in the following studies: Henry Pelling, *The Origins of the Labour Party, 1880–1900* (rev. ed.; Oxford, 1965); A. M. McBriar, *Fabian Socialism and English Politics, 1884–1918* (Cambridge, 1962); E. P. Thompson, *William Morris: Romantic to Revolutionary* (London, 1955); Philip Poirier, *The Advent of the British Labour Party* (London, 1958); Paul Thompson, *Socialists, Liberals and Labour* (Toronto, 1967); Chushichi Tsuzuki, *H. M. Hyndman and British Socialism* (London, 1961); and Peter d'A. Jones, *The Christian Socialist Revival, 1877–1914* (Princeton, 1968).

Robert Blatchford–A. M. Thompson Correspondence. Manchester Central Reference Library, Manchester Public Libraries, Manchester.

John Burns Correspondence. British Museum, London.

Edward Carpenter Correspondence and Papers. Sheffield City Libraries, Sheffield.

Thomas Davidson Papers. Yale University Library, New Haven, Connecticut.

Friedrich Engels Correspondence. International Institute of Social History, Amsterdam.

Fabian Society Correspondence. British Library of Political and Economic Science, London.

Fabian Society Minute Books and Letters. Fabian Society, London.

Henry George Correspondence. British Library of Political and Economic Science, London.

John Bruce Glasier Correspondence. Archives of the Independent Labour Party, Bristol.

Karl Marx Correspondence. International Institute of Social History, Amsterdam.

Alfred Mattison Diaries. Leeds Public Library, Leeds.

Alfred Mattison Papers. Brotherton Library, Leeds.

John Stuart Mill and Helen Taylor Correspondence. British Library of Political and Economic Science, London.

Minutes of the National Administrative Council and other papers of the

Independent Labour Party. Archives of the Independent Labour Party, Bristol.

Passfield Papers. British Library of Political and Economic Science, London.

Andreas Scheu Papers. International Institute of Social History, Amsterdam.

Socialist League Correspondence and Papers. International Institute of Social History, Amsterdam.

Graham Wallas Correspondence and Papers. British Library of Political and Economic Science, London.

P. E. T. Widdrington–Enid Stacy Correspondence. Maurice Reckitt, London.

Index

MARXISM AND THE ORIGINS
OF BRITISH SOCIALISM

Designed by R. E. Rosenbaum.
Composed by Kingsport Press, Inc.,
in 10 point linotype Times Roman, 3 points leaded,
with display lines in Helvetica.
Printed letterpress from type by Kingsport Press
on Warren's 1854 text, 60 pound basis,
with the Cornell University Press watermark.
Bound by Kingsport Press
in Holliston book cloth
and stamped in All Purpose foil.

Library of Congress Cataloging in Publication Data
(For library cataloging purposes only)

Pierson, Stanley, date.
    Marxism and the origins of British socialism.

    Bibliography: p.
    1. Socialism in Great Britain—History. I. Title.
HX243.P52   335'.00942   72–4571
ISBN 0–8014–0746–X